Postmodern

Legal

Feminism

Postmodern

Legal

Feminism

Mary Joe Frug

Routledge · New York and London

Published in 1992 by

Routledge
An imprint of Routledge, Chapman and Hall, Inc.
29 West 35 Street
New York, NY 10001

Published in Great Britain by

Routledge
11 New Fetter Lane
London EC4P 4EE

Library of Congress Cataloging in Publication Data

Frug, Mary Joe, d. 1991.
    Postmodern legal feminism / Mary Joe Frug : with an introduction
by Judith G. Greenberg.
      p. cm.
    Includes index.
    ISBN 0-415-90619-9 (HB)   ISBN 0-415-90620-2 (PB)
    1. Sex and law. 2. Women—legal status, laws, etc. 3. Feminist
criticism. 4. Postmodernism—Social aspects. 5. Feminist theory.
I. Title.
K349.F78   1992
346.01'34—dc20
[342.6134]   92-12539
                                             CIP

British Library Cataloguing in Publication Data also available.

Contents

A Note on the Text

Because this book is being published posthumously, I should say a few words about how it was put together. Shortly after Mary Joe was murdered on April 4, 1991, I began arranging for the publication of her unfinished work. I did so even though I realized that Mary Joe had planned to continue working on all of her essays and thus would not have published any of them in the form in which they then existed. But I was faced with the choice of either letting her ideas die with her or publishing them in their incomplete state. Given the value of what she had already written, the choice seemed to me to be clear.

At the outset I made several editorial decisions about how to proceed. I wanted to let Mary Joe speak in her own voice. Thus I decided that the work would neither be rewritten nor completed; even the half-sentence in Chapter 8 that marks the end of her life would be left as is. Accordingly, only minor editorial changes—substituting the word "chapter" for the word "article," correcting the occasional typo, completing footnotes, and the like—have been made in her manuscripts. I also decided to organize her work into essays, so that texts that seemed connected to each other could be published together. With these guidelines in mind, a number of the chapters in this book were published in law reviews: Chapter 1 and a portion of Chapter 2 in the *New England Law Review*, another portion of Chapter 2 in the *University of Colorado Law Review*, Chapter 3 in the *Harvard Women's Law Journal*, Chapter 7 in the *University of Pennsylvania Law Review*, and Chapter 8 in the *Harvard Law Review*. (Mary Joe herself had published Chapters 4 through 6 in the *American University Law Review* in 1985.) I am grateful to each of these law reviews for their cooperation in the preparation of this book.

The publication of this book required another decision: how to organize the individual essays into a book-length manuscript. At the

viii / Postmodern Legal Feminism

time of her death, Mary Joe had not resolved this issue. I therefore arranged her essays into chapters myself. Although I hope that my organization makes sense, other arrangements were certainly possible. Out of necessity, responsibility for the order in which Mary Joe's essays are presented is mine.

Had Mary Joe lived to publish her own book, I know that she would have dedicated it to our children, Stephen and Emily. I therefore dedicate it to them for her. But this book is not simply written by Mary Joe. It is also being published for Mary Joe. It collects her work, work brutally cut short in the prime of her creative life. It seems equally fitting, therefore, for the three of us to dedicate this book to her: not only for her talents as a feminist, a scholar and a critic— talents amply demonstrated in these pages—but also for her equally remarkable talents as a mother, a wife, and a friend.

Gerald E. Frug
June, 1992

Introduction to Postmodern Legal Feminism

Mary Joe Frug was murdered on the evening of April 4, 1991 as she walked near her home in a tree-lined, well-lit, residential neighborhood.[1] Her assailant has yet to be identified. Mary Joe had spent her adult years as a committed feminist studying the meanings of "woman" and "gender" in American society. Her life and work were dedicated to ending violence against women. It is ironic that she may have been killed because she was a woman. On the other hand, perhaps she was simply in the wrong place at the wrong time.

I have stated these two possibilities as if they are distinct and separate: either she was murdered because she was a woman, or because she was in the wrong place at the wrong time. Mary Joe's own work, including this book, explores whether these statements are really different or whether they are actually the same. What does it mean to be a "woman"? What does it mean to be in the "wrong" place? Is "wrong" itself affected by our understanding of gender? Is it wrong for a woman (but not a man) to be out alone at night? Does the answer depend on whether the neighborhood in which she is "out" is tree-lined and well-lit? Or is she simply not a woman (clearly she is not a lady) if she is out in the "wrong" neighborhood?

Feminists have worked hard to respond to questions like these in describing women's lives and the conditions under which they are lived. In order to improve women's lives we must understand what it means to be a woman in this society and the various forces that constrain and create us. These forces include, but are not limited to, physical violence. Feminists have articulated numerous descriptions or interpretations of our situation. While each of these provides some powerful insights, each also has limitations; the descriptions and interpretations represent a continuing dialogue among feminists as to how to understand the meaning of "women."

Three of these approaches have been particularly important for legal feminists, including Mary Joe. The first of these, which I will label the "sameness/difference" model, compares women to men. According to this model, women are the same as men, except, of course, when women are different from men. These differences are often attributed to culture or biology. The existence and treatment of difference is the focal point of this model. Some feminists have criticized this "sameness/difference" model because it does not address men's pervasive power over women. These feminists see women's subordinate position, women's difference, as a mark of men's domination. Differences, according to the second description—the "dominance" model—derive their meaning from a patriarchal system which places and retains men at the top of the hierarchy.

A third approach to understanding the meaning of women focuses on cultural representation. Postmodern feminists seek to uncover the ways in which "reality" is constituted by language. Like those who subscribe to the dominance model, postmodern feminists recognize the crucial role that male power plays in creating women as different. Postmodern feminists, however, focus on the ways in which this power is itself constructed through discourses—the ways in which it is used, described and thought about. They are concerned with language's constructions of the categories of "power" and "women" and how these meanings construct our identities as women.

Some feminists of color, working within the models and interpretative strategies already described as well as from other stances, have also focused on the meaning of "women." They criticize the essentialist nature of many white feminists' definitions of women—definitions which often merely generalize from the experiences of upper middle-class white women. The position taken by these feminists of color is consistent with postmodern methodologies: they note that generalized perspectives are necessarily partial. They remind us that, while the differences between men and women are significant, so are the differences among women. To define one particular group of women as representing the "essence" of women does violence to and constrains the lives of those women who differ.

Mary Joe Frug was a non-essentialist, postmodern feminist; as such her work is constituted, in part, in dialogue with feminists who use the sameness/difference and dominance models.[2] Mary Joe recognized the theoretical and practical advances that both of these approaches represented for women. She endorsed equality, gloried in women's differences, and believed that male dominance structures our lives in fundamental, invisible ways. But she was not uncritical of these feminist models. She used her commitments to postmodernism, diversity, and feminist politics as a means of critiquing these approaches and thereby advancing our understanding of issues of importance to women. Furthermore, *Postmodern Legal Feminism* is a careful study of the ways in which legal discourses construct the various meanings of "women;" simultaneously, it uncovers the ways in which these discourses are, in turn, constructed by gender. Ultimately, Mary Joe shows us how thinking about the law in a gendered manner may help us to transcend the restricting categories of male and female.

We cannot understand Mary Joe's work without first looking more thoroughly at the various feminist positions with which her work was in constant conversation. Feminists on the "sameness" side of the sameness/difference position, strive to create formal legal equality for women. They argue that women should have the same rights as men. While they succeeded in obtaining a variety of rights for women, their focus has been on equality in the workplace. They recognize that without this crucial right women will never be able to achieve economic independence or to improve their living conditions. White women's wages in 1985 were a mere two-thirds of white men's; women of color received still less. Furthermore, most women are segregated into low-paying women's jobs.[3] Feminist litigators simply asked for the same workplace conditions for women as for men.

This approach won some courtroom victories and for a period of time looked promising. As Mary Joe notes, perhaps its most stunning success was its mere claim to equality; in advocating the "sameness" position, feminists forced others to take seriously the assertion that women were the equals of men.[4] Some of the fruits of this can be seen in the significant increase in the number of women in the legal and medical professions; the smaller, but still meaningful, increase in the number of women in the skilled trades; and the general acceptance of a principle of non-discrimination in access to employment and promotion.

The problem with sameness feminism lies in the very claim to equality that provided the basis for its success. A determination of equality requires a comparison of the subject with a model. When the subject is women and the model is men, the points of comparison are infinite. Which ones one chooses, and thus whether one sees equality or not, will depend on the chooser's point of view. For example, in my initial paragraph describing Mary Joe's murder, I suggested that a man might have been treated just as brutally as she was—that her sex made no difference: perhaps Mary Joe was just in the wrong place at the wrong time. But already in writing that sentence I have undermined the assumption of equality. My use of "perhaps" implies the possibility that her murder was not due to similarities between her and men but rather may have been because of some difference between her and a hypothetical man who might have been in the same place. Perhaps a man would have been stronger—better able to resist or never initially attacked because of his perceived strength. We can view Mary Joe's situation either the same as a man's would have been or different from a man's. The ability to see sameness from one perspective and difference from another shows the limits of the sameness approach. Even feminists advocating that women be treated the same as men recognized women's differences from men. They simply argued that these differences should not matter.[5]

Nevertheless, these feminists' efforts were severely limited by the manipulability of the concepts of "sameness" and "difference". In *Geduldig v. Aiello*,[6] the female plaintiffs argued that a state disability insurance program ought to provide benefits to pregnant women because all conditions that disable men were covered, including conditions that occurred uniquely or primarily to men, such as prostatectomies or heart attacks. Failure to pay benefits to pregnant women treated these disabled women differently than disabled men. Sameness feminists argued that if pregnancy were not treated like other disabilities, women would be forever economically disadvantaged by the fact that *they* became pregnant.

The U.S. Supreme Court did not reject the premise that women should be treated the same as men. Instead, while claiming that the program treated women equally, the Court approved the exclusion of pregnancy. In a now infamous footnote it said that the challenged programs simply "divided potential recipients into two groups—pregnant women and non-pregnant persons." Since women were in both groups, there was no discrimination based on sex! Unlike the plaintiffs, the Court did not see pregnancy as a characteristic that distinguished women from men. Instead, pregnancy simply distinguished some women from other women who were not pregnant (and from all men). According to the Court, all people who were not pregnant were treated the same; only pregnant women were treated differently. *Geduldig* demonstrates the manipulability of equality as a standard. The Court could affirm women's equality with men while rejecting the plaintiff's position; to do so it simply needed to redefine the point of comparison. Since there were many points of similarity and difference between men and women, women could be treated the same as men (according to the Court) and still come out on the short end of the stick (according to the plaintiffs). Or, as Mary Joe said, equality theory with "your fingers crossed turned out not to work."[7]

It should not be surprising that trying to model women's rights on men's does not produce equality. "Woman" is clearly not a synonym for "man" in the modern American vocabulary. Women's differences from men remain, regardless of whether these differences are understood as biological or cultural. American feminists of the late nineteenth and early twentieth centuries often focused on these differences. These feminists, like some feminists today, tended to laud the differences, finding in them a basis for pride in being a woman.

Today, cultural feminists are among those who seek to celebrate women's differences. They argue that a special women's culture exists—one in which women care more about their relationships with other people than men do. For example, Carol Gilligan can be read to claim that women solve problems by thinking about the effects of various possible solutions on others, whereas men solve problems by reference to abstract norms.[8] A possible implication of this is that including women in decision-making institutions would result in different and better outcomes. For example, women might be less prone to engage in war, or more likely as judges to enforce communitarian values over individualistic ones. Some feminists have suggested that not only would women come to different conclusions, but that they would use different processes. Instead of relying so heavily on adversarial litigation, a woman-developed dispute resolution system might emphasize mediation.[9]

One difficulty with defining concern for relationships as the essential characteristic of women is that some women will necessarily be excluded from the category "women" by this definition. For example, what about the large numbers of women attorneys who work very successfully within the present adversarial legal system? Are they any less "women" because they have not moved the system toward mediation? Or because they can succeed within the "male" adversarial system? Or what about women who abuse their children? Are they not women? Or women who abandon their children, husbands or lovers? In some instances this may be an act of self-sacrifice to benefit the other. But in other instances this is very clearly a calculation that the woman will be better off without the one(s) left behind. Slave owners used to believe that their female slaves would not escape because it meant leaving young children behind. Although this was often accurate, does it mean that those women who did escape without their offspring had become men?

Another problem with a cultural feminist approach which defines women in terms of certain characteristics is that this will necessarily affect not only how women are seen, but how they see themselves. Women who understand the meaning of woman to be "one who cares for others" may strive to fulfill that role. But, to see oneself only in terms of others has often been stifling for women. Furthermore, to deprive men of the opportunity to see themselves as caring for others may be similarly limiting. Thus, the identification of certain privileged female characteristics may benefit some women, giving them gender pride, but it simultaneously has negative features in that it excludes some, while constraining others' personalities.

In practice, an emphasis on women's caring role has often meant an emphasis on women's caretaking. Thus, difference feminists have advocated part-time jobs, job sharing, and "mommy tracks" for women. Often, this approach has resulted not in empowerment of women, but rather in their further dependence on men. Part-time jobs, while allowing women extra time with their families, often come at the cost of crucial health care and pension benefits. "Mommy tracks" usually imply reduced opportunities for advancement. Furthermore, difference feminism has provided a basis for the frequently advanced argument that women choose low-paying jobs because these jobs fit better with their "feminine" characteristics.[10]

In *EEOC v. Sears*, the EEOC sued Sears for failing to hire women as commission sales representatives. The EEOC based its case on the statistically low percentage of women who obtained positions in commission sales. In its defense, Sears argued that women chose not to seek commission sales positions. Its claim was that these positions required aggressive, highly informed, self-motivated, risk-takers, whereas women were nuturant, relation-centered and not competitive. Ultimately, Sears won. The emphasis on women as caretakers reintroduced all the negative, subordinating aspects of difference. In *Sears*, difference feminism was subverted from a source of gender pride and power to a conservative force in opposition to change.

Feminist strategies based on women's equality to men or their differences from men have not resulted in the liberation of women that feminists had hoped for. As we have seen, feminists working with these strategies are caught in a never-ending oscillation between sameness and difference. Arguing for the similarities between men and women necessarily implies a recognition of the differences between the sexes, since one would not need to look for similarities if there were not also differences. In contrast, emphasis on the differences necessarily recognizes these distinctions between men and women, but also recognizes that they are dependent on an underlying assumption of sameness. Women's differences are understood as paired with specific characteristics of men: dependence with autonomy, home with work, disability as a result of menses or pregnancy with able-bodiedness, and so on. The mere fact that meaningful comparisons are possible shows a recognition of the way in which home and work, for example, are two sides of the same coin. Each side, however, has a value attached to it, and it should come as no surprise that the male side has traditionally been more highly valued. Whereas difference feminists tried to present women as different from, but on a parity with (or even superior to) men, women's differences have been repeatedly devalued by society. Sameness feminists have been thwarted by the repeated recognition of difference; difference feminists by the devaluing of *women's* difference.[11]

In contrast, the dominance model breaks out of the confines of the sameness/difference dilemma by focusing on men's power over women. In addition to murder, the naked exercise of male power takes the form of rape (within or outside of preexisting relationships), forced prostitution, and sexual abuse or mutilation of female children and adults in both medical and non-medical settings. Often associated with work by Catharine MacKinnon,[12] the dominance approach discloses the politics behind questions of equality and inequality.[13] According to MacKinnon, "an equality question is a question of the distribution of power."[14] What had previously been identified as difference, is not, for MacKinnon, really a difference between men and women, but rather a result of women's subordination to men; in other words, women differ from men in that they are subordinate to men. The dominance model, according to MacKinnon, looks at the world from women's viewpoint with knowledge derived from women's experiences.[15] These show the overpowering effects of male dominance—effects that are invisible when the social system is viewed from the male position of dominance. Whereas in the sameness/difference formulation of women's situation, women's reproductive or parenting roles are often taken as social or biological "facts," the dominance model sees them as indications of male power. The very traits that under a sameness/difference model appear most fundamentally to define difference and thus make women differently situated and unequal, are, for MacKinnon, the ways in which male domination is perpetuated. It is through women's sexual characteristics that men define women and, having defined them, forcibly and legally subordinate them.

The dominance model is particularly illuminating in that it provides a means for analyzing problems that under the sameness/difference model are simply understood as difference and, therefore, not discrimination on the basis of sex. For example, to the extent that rape was primarily committed against women because of their sex, women who were raped could not be thought of as entitled to equal treatment with men. One is stymied by the question of what equality would mean in this context. To be treated as a question of equality, rape would have needed to be reconceived as "similar" to other criminal acts. Perhaps this is what was behind the claim that rape was not a crime of sexuality, but a crime of violence. Violence, presumably, could be done to anyone. But, as MacKinnon points out, rape is not just a crime of violence. It is a violent sexual assault committed against a non-consenting woman because of her sex. The dominance model, by focusing on the sex involved in rape highlights that rape is a crime against women, not random individuals. It puts at issue the hierarchical relations between men and women.

The dominance model also challenges the line between public and private that the sameness/difference model accepts. Rape, by defini-tion, is a violent sexual assault to which consent is not given. The dominance approach forces us to ask what consent means in a social situation in which men dominate women. Is failure to object vocifer-ously an indication of consent (as courts have often seen it) or of lack of consent? What about vociferous objections without a physical struggle? If a woman's silent refusal to consent is not a clear lack of consent, why isn't it? And if it is, how does criminal rape differ from what happens to married women in their bedrooms? The consent recognized by law is, according to MacKinnon, consent from the male point of view. The startling insight of the dominance model is to show the ways in which male power affects every one of us in our most private affairs. Or, in other words, the dominance model asserts that the personal is the political.

In this way, the dominance model enlarged significantly the array of women's issues subject to critical analysis. Under the sameness/difference model, with its acceptance of the line between public and private realms, many issues relating to women's sexuality were not appropriate subjects for the law to consider because they dealt with sex, and sex was something that took place in private. Private deci-sions involving competent adults are traditionally understood to be inappropriate subjects for legal regulation. The sameness/difference model did not challenge this traditional understanding because wom-en's desire for sex, and thus consent to it, was understood to be the same as men's. This meant that a couple's private, "consensual" sexual relations, whether violent or not, would usually be seen as a matter for the couple to handle by themselves. Similarly, the dominance model provided a method for critique of current treatment of prostitu-tion and pornography which had previously been considered to be private "victimless crimes"; the dominance model disclosed their vic-tims to be, overwhelmingly, women. Redefined in terms of their subor-dination of women as a class, issues that had previously been seen as only private and individual could now be understood as public; the pervasive subordination of one-half of the population could not be accomplished without the complicity of public structures.

The cause of action for sexual harassment shows the power of the dominance model to challenge the traditional view of sex as individual and private. The cause of action depends on recognizing an injury when sexual demands are made within the hierarchy of the workplace. From a woman's perspective, there *is* harm simply in being asked; there is harm in being in an environment that treats women as sexual objects. The action also depends on recognizing that sexual demands made on women in the workplace are made because of their sex. The dominance model, with its focus on women's sexuality as the core of women's subordination, allows us to see that sexual harassment is addressed to women as a class. Such harassment does not just happen randomly to workers. Nor is it simply a statement of private desire on the part of one man.

Finally, the dominance model provides a position from which to argue that compliance with sexual demands is not consent. In a stunning victory, the U.S. Supreme Court held that there could be sexual harassment in a case in which a female employee had "voluntarily" engaged in demanded sexual relations with her male employer over a period of years.[16] The Court said that the proper inquiry was not whether the plaintiff had engaged in the relations voluntarily, but rather whether the attentions were unwelcome. Without explicitly saying so, the Court appeared to accept the dominance model's description of a world in which women, because of their sexually subordinate position, are barraged by and submit to unwelcome sexual attentions. The Court recognized an injury that was perceived by women, and held it to be actionable because it was based on women's sex, without allowing the case to be individualized to a simple consensual affair gone wrong between two people.

Feminists working within the dominance model have also focused attention on pornography. Violent pornography, they claim, plays a central role in women's subordination to men. Its images sexualize force and construct the meaning of gender through the association of men with dominance. The dominance model describes pornography as one of the practices through which power is distributed to men in modern America. When pornography portrays men as dominant and engaged in violent sex acts and women as submissive, it defines both male and female sexuality. It is a description, according to feminists like MacKinnon, not of fantasy, but of reality. Male and female sexuality then conforms to the roles scripted for it; men find domination erotic while women's erotic pleasure comes from being dominated.

Pornography is an obvious danger to those women who are coerced into participating in its production and to those against whom violent sex acts are performed based on models from pornography. But dominance theory also makes a much stronger claim about the injury from coercive or violent pornography: such pornography turns domination into sexuality and constructs gender accordingly. What women see as gender, and therefore natural and immutable, is actually a pornographic creation of gender within society. The harm to women from pornography is our inequality.

To give women a legal remedy for the injuries done by pornography, MacKinnon and Andrea Dworkin proposed the adoption of legislation that would outlaw as discrimination on the basis of sex the production or distribution of pornography. Consistent with the view that violent pornography sexualizes the subordination of women, the proposed ordinance defined pornography as "the graphic sexually explicit subordination of women through pictures and/or words" in one of nine scenarios. MacKinnon, Dworkin, and many others organized to put the legislation in front of numerous city legislatures, including the Indianapolis City Council which passed it in 1984; it was immediately challenged in court by media trade groups, aligned with some feminists and traditional civil liberties organizations.[17]

The feminists who joined in the successful court challenge to the ordinance claimed that women, like men, could enjoy pornography. The ordinance, they claimed, was just another in a long line of state efforts to protect "good" asexual women and to ensure that they remain so. Its simultaneously absolutist, but vague, approach to the defined categories of pornography would reenforce the double sexual standard against women. In arguing that women, like men, stood to gain from pornography and an unfettered First Amendment, these feminists reasserted the "sameness" position. While not denying men's power over women, they claimed that the ordinance would promote inequality instead of equality.

Feminists who support the dominance model claim that its description of the situation of women is accurate because it is based on women's "experienced empirical existence"[18] which is understood as the pervasive eroticization of sexual abuse. This methodology, while extremely powerful, produces, however, a certain overdetermination. Given the brute force behind male dominance, its empowerment via the law, and its constant reinforcement through cultural artifacts like pornography, "the truly interesting question" as MacKinnon recognizes, "becomes why and how sexuality in women is ever other than masochistic."[19]

Mary Joe Frug and other postmodern feminists take up this challenge.[20] How can it be that women are different from each other? How can we describe the varieties in women's sexual identities in more nuanced ways? Postmodern feminists investigate the legal, cultural, and political discourses through which our identities are constituted. Whereas MacKinnon claims to describe the realities of women's situations, postmodern feminists emphasize the interpretative nature of all descriptions. For MacKinnon, "Sexual meaning is not made only, or even primarily, by words and in texts."[21] For postmodern feminists, in contrast, women's experiences and relationships do not exist apart from the discourses about them. They are constituted by the discourses in which we think them. These discourses will be interpreted differently in different historical, political, and social contexts. While MacKinnon seeks to present the reality of women's lives, postmodern feminists demonstrate that reality is never present. It can only be (re)presented through language.

Postmodern thought is a response to modern theories like liberalism, Marxism, and the feminist dominance model. These seek to rationalize the social world, often using all-encompassing pairs such as public and private, freedom and coercion, capital and labor, and male and female. While such theories, like the dominance model, claim to "be about what *is*,"[22] and to describe reality, postmodern work is about interpretation. In a reversal of the "modern," postmodern thought focuses on the text instead of on the events that are signified. Interpretation requires a position from which the event is understood, a perspective from which the world is interpreted. The binary pairs of modern theories present particular and partial perspectives. They are discursive strategies for describing the world. They are already interpretations.

In addition to identifying discourses as interpretive of reality, postmodern feminists recognize the partiality and perspectivity of interpretations.[23] For example, in the opening paragraphs of this introduction, I asked whether Mary Joe Frug was murdered simply because she was in the wrong place at the wrong time or whether she was murdered because she was a woman. One way to understand these questions is to see them as posing two diametrically different answers to why she was killed—either it had something to do with her sex or it didn't. The implication is that reality can be captured in the answer. A postmodern reader might ask whether these are really alternatives. What do these questions disclose about the perspective from which they are asked? What does it mean for a woman to be in the wrong place? Are women who go out for walks at night streetwalkers, women of the night? If men represent the model of the erect and upstanding in our society, do women necessarily connote "wrong"? In short, is "wrong" gendered? If it is, then must we think about Mary Joe's murder as other than random? A postmodern feminist might reinterpret "wrong," reading its gender into it and its sex neutrality out. The point is that for a postmodernist, the text that one can read in the murder is simply interpretive. It will simultaneously disclose and mask the reader's interpretive strategies. It cannot make the events of April 4, 1991 transparent to us.

I have described MacKinnon's work as modern, and it certainly is in its claim to portray reality. But, like postmodern feminists, MacKinnon pays careful attention to the role of perspective; she has forcefully asserted the importance of women's viewpoint. Dominance theory is the world as seen from women's viewpoint, not men's. In establishing the importance of women's viewpoint, she asserts the existence of a viewpoint common to all women. She also asserts the primacy of the hierarchy of gender.[24] A postmodern feminist instead might focus on the partiality of all claims to interpret women's realities. A postmodern feminist might try to disclose the discursive practices that create hierarchical differences among women, and between men and women. While MacKinnon stresses the importance of perspective, perspective, for her, is unitary. She certainly acknowledges issues of race and class,[25] but nevertheless believes that she can describe "the realities of women's situation. . . . Comprised of all its variations, the group women can be seen to have *a* collective social history of disempowerment, exploitation, and subordination."[26] In creating *a* collective definition of women's situation, she deemphasizes the ways in which these experiences may have radically different meanings for women of different races, classes, or sexual preferences.

African American feminists have long criticized white feminists for the tendency to generalize the position of women from our own positions. Sojourner Truth's famous "Ain't I a Woman" speech at the Akron, Ohio, Women's Rights Convention in 1851 shows that this type of complaint has a long history. Recent work by Kimberlé Crenshaw shows the ways in which the jurisprudence of Title VII has been constructed to force African American women to choose between being black and being women. Her work also reveals the ways in which misogynist rap lyrics may have different meanings for African American women than for white women. Similarly, other feminists have complained that "feminist" discourse often excludes women who are Canadian, Puerto Rican, lesbian, or otherwise "other."[27]

For postmodern feminists, the discursive practices that create partial interpretations are also constitutive of our identities. Thus, we cannot answer the questions posed at the beginning of this introduction as to who women are and how to improve our situations without reference to the discourses that constitute us. Group identities—including a woman's identity as a member of any particular group of women—are constituted by the multiple discourses through which they are described and recognized. They are not static, but continuously being restated. Postmodern feminist work embraces multiple meanings because the words through which identities are fashioned carry within themselves traces of past usage. Meaning is built on the instability of these past usages. As such, postmodern ideas of identity challenge the conceptions of identity offered by both the sameness/difference model and the dominance model.

Postmodern feminists' readings of erotic texts display several strategies to uncover the multiple, partial meanings assigned to "woman." All of these involve close attention to the ways in which the dichotomous positions on which a text appears to depend dissolve in the text itself. In these texts, we can look at two important binary pairs. The first is the distinction between male and female bodies. Heterosexual texts about sex often involve male-female sex; lesbian and homosexual texts frequently show same sex coupling. It is important to sexual texts that the characters' sex be clear. Secondly, erotic texts are built on assumptions about male and female genders. Men and women are understood to have certain gendered characteristics, like men's sexual aggressivity or women's passivity. The binary pairs of male/female bodies and male/female gender are, on the surface, crucial to pornography and other erotic texts. It is important that the reader/viewer be able to recognize to which side of the pair a character belongs; the pairings are, in this way, essentialist. The postmodern feminists I discuss below show, through their (re)readings of sexual texts ranging from art to pornography, that these dichotomous positions are subverted within the text itself.

Susan Keller's postmodern reading of Madonna's "Justify My Love" exposes the ways in which this erotic video undermines the assumption that male and female *bodies* exist uninterpreted. The film shows people of "uncertain gender; women who may be men, men who may be women." Scenes of apparent heterosexual sex turn into lesbian love-making; "women" display "male" physical characteristics—they wear penciled mustaches or show up bare-breasted in suspenders.[28] Susan Suleiman too explores the way in which bodies in erotic texts exist as male and female only through interpretation.[29] In her reading of Bataille's *Story of the Eye,* she points out that Simone, an apparently female character also is subtly male: the language that Bataille uses to describe Simone resonates with language that Baudelaire used to describe Lola de Valence as painted by Manet. But, this painting depicts a subject who is distinctively "mannish."[30] Like the sex of the characters in Madonna's video, Simone's body does not "exist" as male or female. Instead its sex must be interpreted.

Similarly, Susan Gubar, turns to a discussion of Magritte's *Le Viol* (a painting of a woman from the neck up with "blind nipples replacing eyes, a belly button where her nose should be, and a vulva for a mouth") in order to answer the question of whether an explicitly misogynist image necessarily results in a misogynist ideology.[31] The painting could be understood as one in which the female face is erased by the female torso, suggesting "anatomy is destiny." Furthermore, as Gubar indicates, one need not look far to discover that the "face" is sightless, senseless, and dumb. Yet, Gubar notes that "there is an odd masculine cast" to this painting of a woman: there is a bulge around the waist where a female torso would normally be indented and the pubic hair around the vulva/mouth functions as facial hair. Gubar's work, like Keller's and Suleiman's, emphasizes the way the body exists for us only as it is seen through discourse; it, like everything else, is an interpretation. One way Gubar interprets Magritte's *Le Viol* is as a phallus. The body/face is erect, self-enclosed. As a phallus, this female body represents the male. From this viewpoint, the painting represents the interdependence of images of men and women. Male and female bodies, in postmodern readings of sexual texts, dissolve into each other. Neither is a stable construct; each is constituted by the discourses through which it is understood.

These postmodern feminists also uncover a similar instability in portrayals of gender characteristics. In Bataille's *Story*, Simone's body is not just ambiguously sexed—her character traits are equally unclear. Bataille describes her, according to Suleiman, as " 'a young girl from a good family,' a virginal-looking adolescent"; Suleiman notes, however, that her sexuality could also be described as "male" because of its voraciousness and aggressive nature. Similarly, Keller points out that gender characteristics as well as bodies are often ambiguously sexed in Madonna's videos and pornographic movies. In at least two scenes in "Justify My Love" it is Madonna, not her male lover who appears dominant. In one, they make love with Madonna on top; in another, she leaves him, despite his out-stretched hand. Furthermore, Keller shows how both Candida Royalle, a self-proclaimed feminist pornographer, and more traditional commercial pornography like *Deep Throat* and *The Devil in Miss Jones* explore themes about women's control over sexual encounters.[32]

What does all this mean? Do misogynist images necessarily result in misogynist ideologies? Gubar, having formulated this question about the relationship between misogynist images and discourses, responds by turning to context. The images produced by these texts

have, she says, multiple meanings which must be interpreted in relation to the remainder of the text and the frames through which they
are situated. These frames may be art, literature, history, psychoanalytic theory, or pornographic or racist texts. We must, Gubar argues,
"pay more attention to male . . . traditions in terms of their production
of images of male and female sexuality."

Mary Joe Frug takes seriously law's production of male and female
sexuality. *Postmodern Legal Feminism* rereads legal texts in resistance
to the standard discursive assertions that law is neither constructed
by gender dichotomies nor constitutive of gender. Her claim is that
the law, like other systems of thought, is gendered and that it plays a
significant role in constructing our identities as women.[33] Law and
gender are not two separate, unrelated systems. Each is constitutive
of and defined by the other. Her work pursues two reading strategies.
For each legal or law-related text that she reads, she asks how our
understandings of gender affect our understandings of the law. Repeatedly, using insights from dominance theory, she shows the influence of gender on our interpretations of supposedly ungendered material. Her second, simultaneous strategy is to read the law for the
meanings it assigns to the body and to gender identity. Her methodology throughout is postmodern in its concern for the multiplicities of
language and meaning. In uncovering the power of our constructions
of gender to give meaning to ostensibly ungendered material, Mary
Joe is concerned with the possibility that the use of essentialist categories of gender analysis may limit rather than increase the possibilities
in women's lives. She recognizes this difficulty, asserting that for the
moment, if we are to improve women's situations we must think
within the category woman. But, simultaneously we must reject the
idea that women have a unitary nature. Mary Joe's willingness to
live with and use two contradictory positions, each within a specific
political context, is part of her postmodern methodology.[34]

Repeatedly in this book, Mary Joe shows that our understanding of
gender affects our understanding of the law. One of the ways she does
this is in her analysis of a contracts casebook. Contracts theory does
not overtly discuss gender, yet Mary Joe shows how, given the organizational structure of at least one popular casebook, gender may affect
students' understanding of various doctrines. Casebooks frequently
pair opposite cases or doctrinal approaches. If one side of the pair
involves male parties and the other involves women, students are
likely to read the cases involving women as generating subordinate
holdings and doctrines (exceptions to the rules or doctrines illustrated
by the dominant "male" cases). Students' associations of cases or
doctrines with gender may mislead them into viewing the relations

between dominant and subordinate as more rigidly distinct than they actually are. Male and female, they may think, are, after all, rigid categories that differentiate among people; gender-associated legal positions could be understood in an equally oppositional manner.

Mary Joe's point, of course, is not that certain cases or doctrines are "female" or "male," but rather that given the context in which they are presented, students are likely to associate them with characteristics relating to gender. She makes a similar point about the curricular structure both of contracts law and of most law schools. Thus, doctrines relating to mutuality of assent may be understood as central to contract law because the cases that illustrate these doctrines are primarily drawn from commercial settings in which men predominate. The cases that illustrate the doctrines relating to reliance are more likely to involve personal issues, and women, not men, are associated with the personal. As a result, students may understand reliance doctrines as subordinate to mutuality rules, instead of in tension with them. Similarly, contracts casebooks traditionally do not discuss agreements about reproductive technology, cohabitation, or separation. Discussion of these agreements is usually deferred to other courses. This curricular division does not appear on the surface to be sex-based; many contracts, such as insurance agreements, are assigned to other courses. But, as Mary Joe states,

> This deferral is not neutral. By confining issues that particularly concern women to domestic relations or sex discrimination courses, casebooks combine with standard law school curriculums to perpetuate the idea that women's interests are personal, concerning only themselves or their families. Men, in contrast, are concerned with the rest of life.[35]

Again, she has demonstrated how gender affects our understanding of contract law: commercial contract law is central to the curriculum whereas contract issues within the family or involving relationships are peripheral.[36]

Similarly, Mary Joe's postmodern, feminist reading of impossibility doctrine demonstrates that gender identity establishes roles to which even legal commentary conforms. In defiance of established scholars of contract law, she shows, through a close analysis of language, how two authors' competing approaches to impossibility are gendered. One approach is rigid, and promises to "give content" to impossibility analysis. This approach she terms "phallic." The other is feminine in its attention to multiple sites of knowledge, contextuality, and flexibility. Mary Joe uses essentialist gender traits in analyzing the two approaches. Each approach however falters in its analytic coherence at a particular point; at this spot the authors of each opt for gender integrity, sacrificing a fuller explanation. The "masculine" interpretation responds with a bald, unsupported assertion; the "feminine" interpretation relies on "intuition" and a false denial of conflict. At the moment of maintaining gender integrity, each author marks the partiality of his interpretation. Once gain, Mary Joe has shown the power of gender to construct legal texts.

Mary Joe's careful readings of legal texts not only show the ways in which we use gender categories to help us understand apparently ungendered legal issues; they also disclose the ways in which law constructs gender. Gender identity is a discursive system; like all else, it is constituted by other discourses, including law. The rereading of the contracts casebook illustrates law's construction of gender as well as gender's construction of law. If the core of contracts is commercial cases dealing with the affairs of men, and if contracts relating to issues of concern to women are removed to separate courses, the student's understanding of proper gender roles is likely to be reinforced: "Men . . . are concerned with . . . life"; women appropriately busy themselves with private family problems. Traditional gender identities are further strengthened by the few women's occupations illustrated in the casebook's cases, in contrast to the breadth of men's occupations. Women's contract problems would appear to come only from their positions within the family, or from stereotypically female roles such as fashion designer or welfare recipient.[37]

Mary Joe's claim that law is constitutive of gender identity is not limited to gender statements in obviously constructed texts like casebooks. In the last section of this book she claims that law constructs women as terrorized, sexualized, and maternalized. Using the law of prostitution, she exposes the ways in which these meanings are formed. Prostitution makes certain sex acts illegal; since usually these are women's acts, women's sexuality is understood to be the subject of prostitution. Thus, women must constantly question their sexuality.

> This sexualization of the female body explains an experience many women have: an insistent concern that this outfit, this pose, this gesture may send the wrong signal—a fear of looking like a whore. Sexy talking, sexy walking, sexy dressing seem sexy, at least in part, because they are the telltale signs of a sex worker plying her trade.[38]

Prohibiting prostitution makes each of us potential prostitutes. We are constantly checking ourselves to see if we are prostitutes; our sexuality, regardless of whether we are or are not prostitutes, is constituted by the law's ban on prostitution. The anti-prostitution regulations also terrorize the female body. This occurs because of the relationship between prostitution regulations and other cultural practices such as the infection of sex work with drugs, AIDS, or the inadequate police protection for crimes committed against sex workers.[39] The regulation of prostitution also results in the maternalization of female bodies. Illegal sex is that which is not legal sex and legal sex is tied to reproduction and the legimation of the products of sex. Thus, anti-prostitution laws construct women's bodies as maternal, at the same time as they construct them as sexualized and terrorized.

Mary Joe's discussion of gender identities is carefully non-essentialist. She suggests that women's bodies, as constructed by the laws against prostitution, can be simultaneously sexualized, terrorized, *and* maternalized. They need not be defined in a single, unitary way. In fact, while sexualization, terrorization, and maternalization all describe women's bodies, they may also be in conflict with one another. Mary Joe recognizes that in order to think about women to improve women's condition one must use the category "women." This requires one to be able to define "women." Mary Joe thus uses gendered thinking as part of her strategy of showing how gender constructs law. She is wary however of the ways in which such essentialist positions limit our constructions of ourselves.

In chapter 3, Mary Joe asks whether women have "a different voice." In this chapter she criticizes the conservative reading of Carol Gilligan's *In a Different Voice*, which interprets Gilligan as saying that women make moral decisions based on their concern about relationships and the effects that their actions may have on others. If this is the basis of women's decisions, Mary Joe asks, does it mean that we should read the work of Justice O'Connor through the lens of relationships? The dangers in doing so, Mary Joe shows, are that such a reading may limit our understanding of the Justice's work, "imposing a stereotypically feminine image of womanliness on O'Connor's opinions"[40] and leaving us unable to understand opinions that do not fit the mold.

Essentialist definitions of women may also limit our lives. In her discussion of the Sears case, Mary Joe shows how historians Rosalind Rosenberg and Alice Kessler-Harris both described gender identities in essentialist ways.[41] In *Sears*, the EEOC had sued claiming sex discrimination in decisions as to who received commission sales posts. Rosenberg and Kessler-Harris served as expert witnesses for Sears and the EEOC, respectively. Rosenberg testified that women were less likely to choose commission sales than men because they were "less competitive than men" and "relation-centered" rather than "work-centered." Kessler-Harris claimed, for the EEOC, that women could succeed in traditional "men's" jobs, but she did not challenge their definition as "men's" jobs. Given these two essentialist stances on gender identity, Mary Joe notes that it is no surprise the court found for Sears. As she asks, "Why would we want to encourage women to become . . . [traditional men]?"[42] In this instance, essentialist definitions worked to limit who women could be.

Mary Joe's concern for the adverse affects of essentialist gender definitions led her to be constantly aware of the need to deconstruct gender identities and identities in general. She does this ingeniously in reading the contracts casebook by creating multiple readers and reading through their eyes. The readers vary from "The Feminist" through "The Reader with a Chip on the Shoulder" to "The Reader who is Undressed for Success." While each reader may represent a stereotype, taken together they allow Mary Joe humorously to analyze the casebook from multiple perspectives. Their multiplicity signals to the reader that he or she is not essentialized by this text.

In her reply to Jennifer Wicke's argument that law should not be "married" to postmodernism, Mary Joe shows how gender identities are fluid, not essentialist.[43] In an amusing series of rereadings, Mary Joe asks which would be the bride in such a marriage. First, she identifies law as the bridegroom, because Wicke implies that law is more powerful than postmodernism. But then, in a wonderful twist, Mary Joe suggests that maybe law is actually the bride; Wicke has described law "as a permeable membrane within which . . . struggle can be seen to exist." Each of Mary Joe's gendered understandings of the role of law in Wicke's analysis is supported by considerable evidence. Mary Joe's readings of law as both male and female deconstruct the claim that gender identities are fixed, unitary or essentialist.

Postmodern readings, like Mary Joe's, resist essentialist stances. Postmodern readings, with their twists and turns and doublings back on themselves, are a site for authorial and reader playfulness. They are, for example, a way of fighting the constraining male orientation of "sameness" approaches, the sticky-sweet nature of the image of woman as caregiver or the "vanilla sex Gestapo" stance of some who associated themselves with the antipornography campaign. Attention to multiple meanings helps prevent women from being portrayed as, for example, maternal, but unterrorized and sexless. This very attention of postmodern feminist readings to multiplicity and resistance to a sole definition of women has been criticized as resulting in apolitical stances.[44] In fact Jennifer Wicke's article makes exactly this point. She contends that women, gays, and other members of marginalized groups should not rely on postmodern readings in making their legal claims. As Mary Joe says, adding rhetorical flourish to Wicke's position, "you can't wage a revolution through interpretation

. . . you need tanks."⁴⁵ It was this claim of apoliticism to which Mary
Joe was responding in showing that interpretation is crucial. Without
it, you might think a tank (or a legal doctrine, or women) has only one
meaning. But, a tank may mean war, or a park monument, or a
plaything, or Presidential candidate Dukakis' downfall, or much
more. Tanks, like law, are meaningless without interpretation. Interpretation, the postmodern Mary Joe asserts, is what there is.

Interpretation is not only what there is. It is also a political tool.
Interpretation discloses space for change within established discourses. Part of the genius of this book is in uncovering how this
works. Postmodernism, Mary Joe shows, provides us with methods
for criticizing texts and their "status quo" politics. She dramatically
reconceptualizes *In a Different Voice* by using the relational traits
that Gilligan identifies as omitted from the predominant approach to
moral development as signs to the "location of the silenced, marginalized, or subordinated groups" who are excluded from dominating
discourses.⁴⁶ Mary Joe treats gender difference not as something real
and concrete waiting to be discovered, but as constructed by the
texts and their relationships to each other. Gender difference is thus
interpreted as an indication of what is excluded; its absence serves as
a point of critique. Mary Joe's rereading creates spaces for revision
within the larger body of work on moral development. Postmodern
readings need not be simply a way of providing politically flabby
rereadings *ad infinitum*; postmodernism can be a critical methodology.

The charge that postmodern feminism is not political has often been
tied to these feminists' antiessentialist stances. How can one possibly
act on behalf of women if the meaning of the category "women"
changes from context to context? For example, how can we even think
about strategies relating to pornography if women are simultaneously
understood as in control and as passive, if pornography is at the same
time about women's liberation and their domination? Mary Joe's
critique of the anti-pornography campaign provides an illustration
of how postmodernism can be empowering for women. The anti-
pornography campaign in the U.S. has been stalled, and Mary Joe
suggests that one of the reasons for this may have been its exploitation
of the essentialist male/female dichotomy. While attacking hierarchy
in order to oppose its sexualization, the ordinance campaign utilized
the power of "male" language and male-identified positions.⁴⁷ Pro-
ordinance advocates dismissed their opponents as "individualistic";
they defined pornography as unnuanced, having only one (phallic)
meaning: "rip and slash." In both its subject and its practice, the anti-

pornography campaign reinforced the limiting, dualistic nature of traditional conceptions of sex.

Again, Mary Joe's postmodern methodology is a tool for her feminist politics. By paying careful attention to the discourse of the anti-pornography campaign she is able to provide constructive criticism. If sex is the basis of women's oppression through pornography, then it is sex that must be reconceived. This, she argues, can not be done usefully if the debate simply recreates the traditional categories of sex. Instead, Mary Joe suggests that a "less dichotomized approach to the problem of the oppression of women by sex would have been more likely to change the way we think and act about sex."[48] We should consider the variety of materials that are sometimes called pornographic (not just those involving overt violence against women) and the multiple ways in which pornography users may identify across sexual lines. In complicating the analysis in these, and other ways, we may be able to deconstruct our dichotomous ideas about sex, creating political spaces within which we can recreate ourselves.

Postmodern approaches to feminism have also been criticized for their emphasis on the ways in which gender meanings are constructed by discourse. If our identities are constituted by language and discourse, how is agency possible? Yet, we recognize women as agents, often acting in resistance to the dominant structures. Slave women resisted in innumerable ways, large and small. Battered women's resort to violence or flight from their batterers are modes of resistance. Prostitutes resist through multiple mechanisms, including hiding money from their pimps or leaving the business. We all resist the structures of male domination daily. How can this be possible if we are constituted by the discourses of these structures?

Mary Joe intervenes powerfully at this point to show how postmodern approaches need not be interpreted as erasing agency. Gender, like power or meaning, is not created once by discourse to then exist in a single form forever more. Instead, it is constantly remade, each time in relationship to those that preceeded it. The relationship could be one of opposition, nuanced difference, or an effort at repetition. But no repetition can be exact. Even if the effort is to generate an exact copy, the new version will differ in meaning precisely because it is the newer, not the older, version. There is a difference between a copy and what it copies, between a prior rendition and a present one. Meaning, never static, is recreated with a *différance* in each usage.

Gender is no different. It is constantly recreating itself. It obtains new meanings from continuous efforts to repeat prescribed meanings. Gender is a role that will be played differently each time. As such, agency, or the possibility of resistance to prescribed gender roles, exists as the parody of a past expression of gender. Judith Butler says, "The injunction *to be* a given gender produces necessary failures, a variety of incoherent configurations that in their multiplicity exceed and defy the injunction by which they are generated."[49] It is not necessary to posit a self that exists outside of discourse in order to have agency. Such a self does not exist. Instead, agency can only be "a taking up of the tools where they lie, where the very 'taking up' is enabled by the tool lying there."[50]

Postmodern Legal Feminism illustrates, in the legal context, where the tools lie. They may lie where gender has slipped in its role-play or where it has been supplemented. This is why Mary Joe's gendered readings of legal texts are so path-breaking. They demonstrate for us where the points of agency may exist. Mary Joe has carefully identified these for us in her analyses of the anti-pornography campaign, impossibility doctrine, Jennifer Wicke's work, and *In a Different Voice*. We are left to locate them for ourselves in the many other issues facing women: violence, high infant mortality rates, prostitution, impoverishment, inadequate working conditions and pay, abortion, health care, and so on. What Mary Joe has shown is that the use of gendered analysis sometimes simply perpetuates the rigid categories within which we now live, but sometimes unveils a gender performance that differs from the role set for it. Her readings disclose openings for action.

Mary Joe's work rescues postmodernism from the claim that it is apolitical or worse yet, politically regressive. She demonstrates the gendered nature of legal thought and how law constructs gender, while simultaneously deconstructing the concept of gender. Many understand legal thought as defining our gender and being defined by it. But Mary Joe disputes that dichotomous portrayal of discourse. Gender, she shows, does not exist prior to or outside of legal discourse, to be written upon by it. Instead, what Mary Joe shows is the way that legal discourse is gendered by its own rules which provide meanings in accordance with which both it and we perform. This is already a political statement since it ruptures the boundaries between law and politics. Law, it turns out, is a general in the battle between the sexes.

Mary Joe's work goes farther than this however. While she uncovers through postmodern readings a politics of the law, she also discloses through reading law, a postmodern feminist politics. She shows not only that agency, resistance, and change are possible within postmodern readings, but that gendered postmodern readings can uncover their possible locations. Furthermore, she reminds us that if sex is the basis of our oppression, it is thought about sex and sexual practices themselves that we must change in order to be freed. This she warns will not be possible so long as we reiterate in our own arguments, unconsciously, the markings of gender. Instead, we must consciously deploy language to reveal new strategies of interpreting sex and gender that will display their noncongealed, contingent meanings. "Only," she concludes, "when sex means more than male or female, only when the word 'woman' cannot be coherently understood, will oppression by sex be fatally undermined."

JUDITH G. GREENBERG
*New England School of Law,
Boston, 1992*

Notes

1. For almost a decade Mary Joe Frug was my colleague, feminist sister, source of intellectual stimulation, and friend. My work on this introduction has been a way for me to deny her death and memorialize her life. I want to thank Jerry Frug, Phil Hamilton, Duncan Kennedy, Martha Minow, Anne Simon, Elizabeth Spahn, and especially Ken Greenberg, for their comments on innumerable drafts of this introduction—as well as for their support during this past year.

2. Her dialogues with these other feminists were both academic and personal. Many of them were her close friends; most of the people whose work is cited in these footnotes were influenced personally and in their work by Mary Joe. In turn, she was influenced by them.

3. National Committee on Pay Equity, Pay Equity: An Issue of Race, Ethnicity and Sex, excerpted in Mary Joe Frug, Women and the Law (1992) 141.

4. Postmodern Legal Feminism 333 (hereinafter referred to as PLF).

5. Ruth Bader Ginsberg, Some Reflections on the Feminist Legal Thought of the 1970s, 1989 U. Chi. Legal F. 9.

6. 417 U.S. 484 (1974).

7. PLF 50.

8. C. Gilligan, In a Different Voice (1982).

9. The articles arguing that the legal system might be different if created by women instead of men include Ruth Colker, Feminist Litigation: An Oxymoran?—A Study of the Briefs Filed in *William L. Webster v. Reproductive Health Services*, 13 Harv. Women's L. J. 137 (1990); Carrie Menkel-Meadow, Portia in a Different Voice: Speculations on a Woman's Lawyering Process, 1 Berkeley Women's L. J. 39 (1985); Judith Resnik, On the Bias: Feminist Reconsiderations of the Aspirations for Our

Judges, 61 S. Cal. L. Rev. 1877 (1988). For other cultural feminist positions see Martha Fineman, Dominant Discourse, Professional Language, and Legal Change in Child Custody Decisionmaking, 101 Harv. L. Rev. 727 (1988); Robin West, The Difference in Women's Hedonic Lives: A Phenomenological Critique of Feminist Legal Theory, 3 Wis. Women's L. J. 81 (1987). For a critique of the suggestion that mediation is necessarily a woman-oriented system of dispute resolution see Trina Grillo, The Mediation Alternative: Process Dangers for Women, 100 Yale L. J. 1545 (1991).

10. For critiques of this position see Joan Scott, Deconstructing Equality-Versus-Difference: Or, the Uses of Poststructural Theory for Feminism, 14 Feminist Stud. 33 (1988); Vicki Schultz, Telling Stories About Women and Work: Judicial Interpretations of Sex Segregation in the Workplace in Title VII Cases Raising the Lack of Interest Argument, 103 Harv. L. Rev. 1749 (1990); Joan Williams, Deconstructing Gender, 87 Mich. L. Rev. 797 (1989).

11. Other feminist work recognizes women's differences from men and the necessity for consideration of these differences within the law, but grounds these differences not in culture, but in socioeconomic or biological structures. Mary Joe Frug argued that, given current social and economic structures, equality claims will necessarily result in a demonstration of difference; see Securing Job Equality for Women: Labor Market Hostility to Working Women, 59 B.U. L. Rev. 55 (1979). For an argument that women's differences are based in our reproductive capacities see Sylvia Law, Rethinking Sex and the Constitution, 132 U. Pa. L. Rev. 955 (1984).

12. For the discussion of the dominance model in MacKinnon's books, see Sexual Harassment of Working Women: A Case of Sex Discrimination (1979); Feminism Unmodified: Discourses on Life and Law (1987) (hereinafter referred to as Feminism Unmodified); Toward a Feminist Theory of The State (1989) (hereinafter referred to as Feminist Theory).

13. While MacKinnon's name is often associated with the dominance theory, so is that of Andrea Dworkin. For an example of her work see Pornography: Men Possessing Women (1971, rev'd. introduction 1989). Many other legal feminists have also contributed significantly to the model. See, e.g., Christine Littleton, Reconstructing Sexual Equality, 75 Cal. L. Rev. 1279 (1987); Ann Scales, The Emergence of Feminist Jurisprudence: An Essay, 95 Yale L. J. 1373 (1986); Elizabeth Spahn, On Sex and Violence, 20 New Eng. L. Rev. 629 (1984–85). For a position that uses difference and dominance models, see Leslie Bender, From Gender Difference to Feminist Solidarity: Using Carol Gilligan and an Ethic of Care in Law, 15 Vt. L. Rev. 1 (1990).

14. Feminism Unmodified 40 (1987).

15. The methodology of focusing on experiential knowledge, used by MacKinnon and other legal feminists, has generated significant discussion.

For examples of others who rely heavily on their own experiences, see Marie Ashe, Zig-Zag Stiching and the Seamless Web: Thoughts on "Reproduction" and the Law, 13 Nova L. Rev. 355 (1989); Patricia J. Williams, The Alchemy of Race and Rights (1991). For discussions of the value of experiential knowledge, see Kathryn Abrams, Hearing the Call of Stories, 79 Cal. L. Rev. 971 (1991); Elizabeth Schneider, The Dialectic of Rights and Politics: Perspectives from the Women's Movement, 61 N.Y.U. L. Rev. 589 (1986).

16. Meritor Savings Bank, FSB v. Vinson, 477 U.S. 57 (1986).

17. The ordinance was held unconstitutional in American Booksellers Association v. Hudnut, 771 F.2d 323 (7th Cir., 1985) aff'd, 475 U.S. 1001 (1986). A related statute has recently been upheld in Canada, R. v. Butler, #22191 (S.C.C. February 27, 1992).

18. Feminist Theory 129.

19. Feminism Unmodified 161. Some commentators have speculated that this overdetermination is strategic. See, for example, Frances Olsen, Feminist Theory in Grand Style, 89 Colum. L. Rev. 1147 (1989); Kathryn Abrams, Ideology and Women's Choices, 24 Georgia L. Rev. 761 (1990).

20. For other postmodern legal feminist work, see Marie Ashe, Law-Language of Maternity: Discourse Holding Nature in Contempt, 22 New Eng. L. Rev. 521 (1988); Drucilla Cornell, The Philosophy of the Limit (1992); Drucilla Cornell, Beyond Accommodation (1991); Clare Dalton, An Essay in the Deconstruction of Contract Doctrine, 94 Yale L. J. 997 (1985); Martha Minow, Beyond Universality, 1989 U. Chi Legal F. 115; Frances Olsen, Statutory Rape: A Feminist Critique of Rights Analysis, 63 Tex. L. Rev. 387 (1984); Deborah Rhode, Feminist Critical Theories, 42 Stan. L. Rev. 617 (1990). For a rejection of postmodernism in legal feminism, see Robin West, Feminism, Critical Social Theory and Law, 1989 U. Chi. Legal F. 59.

21. Feminist Theory 129.

22. Feminist Theory xii.

23. For excellent discussions of perspectivity, see Katharine Bartlett, Feminist Legal Methods, 103 Harv. L. Rev. 829 (1990); Mari Matsuda, When the First Quail Calls: Multiple Consciousness as Jurisprudential Method, 11 Women's Rts. L. Rep. 7 (1989); Martha Minow, The Supreme Court 1986 Foreword: Justice Engendered, 101 Harv. L. Rev. 10 (1987).

24. Feminism Unmodified 172.

25. Feminist Theory xi. See also, Catharine MacKinnon, From Practice to Theory, or What is a White Woman Anyway? 4 Yale J. L. & Feminism 13 (1991) (hereinafter Practice/Theory).

26. Practice/Theory 15 (emphasis added).

27. For works by feminists critical of feminist exclusions based on race, ethnicity, nationality, and sexual orientation, see Regina Austin, Sap-

phire Bound, 1989 Wis. L. Rev. 539; Hazel Carby, Reconstructing Womanhood: The Emergence of the Afro-American Woman Novelist (1987); Ruth Colker, The Example of Lesbians: A Posthumous Reply to Professor Mary Joe Frug, 105 Harv. L. Rev. 1084 (1992); Kimberlé Crenshaw, Demarginalizing the Intersection of Race and Sex: A Black Feminist Critique of Antidiscrimination Doctrine, Feminist Theory and Antiracist Politics, 1989 U. Chi. Legal F. 139; Kimberlé Crenshaw, Mapping the Margins: Identity-Politics, Intersectionality and Violence Against Women (unpublished manuscript); Nitya Duclos, Lessons of Difference: Feminist Theory on Cultural Difference, 38 Buffalo L. Rev. 328 (1990); Angela Harris, Race and Essentialism in Feminist Legal Theory, 42 Stan. L. Rev. 581 (1990); bell hooks, Feminist Theory: From Margin to Center (1984); Audre Lorde, Sister Outsider (1984); Celina Romany, Ain't I a Feminist? 4 Yale J. L. & Feminism 23 (1991); Judy Scales-Trent, Black Women and the Constitution, Finding Our Place, Asserting Our Rights, 24 Harv. C.R.—C. L. L. Rev. 9 (1989); Elizabeth Spelman, *Inessential Woman: Problems of Exclusion in Feminist Thought* (1989).

28. Susan Keller, Review Essay, 18 Western St. U. L. Rev. 463 (1990).

29. Susan Suleiman, Pornography, Transgression, and the Avant-Garde: Bataille's *Story of the Eye,* in The Poetics of Gender (Nancy K. Miller ed. 1986).

30. Richard Wollheim, Painting as an Art 175 (1987).

31. Susan Gubar, Representing Pornography: Feminism, Criticism, and Depictions of Female Violation, in For Adult Users Only: The Dilemma of Violent Pornography (Gubar and Hoff eds. 1989). Similarly, Gubar notes the visual play in an image reproduced in *Minotaure* in which four erotically posed female nudes appear as a male profile.

32. Susan Keller, Powerless to Please: Candida Royalle's Pornography for Women, 26 New Eng. L. Rev. (forthcoming 1992). For a further discussion of pornography that involves extreme violence by women as well as by men, see Andrea Dworkin, Pornography: Men Possessing Women 30–36 (1989).

33. For discussions of the ways in which law is gendered, see Lucinda Finley, Breaking Women's Silence in Law: The Dilemma of the Gendered Nature of Legal Reasoning, 64 Notre Dame L. Rev. 886 (1989); Frances Olsen, The Sex of Law, in The Politics of Law (David Kairys ed., rev. ed. 1990).

34. PLF 49; see also Martha Minow, Beyond Universality, 1989 U. Chi. Legal F. 115 (1989). For discussions of using the category "women" while avoiding exclusionary essentialism see, Catharine MacKinnon, Practice/Theory; Diana Fuss, Essentially Speaking: Feminism, Nature and Difference (1989).

35. PLF 71.

36. Since Mary Joe initially began to write and lecture on gender and contracts law other feminists have begun to review other law school fields,

see e.g. Leslie Bender, A Lawyer's Primer on Feminist Theory and Tort, 38 J. Legal Ed. 3 (1988); Lucinda Finley, A Break in the Silence: Including Women's Issues in a Torts Course, 1 Yale L. J. & Feminism 41 (1989).

37. PLF 62.

38. PLF 132; For a description of the particular ways in which law and the media construct black women as prostitutes see Regina Austin, For Mary Joe and Black Women, Sisterhood and the Difference/Deviance Divide, 26 New Eng. L. Rev. 877 (1992), and Mary Joe Frug, Difference, Community and Sexual Politics: A comment on Regina Austin's Black Women, Sisterhood, and the Difference/Deviance Divide, 26 New Eng. L. Rev. 889 (1992).

39. Mary Joe notes that the conflation of sexualization and terrorization would result in a MacKinnonesque position; their radical separation allows Madonna to claim she is "in charge," undominated. Mary Joe's own position on the relationship between sexualization and terrorization is between MacKinnon's and Madonna's, PLF 134.

40. PLF 47.

41. PLF 13 and following.

42. PLF 16.

43. PLF 18 and following.

44. Susan Bordo, Feminism, Postmodernism and Gender-Scepticism, in Feminism/Postmodernism, 133 (Linda Nicholson ed. 1990); Katharine Bartlett, Feminist Legal Methods, 103 Harv. L. Rev. 829 (1990).

45. PLF 20.

46. PLF 48.

47. PLF 152.

48. PLF 152.

49. Judith Butler, Gender Trouble: Feminism and the Subversion of Identity 145 (1990).

50. Id.

Feminist Doctrine

1

Sexual Equality and Sexual Difference in American Law

The problem of the relationship between sexual difference and equality is illustrated for me by a story told by a woman about her reactions to watching a male friend shop for a suit. Although the man chose a suit which was too short in the arms, too long in the legs, and too tight in the pants, he looked at his reflection in the mirror and said with cheerful confidence, "This looks great. Send for the tailor." The woman reported realizing that if she had been in his position she would have looked at herself in the mirror and said, "This looks terrible. My arms are too long, my legs are too short and my rear is too fat."

Feminist legal scholars over the past fifteen years have generated a body of law review articles on the problem of sexual difference and equality which might be read to suggest several strategies for explaining and re-dressing the sad disparity between the reactions of these two people in their suits. For some feminists, the lesson of the story would be that clothing stores should be transformed, so that women could find power outfits as easily as men, so that we would routinely have tailors standing ready to deal with the divergences between our garments and our bodies. For other feminists, the lesson of the story would be that women somehow must learn to feel more comfortable with our actual appearances, that we should give up our desire to conform to the fantasies men have invented for feminine attractiveness. Still other feminists might challenge such conclusions, arguing that integrating men's clothing stores and validating women's bodies constitute strategies which themselves are likely to recreate and perpetuate the problem of the relationship between sexual difference and equality. For these feminists, whom I designate the postmoderns, equality must come to mean something other than a choice between treating people the same or treating them differently.

Since that choice has consistently functioned to require that women either conform to a male standard of conduct or accept inferior treatment as a condition of acknowledging the differences between women and men, the postmoderns maintain that we should try to combat our oppression by avoiding the sameness/difference choice. The tough problem, of course, is how to do that.

The issue of what constitutes equality for women and how they can achieve it is the heart of the feminist legal project. It is implicated by any quest women undertake to combat their subordinate circumstances through legal change. Indeed, although it usually goes unrecognized or unacknowledged, the problem of the relationship between sexual difference and equality is also involved in any efforts lawmakers undertake to structure a just society.

In this chapter, I will describe four approaches feminist legal scholars have taken to the problem of the relationship between sexual difference and equality. This will be a history and a typology of feminist legal scholarship since the early 1970s. Although feminists were actively concerned with the legal treatment of women long before the 1970s, the seventies mark an extraordinary emergence of a significant body of law review articles devoted to the problem of using law either to improve the position of women or to eliminate the constraints of gender on both sexes. I divide the feminist legal scholarship that has been produced since the seventies into four groups of articles, groups which I label equality doctrine, equality theory, feminist theory, and feminist doctrine. These categories roughly but not inevitably coincide with historical divisions. I believe each category of scholarship I will describe has had and retains significant value for women's efforts to fight their oppression. But I claim that the postmodern form of feminist legal scholarship—the version I designate feminist doctrine—currently offers the most promise to women and their cause.

Equality Doctrine

Equality doctrine articles were principally written during the seventies, when the campaign for the Equal Rights Amendment was a spirited and ongoing issue, and sex-based legal classifications restricting women from participation in public life were much more prevalent than they are today. This was the period when the enforcement of state and federal employment discrimination laws was just cranking up, and unanswered questions about how far such laws would change the widespread sex segregation of the work force led to one litigation battle after another. Equality doctrinalists analyzed how the position of women could be improved by using and extending civil rights statutes or the Constitution in their behalf. Indeed, since some of the articles were written by women who were litigating cases of that sort, these scholars often implicitly addressed their arguments to other litigators and to judges who were handling sex discrimination issues.

A dominant doctrinal issue in this period was the scope of the developing equality standard. Litigators and commentators turned to the Equal Protection Clause as a means of combating adverse treatment of women, seeking to bring laws which disproportionately disadvantaged women as well as overtly sex-based laws within its aegis.[1] Under the equality standard as it had been understood since Tussman and tenBroek,[2] the equal protection guarantee required only that similarly situated classes be treated similarly. Believing that legislatures could treat women differently than men only if women were understood to be differently situated, those working to advance women assumed a sex-blind posture regarding sex differences. Equality doctrinalists argued either that there were no differences between women or men, or they argued that sexual differences should be considered legally irrelevant. Attempting to make women and men appear similarly situated in a context of social and economic inequality required equality advocates to assume contorted and unconvincing sex-blind postures.[3] They justified this somewhat hypocritical stance, in my view, because at least one tantalizing Supreme Court decision suggested such a strategy would lead to sweeping legal reforms.[4] In the end, however, in several crushingly disappointing cases[5] the Supreme Court refused to go along. Being sex-blind with your fingers crossed turned out not to work.

Outside the context of their efforts to extend equality guarantees to women, some equality doctrinalists cautiously acknowledged the legal relevance of sexual differences as part of a strategy to extend Constitutional liberty and privacy guarantees to women.[6] At the same time, therefore, that advocates were maintaining an almost sex-blind attitude regarding equality litigation, they were also aggressively assuming a sex-specific attitude toward the relationship between law and reproductive rights in cases involving abortion and pregnancy. Ultimately, however, this doctrinal strategy also fell far short of achieving equality for women, as women won Constitutional protection against the criminalization of abortions[7] but lost their efforts to obtain a Constitutional right to funding for such procedures.[8]

Equality doctrine articles may have helped women secure a number of positive legal changes, but the litigation losses women also suffered utilizing the strategies of equality doctrine indicated that this jurisprudence had certain shortcomings. These shortcomings were analyzed in a second group of articles in feminist legal scholarship, the group of articles I label equality theory articles.

Equality Theory

Equality theorists attempted to account for the doctrinal failures of discrimination law by exploring the origins, the conflicts, or the unstated assumptions underlying conventional interpretations of the equality standard. Their articles are less closely connected to ongoing litigation than are articles in the equality doctrine category, but equality theorists nevertheless implicitly address litigators, judges, and also legislators in their writing, urging them to rethink and reframe equality laws.[9]

Equality theorists claimed that conventional equality has not been calibrated on a neutral principle but has been constructed pursuant to a male perspective. This insight liberated equality theorists from the inhibitions of the sex-blind posture that equality doctrinalists thought they must assume; it permitted them to argue that equality for women should not be predicated on a requirement that women demonstrate their similarities to men. It also permitted equality theorists to confront and debate the issues of which sex differences should matter and how much difference should be tolerated in the interpretation of equality.

Equality theorists have been primarily responsible for the specialized, shifting vocabulary and rationales utilized in challenges to conventional sex-equality doctrine. Thus, it is in this group of articles that one encounters the concepts of equal versus special treatment,[10] equal treatment versus equal achievement,[11] assimilation versus acceptance,[12] and difference versus anti-domination.[13]

In addition to disputing the neutrality of the equality principle, equality theorists also questioned the merit of conventional equality. They questioned whether male privileges and responsibilities were socially valuable and desirable. Rather than apologetically and covertly seeking child care benefits, for example, on the grounds of special treatment or fundamental rights analyses, equality theorists introduced the possibility of gender pride to jurists. They argued that women's needs were noble, significant and worthy concerns which the equality principle should embrace with dignity rather than tolerate with condescension or ignore.

The shortcomings of equality theory and the problems entailed by choosing sameness or difference were illustrated forcefully and publicly by the debate among feminists during the 1986–87 term of the U.S. Supreme Court. In arguments, articles, and briefs connected to *California Federal Savings & Loan v. Guerra*,[14] some feminists argued that since women must be like men in order to have equal status in the workplace they should not seek to obtain childbirth benefits.[15] Other feminists argued that since women have unique reproductive characteristics and responsibilities, equality doctrine should afford them special treatment, in the form of childbirth benefits, even if those benefits might reduce their public stature by flagging women's unique needs.[16] The problem with the arguments about women in the *Cal. Fed.* case was not that one argument was true and the other false. Rather, both arguments were simultaneously true: women can be like men in the workplace, but they can also undergo reproductive experiences which can make them different. *Cal. Fed.* demonstrates the way in which the claim that women are either the same as men or they are different forces decisionmakers into risky choices. Either women get benefits or they don't, depending in large part on what a decisionmaker decides women are *really* like.[17]

Like equality doctrine work, equality theory articles have been important to litigation brought on behalf of women, and they may also be influential in the general jurisprudence of equality. Despite this success, however, equality theorists came to acknowledge the limitations of their own critique. Scholar after scholar has admitted a stalemate in the legal project of seeking women's liberation through an equality strategy.[18] The penetrating criticisms which these articles leveled against equality doctrine were unable to alter the conventional relationship between sexual difference and equality; legislator, litigator, judge, and legal scholar still had to choose between treating women and men similarly or differently, and both choices were apt to produce unsatisfying results, particularly for women.

Feminist Theory

I designate the third group of feminist legal scholarship articles the feminist theory category. Often inspired by feminist theory in disciplines other than law, these articles move beyond arguments relating to the extension of legal doctrine or critiques relating to the equality guarantee. Their subject is the more general question of how legal doctrine works in conjunction with other systemic factors to keep women oppressed. It is under the influence of this scholarship that I can evaluate the problems I will shortly identify in the previous groups of feminist legal scholarship.

Catharine MacKinnon, a principal author of the Minneapolis anti-pornography ordinance and the architect of current sexual harassment law, is a particularly trenchant and significant feminist theorist.[19] Under her influence, articles in the feminist theory category of feminist legal scholarship have identified a politics of gender which infests and contaminates not only conventional equality doctrine but other law as well. MacKinnon argues that focusing on the difference between women and men as a way to obtain equality for women is a doomed enterprise in a society in which power is distributed unequally between the sexes. Indeed, this form of legal analysis perpetuates male oppression of women. "[D]ifference is abstract and falsely symmetrical," MacKinnon has written. "[A] discourse of gender difference serves as ideology to neutralize, rationalize, and cover disparities of power, even as it appears to criticize them. Difference is the velvet glove on the iron fist of domination."[20]

The critique of sexual difference and the shift to a focus on power— the politics of gender, as I am calling these ideas—has had significant implications for the agenda of feminists working in law. This aspect of feminist theory substantiates and furthers the equality theorists' charge that the equality standard is based on a false neutrality. In addition, embracing the politics of gender has encouraged legal feminists to look beyond equality doctrine in order to locate and develop challenges to other centers of power which are closely related to male dominance. By pointing out new law-related arenas of struggle— domestic violence programs, divorce reforms, and the anti-pornography ordinance campaign are examples—this group of articles has offered transformative guidance as well as illuminating criticism to feminist legal scholars.

In addition to the politics of gender, feminist theorists have also questioned the epistemology of gender. That is, in addition to analyzing the allocation of power between the sexes, feminist theorists have also written about the meaning of gender; they have addressed the issue of how sexual difference is constructed and perpetuated by complex social practices, including law.[21] I find the feminist theoretical critique of the epistemology of gender particularly useful in evaluating the assumptions about sexual difference that underlie equality doctrine and equality theory. Indeed, although the analysis that follows is my own, I associate it with feminist theory scholarship and elaborate it in this section of the discussion because feminist theory has been critical to my development of these views.[22]

As I suggested in my description of equality doctrine and equality theory, scholars in both groups argue that the law should either ignore or accommodate sexual differences. The assumption underlying these arguments is that sexual difference can be defined by reference to two separately defined bundles of "feminine" and "masculine" characteristics. Because these bundles are generally understood to contain a predictable or essential group of traits which are relatively intractable, this attitude toward sexual difference is sometimes referred to as "essentialist."[23] Although an essentialist stance toward sexual difference unites a number of scholars writing in several different genres of feminist legal scholarship, there are distinctions among them regarding the value of femininity and the degree to which sexual differences may be modified by changes in the law. I refer to these distinctions by the categories of negative and cultural feminisms.

Negative Feminism

The group of feminists I designate as negative feminists believe that women are defined as what men are not, as in: "(unlike men) women are not active, not rational, and not aggressive." Negative feminists acknowledge the degraded character which this negative definition casts on our sexual identity, but they believe that sexual difference is a consequence of the superior social and economic power of men over women. Under this etiology of sexual differences, women are what the pornography industry implies: we are holes. Zeros. Ciphers. Because our identity has been wholly constructed by men, we cannot know what a true feminine identity might be. Nevertheless, negative feminists actively oppose the negative sexual identity that has been imposed on women. They seek to change the social order so that women can be whole. Like men. This aspiration is somewhat problematical, because if women are either not-men or what-they-make-us we cannot know what form our self-actualization might take in the absence of male control.

Cultural Feminism

Like negative feminists, cultural feminists also describe sexual difference in oppositional terms. Women are what men are not. But in contrast to negative feminists, cultural feminists appeal to more positive, stereotypically female terms in their description of women's characteristics. Their position about sexual difference is that although men often mistakenly describe women pejoratively by comparing them unfavorably with themselves, the qualities commonly linked with our sex—qualities such as passivity and emotionality—are noble characteristics. These qualities make us nurturing, attentive, and selfless—traits which should be affirmed, rather than denigrated. Cultural feminists believe that women have a unique, feminine identity which men have prevented them from fully developing. They seek, therefore, to challenge the social constraints which devalue and suppress femininity.

Both negative and cultural feminisms have powerful evangelical potential as political organizing themes, although I believe the anger and pessimism connected with negative feminism produces a more positive political residue than the form of sentimental boosterism that often accompanies cultural feminism.[24] Both feminisms, however, represent stances toward the construction of sexual difference which can pose harmful consequences for our common cause. Both attitudes confuse the commonality of women with a universal woman, and both define the content of sexual difference in polarized, dichotomous terms which imply an essentialist gendered selfhood. The inability of equality doctrine and equality theory scholars to break out of the sameness/difference paradigm is directly linked, in my view, to the similarly dualistic or essentialist framework in which sexual difference is deployed in their work.

Feminist theory is still an active, lively genre of feminist legal scholarship, but to the extent that this work is elaborately self-referential and abstract, to the extent that it seeks to account decisively for a single cause of women's oppression through law, or to the extent that it neglects to attend to its own insights regarding the epistemology of gender, its analytical and political force is jeopardized.[25] The articles I assign to the category of feminist doctrine are heavily dependent on the critiques developed within feminist theory, but this scholarship is distinguished from feminist theory by its integration of theory and doctrine and by its anti-essentialist attitude toward women in relation to law.

Feminist Doctrine

Scholars writing in this category of feminist legal scholarship explicitly acknowledge differences among women. Rather than adopting a static or fixed definition of femininity, they define sexual difference by the relationships or context in which sexual difference is asserted. This stance toward sexual difference leads them to explore concrete, specific legal rules or doctrines that are of interest to particular groups of women; it also leads them to analyze the complex social practices in which laws are taught and used. The significance of shifting points of view and the commitment to an anti-essentialist depiction of human nature within this scholarship are the characteristics that make me link feminist doctrine with postmodern scholarship.[26]

Feminist doctrinalists do not depend on a single doctrinal standard to define equality. Rather, these scholars seek equality for women through law by questioning, recontextualizing, and attempting to unsettle existing laws in a wide range of areas. Because, unlike feminist theorists, they avoid the dichotomous imagery associated with cultural and negative feminisms by invoking diverse, multiplicitous images of women in their work, I believe that feminist doctrinalists offer constructive promise for breaking through the doctrinal impasse of traditional sexual equality doctrine.

In order to indicate more concretely the character of feminist doctrine, let me now turn, for an illustration of this genre, to the discussion of some specific examples.

2

Feminist Doctrine

The Sears Case

In 1973 the Equal Employment Opportunity Commission (EEOC) brought charges of sex discrimination against Sears, Roebuck and Co., the "largest retailer of general merchandise" and the largest civilian employer of women in the United States.[1] After eleven years of investigation and a ten month trial before a U.S. federal district judge in Chicago, the charges against Sears were dismissed in an opinion issued in 1986.[2] This decision was affirmed by a divided panel of the U.S. Court of Appeals for the Seventh Circuit in January 1988.[3]

My reason for discussing this complex litigation is the EEOC's claim that Sears discriminated against women by failing to hire and promote proportionate numbers of women in commission sales positions. The EEOC based this claim on statistics which showed roughly that although two-thirds of the applicants and promotion candidates for commission sales positions were women, women constituted only one-fourth of those actually hired or promoted.[4]

At the time when *Sears* was litigated, employment discrimination law provided that once a complainant demonstrated disproportionate statistics, the employer was allowed the opportunity to come forward with a nondiscriminatory explanation to justify imbalance in the company.[5] Sears explained the low number of women in commission sales by introducing evidence which described commission sales work and which set forth the personality traits the company considered commission sales workers needed in order to be effective. Specifically, Sears described commission sales work as: (1) the sale of "big ticket" items, such as major appliances, roofing, air conditioning, and sewing machines; (2) work which was compensated by commission or a combination of commission and flat sum; (3) work which, despite the "risk" inherent in compensation by commission, is more highly paid than straight saleswork; (4) work which could take personnel away from the stores and which could, therefore, feel more isolated and require more independence than straight saleswork; and (5) work which sometimes required technical knowledge.[6] Sears officials testified that effective commission sales workers should be (1) aggressive, (2) outgoing and good with people, (3) highly motivated, (4) already informed about their products, and (5) "leaders."[7]

Having described commission sales work and commission sales workers' ideal personality traits, Sears then continued its explanation for the disproportionately low number of women in commission sales by introducing testimony which described commonalities among women in relationship to their work.[8] Sears called upon feminist historian Rosalind Rosenberg for evidence drawn from social history that women have traditionally subordinated their paid labor activities to their domestic responsibilities.[9] In rebuttal, the EEOC called upon feminist historian Alice Kessler-Harris to testify that women have successfully undertaken "nontraditional" paid labor on the unusual occasions when employers allowed them to do so.[10] Relying on these historical claims, the witnesses then reached opposite conclusions on whether Sears should be considered responsible for the low number of women in commission sales.[11]

My argument is that in reaching their conclusions both feminist historians masculinized the traits needed to work in commission sales. That is, they interpreted Sears' description of the ideal commission sales worker by reference to a particular masculine stereotype. In addition, the historians' descriptions of women in the paid labor force suggested two opposing feminine stereotypes, neither of which fit the stereotypically male model of sales worker. The social history on which the historians relied did not require the essentialist stance toward women which the witnesses, particularly Rosenberg, adopted in their testimony. Similarly, if the historians had relied on a less stereotypically male image of the successful commission sales worker in drawing conclusions about the relationship between the social history of women workers and women's general aptitude for commission sales, Sears' explanation for the lack of women in commission sales might have seemed less convincing. Relying fully on the advantages of hindsight, therefore, I would like to propose both an alternative interpretation of the evidence that the feminist historians used in their testimony as well as a less stereotypically masculine depiction of the successful commission sales worker. My objective is to demonstrate in a concrete situation how sexual difference can be discussed without resorting to dichotomized description in which

maleness and femaleness are presented as rigidly opposite characteristics.

Sears' witness Rosalind Rosenberg,[12] relying on Carol Gilligan's
work as well as others', testified that because women as a group
tended to subordinate their careers to the needs of their families, they
were less likely than men to *choose* commission sales work.[13] She
described women as "feminine," "nurturant," and "selfless"; "relation-
centered" rather than "work-centered," and "less competitive than
men."[14] She asserted that employers should not be blamed for these
traits,[15] although she also indicated that women themselves were not
responsible for their attitudes toward work. She argued, rather, that
women have been "trained," "exhorted," and "socialized" to be the
way they are.[16]

EEOC's witness, Alice Kessler-Harris,[17] disputed Rosenberg's position that women "have" different interests which lead them to "choose"
other jobs over commission saleswork. She claimed that women's
qualifications for and attitudes toward work depend on the "framework of available opportunity."[18] "What appear to be women's choices
and what are characterized as women's interests are, in fact, heavily
influenced by the opportunities for work made available to them."[19]
Having argued that women and men can adapt their personalities to
their circumstances, Kessler-Harris then recounted many examples
of women successfully undertaking traditional men's work—she mentioned welders, crane operators, and typesetters, as well as insurance
and real estate workers and others.[20] Unfortunately, although she
asserted that "women's traditional roles are neither deeply rooted in
women's psyche nor do they form a barrier that inhibits women's
work force participation,"[21] she did not acknowledge how few women
had undertaken the "men's" jobs she described, and she did not dispute Rosenberg's essentialist depiction of domestic women.

Just as Kessler-Harris failed to dispute the feminine attributes
which Rosenberg attributed to the many women who have been primarily engaged in domestic labor, Rosenberg did not directly dispute
Kessler-Harris' testimony that women have successfully undertaken
"men's work" when it was made available to them. Because they
ignored each other's contentions about what women are like, the
testimony of both historians conveyed the impression that women
conform to one of two particular, yet quite different, images. Indeed,
Rosenberg's focus on women's domestic concerns aligned her with
the cultural feminist position that women have a unique, feminine
identity which should be protected and preserved. In contrast, Kessler-Harris' focus on the constraints which have restricted women's
full participation in the paid labor force aligned her with the negative

feminist position that the identity of women is constructed by and in relation to men. Despite Kessler-Harris' assertions that gender differences are a function of social circumstances, her detailed exposition of the "men's work" women have done suggested an image of the typical woman as capable-of-being masculine. Because Rosenberg's testimony contained an essentialist depiction of women as stereotypically feminine, read together the testimony of both historians presented the judge with the choice of one stereotypical image of woman over another.

Both of the witnesses' claims about the history of working women are undoubtedly true. Women have been disproportionately underrepresented in wage labor, just as Rosenberg suggested, and women have been able to undertake "masculine" work, just as Kessler-Harris testified. The problem with their testimony lies in the dichotomized image of femininity and masculinity which they conveyed in their interpretations of this history. The stereotypical feminine traits explicitly invoked in Rosenberg's testimony do not fully or adequately describe the personalities of actual, historically situated women. Such stereotypes belie the complex, contradictory, and highly nuanced character of women who are primarily homemakers. It is not surprising that the court selected the image of a "typical" woman which let the nation's largest civilian employer of women off the hook, but such a conclusion would have been more difficult if Rosenberg had acknowledged the complications and contradictions contained in the domestic social history upon which she relied, and if Kessler-Harris had not conveyed in her testimony the impression that traditional "men's work" was somehow masculine.

My argument thus far has been that Rosenberg and Kessler-Harris were guilty of silence, of conveying a false simplicity and uni-dimensionality in their testimony regarding the content of sexual difference. My additional criticism of the historians is that in reaching their conclusions about Sears' responsibility for the disproportionately low number of women in commission sales, both scholars based their judgments on an implicit comparison between the composite woman each had described and a particular male stereotype. That is, Rosenberg's conclusion that Sears should not be held responsible for the low number of women in commission sales was based on her assumption that women are too feminine for that kind of work. In contrast, Kessler-Harris' conclusion that Sears had been discriminating against women was based on her assumption that women could be masculine enough if they were given the chance. Underlying both judgments, I think, is an unnecessarily masculinized image of a successful commission sales worker.

Recall that Sears' personnel testified that effective competitive sales personnel were "aggressive," "outgoing," "highly motivated," and "leaders."[22] The stereotypical masculine image commonly associated with these traits in our gender culture is the image of a back-slapping, joke-telling, arm-twisting, used-car salesman, a man who may have played high school football or been a marine, an individual accustomed to winning confrontations under challenging conditions. This image is also suggested within the opinions by the repeated use of the word "risk" in the descriptions of commission sales work. Commission sales work is considered risky because compensation is predicated on the number of sales an employee makes. But since commission sales workers undisputedly made significantly more money at Sears than salaried employees, the "risk" inherent in commission sales work was not actually a *danger* that employees would be *uncompensated* or *discharged*, but an *uncertainty* regarding the *amount of money* they would earn. By using the word "risk," the parties invoked a particular masculine stereotype: Rambo precariously but triumphantly selling washing machine after washing machine despite the vicious advertising techniques and desperate sales tactics launched against him by the bad guys, the competitors.

If one envisions the battling male warrior as a model for the ideal commission sales worker, then one can understand why Rosenberg's claim that women are unsuited for commission sales because they are nurturing, selfless, and relation-centered may have sounded persuasive to the Court, whereas Kessler-Harris' claim that women could do commission sales if they were permitted to undoubtedly sounded unappealing. Why would we want to encourage women to become like that sort of man?

Although the warrior image of the commission sales worker may have captivated the participants in the *Sears* case, I doubt the commission sales force at Sears actually conformed to such a stereotype. It seems evident to me—avoiding, to the extent I can, exactly that sort of sales person when I buy my washing machines—that no company would or should want its commission sales workers to act in the stereotypical way we think marines or linebackers act. Moreover, I believe that female sales workers are quite capable of exhibiting the traits Sears claimed that commission sales workers need in order to be effective. Trying to sneak past department store cosmetic counters, for example, without spending twenty-five dollars I don't want to spend, reminds me that women who work in those locales could easily be described as "aggressive," "outgoing," and quite informed about their business.

Other "women's" work also entails the traits Sears ascribed to effective commission sales workers. Think, for example, of a nurse who can coax a depressed patient to eat, of a teacher who can induce a shy child to speak up, of a social worker who can convince a reluctant client to participate in community services. Each of these traditional women's jobs requires individuals to be "aggressive," "outgoing," "highly motivated," and "leaders" in relation to their work. Indeed, if the historians had interpreted the risk individuals must tolerate in commission sales as uncertainty, then they would have been able to link that problem in commission sales with a situation many women have commonly confronted in order to be successful in the psychological aspects of their domestic responsibilities.[23] They might have argued, in other words, that *because* of women's domestic responsibilities they are *more* likely rather than less likely to be able to adapt to the confused, conflicting, or changing responses of sales customers. Thus, Rosenberg and Kessler-Harris might have concluded that the qualities commonly associated with traditional women's work are similar to those required for commission sales. Instead, Rosenberg assumed that women's "feminine" qualities disable them from effectively selling on commission, while Kessler-Harris based her claim that women are able to do commission sales on the men's work women have sometimes done, rather than the women's work they have mostly done. Both historians therefore undersold women in the interpretations they offered about the meaning of women's history in the work force.

Many feminists have criticized Rosalind Rosenberg's conduct in the *Sears* case, suggesting that if she were genuinely interested in advancing the cause of women, as she claims she is, she should have declined to testify. I myself, however, do not criticize Rosenberg for testifying that women have historically done more domestic labor than paid labor, since that generalized statement seems indisputable. Nevertheless, I do criticize Rosenberg for mistaking women's common social history regarding paid work for a low aptitude or interest in commission sales or other nontraditional women's work. Rosenberg's dualistic, reductive attitude about what most women are like constitutes an essentialist picture of women that is false to the more complicated selves I recognize in both women and men. In addition, Rosenberg's claim that women's feminine traits are so deeply *internalized* by socialization processes that they can not easily be overridden by an employer's conduct[24] belies the way in which I believe women and men are continually responding to their economic and social conditions.

In contrast to their criticism of Rosenberg, many feminists have widely praised Alice Kessler-Harris for her testimony in *Sears*. I believe this praise is particularly appropriate for the position Kessler-Harris took in her testimony regarding the possibility of challenging gender differences. Thus, in contrast to Rosenberg, Kessler-Harris claimed that since women's masculine inhibitions are *externally* imposed by socialization processes, they might realistically be changed by modifying an employer's employment policies.[25] Her confidence that women can acquire the personality traits we need to undertake traditional "men's" work corresponds to the multiplicitous, shifting, socially constructed definition of sexual difference I have used to critique not only Rosenberg's testimony but also Kessler-Harris'. Unfortunately, Kessler-Harris' testimony is vulnerable to the criticism that she implicitly adopted a stance in her testimony that commission sales work *is* masculine. As I have tried to indicate in the preceding critique, masculinity, like femininity, has no inherent, fixed content, and insofar as Kessler-Harris even inadvertently suggested that it did, that essentialist assumption contributed to the either/or choice the judge in the *Sears* case believed he had to make.

My critique of the *Sears* case is partial at best. In a longer piece I would want to move beyond my criticism of the feminist historians and try to elaborate an alternative solution to the doctrinal problem in the case. Despite its partiality, however, I propose that my *Sears* discussion is an example of feminist doctrine, or postmodern feminism, because of its focus on a particular doctrinal issue rather than a more generalized and abstract examination of women in relation to law; because of its reliance on contested interpretation as a significant legal strategy; and because of its claim that sexual difference is a complex, ever-shifting social practice rather than two rigidly circumscribed and essentialist bundles of traits. By challenging dualistic attitudes toward sexual difference, attitudes such as those Rosenberg and Kessler-Harris exhibited in their testimony, postmodern feminists seek to extend their political goals for women through law beyond the single, amalgamated image of women which other forms of feminist legal scholarship have tended to invoke. By deliberately invoking differences among women—differences such as race, class, sexual preference, and age, as well as the conflicting work histories I have alluded to above—postmodern feminism constitutes, in my view, the most promising strategy available to feminist legal scholars for breaking away from the constraints which the sameness/difference paradigm has imposed on women's equality.

The Politics of a Marriage

In her recent article "Postmodern Identity and the Legal Subject,"[26] Professor Jennifer Wicke builds a case against legal postmodernism

by invoking some of the problems that women, gays, and other members of disadvantaged groups encounter when they turn to law for
assistance. If, as Professor Wicke suggests, legal rules grant rights or
privileges only when those who seek legal protection are able to exhibit a coherent subjectivity, then members of subordinate groups
should be very wary of postmodernism and its critique of the unified,
coherent subject. Extending this critique to the position of the legal
claimant could jeopardize the power of legal rules to improve the
conditions of the disadvantaged in our society. What good is postmodernism if it undoes the lifelines of liberation?

The case studies in Professor Wicke's paper seem tailor-made for
demonstrating how disabling the lack of a particular coherent identity
can be, in a legal context, for people in subordinate groups. Three of
her references seem especially compelling. The multiple personality
disorder of the victim in a recent Wisconsin rape trial, for example,
allowed her assailant a much greater opportunity to defend his assault
than he would have had if the victim could have presented a singular
response to the incident.[27] Similarly, the campaign which a number
of gays have undertaken to obtain the benefits of marital status for
monogamous relationships between homosexuals has been hampered
because gays do not have the particular sexual preference that legal
rules prescribe for marriage;[28] according to prevailing legal standards,
their sexual identity is legally unrecognizable, or incoherent.[29] Finally,
the attempt by the Mashpee Indians on Cape Cod to reclaim land from
the New Seabury Corporation was unsuccessful, in a 1976 decision,
because the Mashpees, having been transformed over the years by
their interactions with others, were unable to demonstrate to legal
authorities that they satisfied the arbitrary definitional requirements
the law demanded of "tribes" seeking to qualify for Native American
status and legal protection.[30]

Professor Wicke appeals to our sympathy for these subordinate
groups, in building her case against legal postmodernism. Each of her
case studies suggests that members of underprivileged social groups
can be significantly disadvantaged by their inability to assume the
identity the legal system favors. As claimants they are "postmodern-
ized" before they even approach the legal system for admission; because this condition jeopardizes their chances for legal protection,
postmodernism is dangerous for subordinate groups who need legal
assistance.

Professor Wicke's case against legal postmodernism relies on an
assumption that law is more powerful than postmodernism, that it
has more to offer these groups than postmodernism. This attitude is
signaled by the language of her paper associating law with "ammunition"[31] and postmodernism with "tools," "elastic bands," and "adhe-

sives."[32] (Ammunition is much more likely to be effective against the Scuds that are deployed against subordinate groups than rubber bands.) But the paper also directly criticizes the liberating potential of postmodernism as a political strategy. Professor Wicke argues that postmodernism represents "an overinvestment in discursive gestures, the often fatuous assumption that an alteration of textual style or nomenclature will send shock waves to the heart of social domination."[33]

In other words, you can't wage a revolution through interpretation. If you're going to wage a revolution, you need tanks. For Professor Wicke, this means that subordinate groups need law, law which is uncontaminated by postmodern "theoretical suppositions about the nature of language, texts and human subjects within the lens of the social."[34]

Professor Wicke regrets her conclusion that progressive politics require a barrier between law and postmodernism. Near the end of her paper she writes approvingly of "the attempt to save the Brazilian rain forest by the marketing of Ben and Jerry's Rainforest Crunch ice cream."[35] She praises that combination, of politics and commerce, as a postmodern enterprise that might inspire "a postmodern identity which can also be the legal subject."[36] Nevertheless, she insistently cautions against a law and postmodernism union. Recognizing the limitations of the unified legal subject, she also believes that her political convictions require that law must be shielded from postmodern infestation.

In the course of making her case against legal postmodernism, Professor Wicke invokes the trope of heterosexual intercourse to depict the relationship between law and postmodernism. In a striking array of images at the outset of the paper, Professor Wicke talks about "a dynamic coupling," a "dalliance," an "ambivalent embrace," "bedfellows," and "the costs of a shot-gun marriage."[37] Although Professor Wicke decides that she has to call this marriage off, an analysis of her imagery suggests reasons why she might not have to. The particular question I want to focus on is: Who's the bride and who's the bridegroom in this heterosexual relationship; who's the guy and who's the gal here?

Judging by the conclusion that law must triumph over postmodernism, and associating this triumph with stereotypical masculine hegemony, it might seem that law is meant to be the bridegroom. In addition to arguing that law is more powerful than postmodernism, as described above, Professor Wicke refers to law in terms of "rigor"; she cites the "fixity of the body of law."[38] Postmodernism, in this reading, is the bride. Postmodernism is linked with stereotypical feminine wiles in the text—with "all the significations of glamour and seduction."[39] And like a bride who loses her name, postmodernism is effaced in the end when Professor Wicke's commitment to subordinate groups requires her to argue for the retention of the unified legal subject.

An alternative interpretation of the heterosexual imagery suggests that law may be the bride, rather than the bridegroom. Law is described in the beginning of the paper as "unwilling," as the "staid partner."[40] And near the end of the paper Professor Wicke urges the legal subject to be understood "as a permeable membrane within which innumerable sites of conflict and innumerable forms of struggle can be seen to exist."[41] Having cast the issue of the relationship between law and postmodernism in the rhetoric of heterosexual intercourse, this reference to a "permeable membrane" suggests the hymen of a bride; it invokes an image of law waiting to be penetrated by what the paper refers to as "the activated discursive shards of the postmodern subject."[42]

Identifying law as the bride could explain the urgency of Professor Wicke's case against a law and postmodernism marriage. Marriage would require law to lose the value an intact membrane has traditionally given women. Pursuant to this interpretation of the paper's heterosexual imagery, it's not surprising that Professor Wicke argues, as many feminists have, against marriage.

There is conflict, within feminism, about the politics of marriage. Marriage seems quite problematic for both partners when it requires them to merge into a single identity, and it seems particularly problematic for a woman if the identity she must assume is her husband's. My own view is that feminists don't have to boycott this marriage (or others) for political reasons, that successful political struggle can occur within heterosexual relationships, and within a union of postmodernism and law. If this is so, then understanding the relationship between postmodernism and law as a romantic tragedy in which Romeo and Juliet must be separated in order to avoid damaging their families and the overall social fabric would be a mistake. It relies on a construction of marriage that should be resisted.

It seems to me that subordinate groups could be significantly empowered by using postmodern theories in legal contests. Indeed, I suggest that the coherent subject position Professor Wicke thinks she must defend is actually a critical obstacle to legal protection in the case of the Mashpee Indians and in the campaign to extend gays the benefits of legal marriage. Professor Wicke's use of these cases in her argument indicates to me an exaggerated respect for the reliability of legal rights as well as a mistaken impression that change would necessarily make law less potent. In two of the three cases I've drawn from her paper progressive outcomes were sabotaged by the current legal structure; under these circumstances change seems worth a try.

Law requires all legal claimants to assume a particular posture—a partial identity—in seeking judicial assistance; we must leave aside much of the multiplicity and complexity of our lives in order to engage in legal discourse. Injustice occurs, as in the Mashpee case and the gay marriage campaign, when legal rules structure these particular postures in such a way that subordinate groups cannot squeeze into them at all. In these situations, legal rules need to expand the narrow and rigid character of the subject position they impose as a condition of admission to the legal arena. Law might indeed have benefitted, in the Mashpee case and the gay marriage campaign, from "challenging the theoretical suppositions about the nature . . . of human subjects within the lens of the social."[43]

The victim in the recent Wisconsin rape trial was lucky, not because a postmodern critique was rejected but because her objection to having sex was vindicated. It might not have been. As Fran Olsen has eloquently pointed out in her analysis of statutory rape, women who lack sufficient social and physical power to determine the circumstances and character of their sexuality, who want but also don't want to have sex, are not satisfactorily protected by current legal rules regulating rape.[44]

The rhetoric of heterosexual intercourse that Professor Wicke provides in her paper supports her case against legal postmodernism by appealing to a traditional form of marriage which feminists oppose. However, it can also support a case in favor of this union, if the relationship between law and postmodernism is understood as a reconstituted notion of marriage in which neither partner is required to fuse with or become dominated by the other. Professor Wicke herself suggests this, I think, by the shifting character of the paper's heterosexual references. If it's not clear who's the bride and who's the groom, aren't the dangers of domination that feminists fear in marriage far less likely to occur?

Professor Wicke's reference to law as a "permeable membrane" is also consistent with a reconstituted notion of heterosexual relations. Such a notion is currently being promoted by "Madonna in any of her endless incarnations," as Professor Wicke depicts her in describing "the valences within . . . the umbrella of postmodernism."[45] I have in mind, however, a video that seems particularly relevant here. In "Like a Virgin" Madonna sings of being "touched for the very first time," but the character she plays in the video leaves no doubt that this is a woman who has been touched before. She is not a virgin. She wears a gown with a neckline and hemline that are cut like a nightclub dress, although it is white, long-sleeved, and has a train and a veil. She is sultry and naughtily seductive, but she is also wistful and yearning. She is not a virgin; she doesn't say that she is. She is *like* a virgin.

Women are cruelly restricted by the convention that their social value depends on having an intact membrane, just as they suffer deeply from coerced or brutalizing sexual relations with men. However, if heterosexual women have control over when, how, and with whom they have sex—if they are economically and physically secure—sexual intimacy can offer them a complex constellation of experiences, experiences that include intense pleasure, and rejuvenation as well as disappointment and sadness. These experiences are life enhancing; they do not entail a loss of power. If a union between postmodernism and law were informed by a positive model of heterosexual relationship, then a marriage between law and postmodernism might be quite promising.

Professor Wicke states in her paper that postmodernism's significance for law is its critique of the unified, coherent subject. I suggest that neither the politics of marriage nor the importance of legal protection for subordinate groups needs to prevent us from pursuing the promise of that critique.

Difference Models in the Study of Women in Law

The Michigan Survey

In 1967 the *Michigan Law Review* published James White's seminal survey of women in the legal profession.[46] Based on questionnaires returned by over 2700 male and female graduates of 108 law schools, the first quarter of the Michigan Survey compares the income, job profiles, work descriptions, and family status of men and women who graduated from law school between 1956 and 1966. It also compares the graduates' views regarding sex discrimination in the profession and their motives for studying law. The data Professor White reports reveal that in contrast to the men the women who responded to his questionnaire had different job profiles,[47] different work descriptions,[48] and different family relationships.[49] Professor White's principal focus, however, is the marked discrepancy between the incomes of male and female respondents. Three-quarters of the article is devoted to analyzing the reasons for the income differential between the sexes and to discussing how the differential could be challenged.

Professor White rejects any explanation for the income differential women lawyers suffer other than overt discrimination against women. Specifically, he examines his data to determine whether any purported differences between the sexes might account for the wage discrepancy—purported differences such as: fewer women make law review, work full-time, work in more highly compensated jobs, or care about higher compensation. None of these explanations pan out. White decisively concludes that differences between male and female lawyers do not account for the surplus money men earn. The reason for the income differential, White sternly and stirringly asserts, is prejudice within the profession. Women lawyers are not to blame.[50] The solutions he recommends, therefore, are measures that he thinks will eliminate the profession's wrongful treatment of women.[51]

Although the Michigan survey relates a substantial number of differences between the circumstances of female and male lawyers, I believe the author of the survey would claim that he had a neutral or sex-blind position regarding sex differences. I imagine he would argue, with justification, that when he solicited and collected the data for his article he was not committed to finding any particular differences between male and female lawyers. He was prepared to let the data speak for itself.[52] Moreover, despite the numerous sex differences his data revealed, Professor White perseveres in a neutral stance toward such differences by arguing that they should not prevent women from assimilating into the profession. Women should be permitted to function like men, should they choose to try.

The sex-blind position Professor White implicitly claims for himself and which he seeks to secure for the profession does not uniformly characterize the attitudes toward difference exhibited in the Michigan survey. For example, the survey's appendix reveals that the questionnaires which were sent to women were slightly different from those sent to men. Both men and women were asked if they had ceased practice, and if they had, whether they had done so simply because they had lost interest in the law or for more interesting or remunerative work,[53] but only women were asked if they had ceased practice in order to "get married," "have a baby," or "devote time to [their] famil[ies]."[54] Moreover, in a postscript to the follow-up letter sent to male lawyers who had not responded to an initial request for cooperation, Professor White candidly states his view that even the questions asked of both sexes were not sex neutral.[55]

There are a number of places within the article where Professor White indicates that, although willing to be convinced otherwise, he assumes female lawyers are different from male lawyers. In addition, the language of the separate letters sent to the men and women who were asked to complete questionnaires indicates that White held different personal attitudes toward the sexes. The women's letter is written in a gentlemanly, courtly, and somewhat formal tone, while the men's letter is jocular, self-mocking, and somewhat conspiratorial. "[W]e *beseech* you," White wrote women alumnae; "We enlist your support in a common cause."[56] To the men he wrote, "I'm certain that you have nothing better to do than to fill out questionnaires for crackpot professors. . . . Needless to say, your response as a member of [our control group of men] is more important than the response of any individual among the female group. . . . We ask . . . that you indulge this one crackpot scheme."[57]

Just as the author's ambiguity toward sex differences undermines his implicit claim that he is neutral with respect to his data, so his efforts to persuade readers that the profession should take steps to prevent "discrimination" are qualified, in this instance by the narrow scope of discrimination he in fact is willing to eradicate. Thus, although Professor White defines discrimination broadly to include "every differentiation, whether or not it is rational or functional," he argues that only functional discrimination (discrimination which produces an economic gain for an employer) should be unlawful.[58]

The particular attitudes displayed in the survey had an impact on the research product which was produced. The data White obtained about women lawyers in law did not emerge from the women untainted; rather, Professor White's attitudes toward his subject unavoidably infected the data he received. Since the Michigan survey was published almost a generation ago those attitudes may seem more exposed than in contemporary work, but I maintain that current scholars will be as unable to sustain a neutral stance toward sex differences as Professor White was. It seems obvious to me, for example, that failing to ask male lawyers whether the birth of children affected their work perpetuates the ideology that parenting is a woman's responsibility. Both women and men are parents, but the questionnaire is drafted on the assumption that women have day-to-day responsibility for child care which men do not have. The questionnaire reminds women lawyers of their parental obligations but it neglects to remind men.[59] The result of this polarized assumption regarding the relationship between the sexes with respect to child care is that the questionnaire furthers differences between the sexes.

The different tones which Professor White adopted in his letters to male and female lawyers also assume and then create polarized differences between the sexes. In my view either letter could have been sent to all the respondents without jeopardizing their responses.

Professor White might also have sent the informal letter to men and women whom he already knew, while the more formal letter could have gone to the lawyers with whom he was unacquainted. However, once we stipulate that there are different letters and one is to be sent to women and the other to men, it seems clear which letter went to which sex. Professor White measured his feelings toward women lawyers by comparing them with his feelings toward male lawyers; women were stranger to him than men. Since Professor White was writing an article in which he sought to "narrow . . . the gap which exists between female and male status,"[60] it is likely that his use of letters which furthered the emotional separation of women and men as groups was an inadvertent result of his insensitivity to the slightly more distanced reaction women would have to their letter. But the different letters which were sent to women and men constitute a mechanism, if only a small one, by which discourse perpetuates sexual difference.

This polarization of the relationship between men and women tends to sweep away from consideration inconsistent, marginal distinctions. Eliminating these distinctions may be a significant loss in the study of women in law. For example, there may have been men among those whom Professor White surveyed who shouldered substantial parenting duties. Because this information was not obtained or reported, the image of parenting as a woman's responsibility remained intact in the Michigan survey. Moreover, no matter how many more women than men have primary childrearing responsibility, aligning this responsibility exclusively with women contributes to the continued characterization of childrearing as a woman's issue, rather than a communal concern.[61] This is likely to deter consideration of institutional changes that would alter the current privatized structure of child care.

Similarly, Professor White used income as the predominant measure of a lawyer's success. This may have been, as he asserted it was, "the most universally recognized single measure of success in American society" in 1967. But at that time women were legally excluded from many paying jobs and were legally paid less than men for similar work. Selecting the income standard, therefore, did not take into account the measures by which women, convinced of their self-worth despite their restricted incomes, evaluated their success. Those measures—effective problem resolution, integration of work and family life, creativity, social contribution, and there are surely other possibilities—are hidden from consideration by the polarizing effect of the male standard.

The Chicago Alumna Letter

An issue of the University of Chicago Law School's *Law School Record* contains a letter written at the invitation of Dean Richard Badger by Elizabeth Gorman Nehls, a 1985 graduate of Chicago.[62] The letter stemmed from a series of conversations between Ms. Nehls and two Chicago deans on "the subjects of discrimination and the experiences of women in law school," and it sets forth the author's analysis of why women graduates are not achieving as much "academic and professional success [as] might be expected."

Although Ms. Nehls acknowledges the "real effect" which both blatant and subtle forms of discrimination or prejudice have on women, the focus of her letter is on the problems within women which impede their success in the profession.[63] Drawing support from Carol Gilligan, Cynthia Fuchs Epstein, Colette Dowling, Matina Horner, and Virginia Woolf, Ms. Nehls singles out for discussion three attitudes which particularly characterize and disadvantage women: "the Ethnic of Selflessness," "the Link between Femininity and Passivity," and "The Expectation of Failure." Ms. Nehls not only claims that selflessness, passivity, and insecurity inhibit women in their pursuit of success as lawyers; she also assumes that *men* do not have such characteristics.[64] Indeed, Ms. Nehls not only generalizes the sex differences she identifies in men and women, but she also treats the characteristics she discusses as oppositions. That is, rather than arguing, as she might have, that male lawyers are *very* selfish, *very* active, and *very* self-confident, whereas female lawyers are like that but less so, she describes the differences between male and female lawyers in oppositional terms: men are selfish/women are selfless; men are active/women are passive; men are self-confident/women are self-defeating. These generalized and polarized differences which Ms. Nehls sympathetically describes form the basis for her recommendation that Chicago consider instituting several remedial programs which might help women compensate for or adjust to their differences.[65]

In contrast to Professor White's implicit efforts to be sex-blind in the Michigan survey, the author of the Chicago alumna letter is firmly committed to the position that women are different from men. She does not cite any research which challenges her claim that there are generalizable and oppositional differences between the sexes, and unlike Professor White she does not betray any internal ambivalence in the letter about her position. Ms. Nehls displays a similarly inflexible attitude toward the structure of the legal profession, implying that women, not law practice, must be transformed if women are to advance. Thus, whereas Professor White argued that some but not all discrimination in the profession should be outlawed, Ms. Nehls does not consider any changes in the structure of law practice. Her recommendations for changes at the University of Chicago relate to counseling programs and workshops which would either insignificantly or imperceptibly alter the teaching and classroom socialization patterns prevalent in legal education.[66]

Ms. Nehls' recommendations for remedying the obstacles women face do not seem to be dictated by her attitude that there are firmly entrenched differences between the sexes. Thus, while the particular objective she articulated in the letter was to help women assimilate more effectively into the legal profession, logically she could as easily have pursued an alternate objective of attempting to change the legal profession rather than the women who seek to enter it. For example, she might have argued that even though women and men have different and opposite personality traits regarding their concern for others, their aggressiveness, and their self-regard, female traits are more desirable than male traits. Therefore, the legal profession should be transformed so that lawyers would become less competitive, more sensitive to their clients' concerns, and more open to change. More like women.

My concerns about Ms. Nehls' stance toward sex differences relate not to the objective she pursued in her letter, although I would have preferred that she seek the one I have just articulated, but to the incredibility of her attitude and its negative consequences for women. Ms. Nehls' attitude toward the differences between male and female lawyers is unconvincing to me because it ignores differences I have observed among women and among men. Some women may be as selfless, passive, and self-defeating as she claims, but I have taught men and known male lawyers who exhibited those same characteristics. I have also taught women and known female lawyers who could be as selfish, active, and self-confident as Ms. Nehls suggests male lawyers are.

It may be courteous to overlook exaggeration for effect in some circumstances, but not, I think, when the exaggeration produces undesirable consequences. Such an unqualified assertion regarding female characteristics seems likely to disadvantage women who are inaccurately described by such characteristics. Drawing the characteristics in oppositional terms, thereby magnifying the differences between the sexes, exacerbates this danger.[67] Moreover, if one accepts Ms. Nehls' position that there are deeply established differences between the sexes, then the question of how women might change the profession seems more acute. Assuming an analysis of that issue requires some sense of who women are, a generalized and oppositional description which seems false is likely to sabotage such an effort.

I believe Ms. Nehls' attitude toward women has enormous appeal for scholars studying women in law. The power such an attitude exerts, I claim, stems from the way in which it parallels familiar doctrinal disputes involving gender equality. In the next chapter, I address the relationship between a doctrinal dispute over sex-segregated education and the book that most influentially captures Ms. Nehls' (and Rosalind Rosenberg's) attitudes toward women, Carol Gilligan's *In a Different Voice.*

3

Progressive Feminist Legal Scholarship: Can We Claim "A Different Voice"?

Feminist psychologist Carol Gilligan published her book, *In a Different Voice*, in 1982. Justice Sandra Day O'Connor wrote her first major sex discrimination opinion, a decision that held Mississippi's refusal to admit Joe Hogan to its women's nursing school was unconstitutional, in the same year.[1] A number of themes lie in the coincidence of these two events, themes such as the relationship between Gilligan's claims regarding women's difference and O'Connor's assertion of formal equality between the sexes,[2] the "different voice" of Sandra Day O'Connor, and the caregiving aptitude of women and men. Although O'Connor's opinion in *Hogan* is understood as the decision which finally secured substantial Constitutional protection against gender-specific laws,[3] the case did not bring feminist legal scholars home from the ramparts. Feminist lawyers are in favor of formal equality, of course, but they are conscious of its limitations as an empowering strategy for women. They are skeptical of how much women gain from equal treatment in a society in which social power and physical security are unequally distributed between the sexes.[4] Under the formal equality attained in *Hogan*, for example, Mississippi was required to adopt sex-neutral admission standards for its School of Nursing, despite arguments that sex-segregated education liberates women from the "sociological fact" of their role as "the pursued sex" and enables them "to function and achieve in the still male dominated economy."[5] Feminists admittedly have conflicting views regarding sex-segregated education, but the feminist critique of formal equality cannot be limited to the debate surrounding that particular issue. Feminists have been critical of the application of the equality guarantee in numerous other contexts as well, as illustrated, perhaps most familiarly, by the extensive literature exposing the shortcomings of formal equality as a strategy for restructuring conditions that particularly burden mothers in the work force.[6] In this chapter, I shall analyze Justice O'Connor's opinion in *Hogan* in order to indicate the limits of the concept of formal equality, and I shall offer a reading of Carol Gilligan's *In a Difference Voice*. My principal purpose is to assess the use of Gilligan's book by feminist lawyers as they increasingly pursue what I term a "strategy of difference," rather than formal equality, in their post-*Hogan* efforts to advance the position of women through law.

Mississippi University for Women v. Hogan: Liberalism and Its Shortcomings

Justice O'Connor's Opinion in Hogan

In *Mississippi University for Women (MUW) v. Hogan* a male nurse, who wanted to supplement his nursing credentials by attending school in his hometown, challenged the legality of the woman-only admissions policy at MUW's nursing school. By a five to four vote, the Supreme Court held that under the equality guarantee of the Federal Constitution, the single-sex admission policy was unlawful. Although the Supreme Court has not decided a sex-discrimination case on equal protection grounds since *Hogan*, *Hogan*'s test for gender equality review remains the governing standard for the Court.[7] *Hogan* strongly suggests that except in exceptional circumstances statutes that explicitly treat women and men differently are impermissible under the Federal Constitution. As O'Connor explains it, the federal equality guarantee imposes a burden of "exceedingly persuasive justification" on gender specific laws.[8]

Because the burden of justification in this case was triggered by a male, the Court's interpretation of the equality guarantee in *Hogan* is rigorously neutral.[9] It rejects a more paternalist approach that would restrict equal protection to claims brought by women. Moreover, the Court specifically rejects Mississippi's defense of its single-sex policy as compensation for past discrimination against women;[10] according to the Court's opinion, the nursing school's policy "excluding males . . . tends to perpetuate the stereotyped view of nursing as an exclusively woman's job."[11] "The purpose [of the heavy justification burden imposed by the equality guarantee] is to assure that the validity of a classification is determined through reasoned analysis rather than through the mechanical application of traditional, often inaccurate, assumptions about the proper roles of men and women."[12]

As a definitive statement regarding the prohibition of legally imposed, sex-based treatment, O'Connor's opinion in *Hogan* depicts the

Constitution as an engine of liberation with respect to sex differences. Like much anti-discrimination law, the Constitutional equality guarantee can break down economic, employment, and educational barriers that explicitly prevent either sex from acquiring the benefits available to the other in society. Of course, historically such barriers have disproportionately been erected against women, not men, so that extending the benefits of liberation even-handedly to men as well as women seems *un*even. Or ironic. Or a reason to be suspicious.

Indeed, Justice O'Connor's opinion in *Hogan* is both frustrating and unsatisfying. There are obvious shortcomings that arise from the approach to the relationship between law and sex differences which the *Hogan* equality guarantee represents, the relationship referred to above as "*un*even" even-handedness. Together with earlier decisions specifically refusing to extend the equality guarantee to facially neutral laws which disproportionately disadvantage women,[13] *Hogan* confines the equality guarantee to specifically sex-based rules. The law will lower formal barriers, so that women—like Joe Hogan—can be free to choose how to make their lives. But the equality guarantee is not responsive to or useful against many factors affecting women's "choices" in life, factors relating to workplace organization, cultural expectations, or family socialization.

This interpretation of the equality guarantee produces a real shortfall for women. Invalidating sex-specific laws in a context of social and economic inequality will not produce substantive equality between the sexes. Nor will it help most women improve their life chances. Thus, eliminating sex-based barriers in the wage market reduces some restrictions on women but does not disturb sex-neutral work structures that conflict with the significant parenting responsibilities which women workers disproportionately bear.[14] Similarly, eliminating sex-based distinctions in the laws governing alimony and distribution of property on divorce will not reduce and may even exacerbate the disproportionate economic impact of marital dissolution on women and men.[15] As a wide range of feminist legal scholars have argued,[16] restricting the liberatory reach of the equality doctrine to sex-based laws insulates a large chunk of male power from legal attack.

Hogan's liberatory promise is further undermined by the well-entrenched qualification that the equality guarantee extends only to similarly situated classes.[17] Because the Supreme Court has unambiguously stated that women and men are *not* similarly situated in all respects—more specifically, that women and men are differently situated with respect to reproductive issues such as pregnancy, childbirth, and abortion[18]—this turns out to be a substantial qualification. However "natural" it may seem to assert that women and men are different with respect to reproduction, a gender equality doctrine that does not extend to reproductive issues significantly reduces the impact the legal engine of liberation might have on women's lives. In the fetal protection policy recently challenged before the Supreme Court, for example, a nationwide company sought to defend a rule that would exclude all "fertile women" from jobs in which they would be exposed to a significant amount of airborne lead.[19] If this policy had been upheld, by one estimate as many as twenty million industrial jobs would have been closed to women.[20] Fertile men would not be excluded from these jobs, because of the excuse that maternal reproductive organs subject fetal health to greater risk from hazardous working conditions than paternal organs.

Like the more general liberal stance toward law, the limits on the gender equality guarantee utilized in *Hogan* are justified by an appeal to neutrality or even-handedness, by a respect for individual self-help and the usefulness of legal restraint. But the shortcomings just ascribed to the equality doctrine suggest that these values are foiled rather than served by this doctrine. By restricting its protective scope to situations in which the sexes are similarly situated, the equality guarantee extends legal assistance to women only when they are able to demonstrate that they are like men. Although neutral in form, the equality guarantee is functionally male-biased. In addition, by restricting its protection to formal, sex-based laws, the equality doctrine fails to redress the residue of a history of social and economic imbalances that handicap individual women seeking to improve their lives. By supporting the power imbalance of the status quo, this kind of legal restraint aggressively undermines individual self-help efforts.[21]

And yet, *Hogan*'s even-handed, gender-blind approach to equality does represent an important achievement. Constitutional neutrality vindicates the claims women have insistently made that our sex should not be used against us. As a result, the liberal commitment to "not taking gender into account" has real appeal for feminist legal activists. Whether feminist-driven reforms to benefit women are aimed at explicit sex discrimination or whether they seek sex-neutral changes narrowly designed to correct social conditions that presently disadvantage women, there is a concrete danger that even well-intended changes may reproduce new social conditions that disadvantage women in fresh ways. This "dilemma of difference"[22] is very real.

An example of the dilemma is the "mommy track," an adjustment in labor market work designed to reduce the conflict between labor market and childrearing responsibilities by structuring jobs to accommodate parenting duties. Although the mommy track does alleviate such pressure, in many cases it also institutionalizes yet another marginalized and subordinate set of workplace positions, positions which women disproportionately assume.[23]

Another example of the difference dilemma became apparent after the feminist campaign to mitigate the confining and victimizing effects which fault-based divorce systems had on women. Although some women benefited from the provisions of no-fault divorce reforms that make divorce more accessible and that subject marital property to equitable division, other women, particularly those in long-term marriages and having very little wage market experience, have not benefited. They are less likely to get alimony under the reformed laws, and, in contrast to their husbands, awarding them half of the marital property may not protect them from impoverishment after divorce. Thus, whereas under a fault-based system women were subtly encouraged to become full-time homemakers, under a no-fault system they may be discouraged from doing so. This consequence has both surprised and dismayed feminist legal commentators.[24]

The dilemma of difference is also illustrated by the issue of Sandra Day O'Connor's voice in *Hogan*. O'Connor does not write as a woman in *Hogan*. She does not, for example, "emphasize the 'specificity' of female sexuality," in a "rigorously analytical and highly poetic" style.[25] Nor does she evidence a moral concern to use her "decision-writing [to] explore . . . and fulfill . . . the responsibilities as well as the rights of liberalism."[26] She makes no apologies whatsoever in *Hogan* for the traditional shortcomings of liberalism.

It is also hard to say that Justice O'Connor speaks on behalf of women in this decision. Women receive surprisingly slight attention in her text. Although Justice Powell, in his dissent, states that the purpose of the gender equality standard has been "to free women from 'archaic and overbroad generalizations,' " Justice O'Connor uses gender neutral terms to state the standard quoted earlier, and she refers to the historical legislative (mis)treatment of women only briefly.[27] Unlike Justice Blackmun, who would have upheld the women-only admission policy but who chides the university for the "embarrass[ing]" "historical anachronism" in its corporate papers, Justice O'Connor discreetly tucks the university's corporate aim, to advance "the girls of the state," into a footnote, and then diplomatically describes MUW as an "all-female college," "which limits its enrollment to women." She also uses gender-neutral terms to state the legal standard for judging legislation that purports to compensate women for past discrimination. Since it's hard to imagine sex-specific legislation which a state would seriously attempt to defend as compensating men for past discrimination, this usage also makes O'Connor look as if she is straining to reduce the appearance of women in her opinion.

Although the question of single-sex education for women tends to be of particular interest to women, Justice O'Connor's text accords much less attention to this issue than either Justice Blackmun or Justice Powell writing in dissent. Indeed, Justice O'Connor's opinion invalidates the women-only admission policy at the request of one man who complained that the nursing school's policy would require him to travel an "inconvenient distance" from home to further his nursing education. In their dissents, Justice Blackmun and Justice Powell argue that the validity of single-sex education for women involves not just the inconvenience of one man, but "values," "diversity," "honored tradition," and the "preferences" and individual choices of many women. I do not suggest that the dissenting Justices have captured the woman's point of view in their opinion, because there is no single woman's point of view of the issue of single-sex education.[28] But insofar as single-sex education is a woman's issue, the dissenters are more engaged with it than O'Connor.

Thus, in a case specifically involving sex discrimination, Sandra Day O'Connor neither writes as a woman nor speaks on behalf of women. The unsatisfying and frustrating character of *Hogan*, for me, is partly associated with the sexual flatness of its text. On an initial reading, this is a dull decision; there is no "different voice" speaking, I decide. However, pursuant to the liberal interpretation of equality in *Hogan*, there shouldn't be. There should be no relationship between O'Connor's gender and the text of her opinions. Whatever arguments there may be for diversity in judicial appointments—or for diversity in other institutions, for that matter—sex differences should be irrelevant to legal decision-making. Yet O'Connor's appointment to the Supreme Court was heralded because she would be the first woman there.

This statement of the dilemma of difference in terms of O'Connor's voice bristles with problems for me. I acutely want to interrupt the argument of the paper and to articulate, elaborately (and eloquently), why diversity is critically important to women in law. At the same time, I am falling into a quicksand of internal argument about my claim that there is no different voice in O'Connor's decision.[29] Having turned to the issue of O'Connor's "voice" in order to illustrate, again, how liberalism avoids the problems associated with activism based on women's differences, liberalism's appeal seems almost inaccessible as I write this; like most feminist legal scholars I am ready to turn away from liberalism as a strategy for what can be done to improve the condition of women in law. What is the meaning of a different voice for Sandra Day O'Connor? Is it possible that the constraints of legal discourse and institutional culture silenced O'Connor's femininity, which a freer, less sexist world would liberate?

Feminist Reaction to Hogan: *The Strategy of Difference*

The *Hogan* decision marks the beginning of a shift in feminist legal efforts on behalf of women away from legal claims involving Constitutional or discrimination law.[30] Feminists have sought, increasingly, since the early eighties, to develop other means by which to challenge sex-neutral laws that reinforce women's inequalities. The nature of these challenges varies. Some tend to be theoretically motivated efforts to re-interpret conventional legal rules, such as the critique of self-defense laws generated on behalf of battered women,[31] and the attack on common-law doctrines in tort and contract[32] and on the rules involving rape.[33] Other efforts reach for more radical transformations in legal structures, such as the pornography reform campaign informed by Catharine MacKinnon's claims regarding the sexualization of power,[34] or the attempts to transform traditional analyses and discourse in reproduction and employment law.[35]

I label the stance uniting these various efforts the "strategy of difference," because all of them depend, to some degree, on claims regarding differences between the sexes. That is, these challenges are predicated, at least in part, on assertions that women have different needs than men, that we have different historical traditions, different perspectives, and, sometimes, different "experiences."

The strategy of difference pursued in these claims is epistemologically crucial to the ability of feminists to identify the particular interests of women, and it is politically crucial to our ability to mobilize in those interests. The strategy of difference may also prove instrumental to circumventing the shortcomings of changes premised on formal equality doctrine. However, a danger underlies the strategy of difference, a danger that deploying commonalities *among* women unavoidably embeds such traits *within* women. Thus, feminist efforts to transform differences between women and men, differences we have assumed are socially constructed and therefore subject to change, may have the unwanted effect of perpetuating gender as an essential, irreducible part of identity.[36]

For feminist legal activists the danger underlying the difference strategy raises practical issues regarding the consequences of legal change. A principal concern is that making sex-neutral legal changes that will correct social conditions presently disadvantaging women may reproduce new social conditions that disadvantage women in fresh ways. Making sex-neutral legal changes designed to take women or our interests into account may mask the ideological impact of the strategy of difference. That is, insofar as law influences our ideas about appropriate sex-role conduct, sex-specific laws more obviously signal the effect of law on the construction of gender identity than sex-neutral laws. Thus, the strategy of difference may alter, but by no means eliminate, law's gender-formation functions. Indeed, the ideological effect of legal changes predicated on the strategy of difference may be difficult to foresee, and therefore difficult to regulate. This problem is illustrated by the feminist campaign to mitigate the confining and victimizing effects which fault-based divorce systems had on women, as described above.[37]

It is not surprising that feminist legal scholars pursuing the strategy of difference would turn to Carol Gilligan's book, *In a Different Voice*. Although Gilligan's claims about sex differences are presented in the context of her challenge to psychological moral development discourse, the dominant standard Gilligan challenges, the ethic of rights, is familiar to lawyers from the rhetoric of liberal jurisprudence. Moreover, in her anecdotal presentation of the three research projects that inform the book, Gilligan relies heavily on responses her participants gave to a hypothetical conflict between law and morality. (This is the Heinz dilemma, the question of whether a man should steal a drug he cannot afford in order to save his desperately sick wife's life.)[38] Undoubtedly Gilligan's book is also appealing to feminist lawyers (and to others) because of its refreshing gender-pride. Gilligan is not only unapologetic about the gender differences she presents from her research, but she is very upbeat about women.[39]

Gilligan's book has been approvingly used and frequently cited by feminist legal scholars.[40] However, her work has also provoked very critical reactions.[41] These intense but contradictory responses to Gilligan's work are explicable, in my judgment, because *In a Different Voice* is susceptible to multiple interpretations.

I claim, however, that there is even more at stake in these conflicting readings of Gilligan than a contest over interpretation. In the following section I argue that the differing interpretations of *In a Different Voice* have significantly different implications for the advancement of women through law. More specifically, I argue that there is a progressive interpretation of Gilligan's book which is less problematic for a feminist legal agenda than the conservative interpretation I offer. My claim is that feminist legal activists who rely on a conservative interpretation of *In a Different Voice* are more likely to aggravate the danger posed by the strategy of difference than those who rely on a progressive reading.

I am writing this book as a feminist legal scholar concerned about a feminist legal agenda, and yet I do not mean to suggest that the effect of competing Gilligan interpretations is limited to readers in my position. Because of the affinity between Gilligan's work and law, or perhaps for reasons I haven't identified, some version of Gilligan's argument seems to constitute the definition of legal feminism for a number of armchair feminists, readers for whom the political stakes of interpreting Gilligan may not be particularly important. I believe that feminists should pay attention to these casual readers. Although in my circle the reductive popularization of Gilligan's argument is almost always drowned by the epithet "crude Gilliganism," our ritualistic denunciations cause me to suspect that the dangers posed by conservative readings may be masked, for feminists, by our teasing, know-it-all dismissals and also, in some cases, by our desires to avoid examining too closely the question of our own "feminine" identities.

The question of what difference means for feminists has been an important concern for me, and yet until now Gilligan's book has not figured in my construction of ideas around this question. Indeed, my negative reaction to "crude Gilliganism" has been so heated that I assumed, before undertaking this project, that Gilligan's book had relatively little to contribute to solving the problem of how gender differences are constructed and replicated. I have found, to my surprise, that I was wrong. In the course of presenting different interpretations of Gilligan's book, therefore, I also seek to convey something about the ways in which my readings of her book have affected my views about the question of whether progressive feminist legal scholars can claim "a different voice."

Reading *In a Different Voice* Differently

Progressive and Conservative Readings: An Introduction

For those unfamiliar with *In a Different Voice*, the following description provides a brief and uncontroversial statement of its contents:

> *In a Different Voice* is based on three research projects involving moral choice that were conducted by the author, feminist psychologist Carol Gilligan. More than half of the individuals who participated in Gilligan's studies were women.[42] Based on an analysis of the language used by her research subjects in responding to her

questions, Gilligan constructs a new model of moral development. This model, which is labeled the ethic of care, or responsibility, is associated with women,[43] and with problems in "affiliative relationships."[44]

Gilligan contrasts the ethic of care with a model of rights, or justice, which she attributes to the "critical theory-building studies" of such prominent male theorists as Freud, Erik Erikson, Jean Piaget, and Lawrence Kohlberg.[45] The model of rights is more identified with problems of self-actualization than relational issues, and with a "just resolution to moral dilemmas," as determined by objective standards.[46] The book reveals that Kohlberg did not include any females in the primary study which led to the formation of his six-stage theory of moral development,[47] and the book criticizes Freud, Erikson, and Piaget for subordinating women and feminine developmental issues in their work.[48]

While this description indicates that sex differences play a significant role in Gilligan's book, the principal distinction between a conservative and a progressive reading of *In a Different Voice* lies in the interpretation of that role.

For conservative readers, the sex differences Gilligan discusses in the book *validate gender differences*. Pursuant to this reading of Gilligan, her book constitutes evidence that women are contextually focused, relationship-oriented, and care-giving, whereas men are abstract, individualistic, and dominating. Gilligan's sympathetic presentation of women and her generalizations about the sexes are important to the conservative conclusion that, although Gilligan draws the cluster of sex-linked traits she discusses from the discourse of moral choice, these traits are universal characteristics of the sexes.

Susannah Sherry, for example, in an article about civic republicanism which I will discuss at greater length later in this chapter, decontextualizes Gilligan's descriptions of women and men. Thus she writes, citing *In a Different Voice*, that the difference between women and men "is captured in the tension between women's primary concern with intimacy or connection and men's primary focus on separation or autonomy."[49] Unlike Sherry's approving use of Gilligan, Joan Williams' reading of Gilligan is the basis for a sustained critique. Her passage summarizing Gilligan's attitude toward women indicates, however, that, like Sherry, she also assumes that Gilligan was making universal statements about the sexes in her book:

Women are portrayed as nurturers, defined by their relationships and focused on contextual thinking; men are depicted as abstract thinkers, defined by individual achievement. We should listen to women's "voice," argue[s] Gilligan . . . because women's culture offers the basis for a transformation of our society, a transformation based on the womanly values of responsibility, connection, selflessness, and caring, rather than on separation, autonomy, and hierarchy.[50]

In contrast to the conservative position, a progressive reading would interpret Gilligan's use of sex differences as a methodology for challenging gender, as an example of how contingently-formed gender differences can be strategically deployed to unsettle existing inequities between the sexes.[51] Sex differences, pursuant to a progressive reading, are context-bound. They are associated with language, more than individual identity, so that to the extent language can be changed, gender identity can also be transformed. Progressive readers ground the sex differences Gilligan identifies in the context of the moral development theory she sought to change, overlooking the many instances where Gilligan seems to speak of sex differences as if they are universal.

Marie Ashe associates a methodology similar to a progressive Gilligan reading with a "model of public policy-making" within contemporary critical theory and philosophy, whereby, in the language of feminist jurisprudence, "the silencing of female voices in the public discourse [is attributed] to . . . the cultural valorization of modes of discourse which negate or distort certain realities of female experience."[52] In the next three chapters, I implicitly follow a progressive Gilligan methodology in arguing that the editorial placement of contracts cases involving women, in the fourth edition of the Dawson, Harvey, and Henderson contracts casebook, conveyed messages regarding the subordination of particular contract rules. That is, like Gilligan, I identify sex-related traits in my research (for me, differences between textbook cases involving women and those that did not), and then treat the differences as clues to a critique of the dominant interpretation of contract law.[53]

There is support in Gilligan's book for both a conservative and a progressive interpretation. In the following subsection, I present conflicting evidence on the question of whether the sex-linked traits Gilligan discusses should be understood as an essential part of gender identity. In the succeeding subsection, I discuss the book's conflicting evidence regarding Gilligan's validation of the traits conservative readers link to women.

Inherent Differences

A conservative reader's conviction that the sex differences Gilligan describes can be severed from the context of moral development structures is supported by an introductory statement to *In a Different Voice* which emphasizes Gilligan's intention to focus her work on women. From the conservative reader's perspective, if *In a Different Voice* is primarily about women, rather than moral development models, then it is reasonable to loosen the sex-linked traits Gilligan describes from their moorings in the book. In contrast to the conservative statement of the book's theme, a concluding statement of purpose is more compatible with the progressive interpretation that Gilligan's objective in the book is to reform the content of moral development theory.

Conservative Purpose:
In presenting excerpts from this work, I report research in progress whose aim is to provide, in the field of human development, a clearer representation of women's development which will enable psychologists and others to follow its course and understand some of the apparent puzzles it presents, especially those that pertain to women's identity formation and their moral development in adolescence. For women, I hope this work will offer a representation of their thought that enables them to see better its integrity and validity, to recognize the experiences their thinking reflects, and to understand the line of its development.[54]

Progressive Purpose:
Since this dialogue contains the dialectic that creates the tension of human development, the silence of women in the narrative of adult development distorts the conception of its stages and sequence. Thus, I want to restore in part the missing text of women's development, as they describe their conceptions of self and morality in the early years. In focusing primarily on the differences between the accounts of women and men, my aim is to enlarge developmental understanding by including the perspectives of both of the sexes. While the judgments considered come from a small and highly educated sample, they elucidate a contrast and make it possible to recognize not only what is missing in women's development but also what is there.[55]

Notice that the conservative version of purpose refers to women's thought, identity formation, and moral development in singular terms ("*its* integrity," "the line of *its* development"), as if women are interchangeable. Gilligan uses singular terms to describe women elsewhere in the book, most noticeably in the title of her first chapter, "Woman's Place in Man's Life Cycle," and in her failure consistently to qualify references to women, either by using limiting adjectives, such as "some" or "many," or by linking the word "women" in the text to the individuals she interviewed in her research.[56] The repetitive references to women as if they are identical furthers the conservative interpretation that the sex differences Gilligan discusses are inherent in all women.

In contrast to the conservative statement of purpose, the progressive version contains a statement in which Gilligan explicitly acknowledges the partiality of her research sample. Her admission suggests to the progressive reader that Gilligan does not assume women are identical, that she is aware of differences among women which might have altered her research.

Gilligan overtly supports the progressive interpretation that the sex differences she identifies are not inherent in the sexes in at least two separate passages:

> The different voice I describe is characterized not by gender but theme. Its association with women is an empirical observation, and it is primarily through women's voices that I trace its development. But this association is not absolute, and the contrasts between male and female voices are presented here to highlight a distinction between two modes of thought and to focus a problem of interpretation rather than to represent a generalization about either sex.[57]

> The choice of a girl whose moral judgments elude existing categories of developmental assessment is meant to highlight the issue of interpretation rather than to exemplify sex differences per se.[58]

However, other evidence in the book supports a conservative interpretation that Gilligan believes the sex differences she discusses are universally linked to women. For example, with the exception of a short account of psychological research on the relationship between sex roles and violence,[59] most of the thirty-nine pages in Gilligan's second chapter are devoted to extensive quotations from two eleven-year-old children and one twenty-seven-year-old woman. At the conclusion of the chapter, Gilligan abruptly employs unqualified statements about women[60] in two rhetorically critical paragraphs that summarize the major theoretical model of her book, the ethic of care.[61] These passages might be read to contain an overly enthusiastic but pardonable proposal that Gilligan's model of moral development is a model all women will find appropriate. But a conservative reader could reasonably infer that Gilligan's shift from particular research subjects to generalized statements about the sexes also implies that Gilligan believes that the traits she depicted in her female research subjects are a fundamental part of the identity of all women.

By choosing an anthropomorphism ("voice") to entitle a book describing a theoretical model of moral development, Gilligan ingeniously refers both to the ethic of care and to herself, since her book is in the "voice" of (written by) a woman, "different" from (unlike) other moral development scholarship. However, the title of the book also supports the conservative impression that Gilligan's book constitutes evidence of universal sex differences. Gilligan repeatedly uses the word "voice" in her book as a synonym for the feminine self.[62] Moreover, because much of the book's argument is presented through quotations from research interviews, the "different voice" metaphor hovers over the entire book, connecting each of the women Gilligan interviews with "a different voice." These clues within the book suggest, then, that Gilligan's title also refers to "a" female research subject, an exemplary model of womanhood from whose representative discourse the ethic of care was developed. Thus, the title *In a Different Voice* subtly suggests the ethic of care is an essential feminine trait.[63]

Some of the conflicting evidence I have just presented regarding the book's position on the universality of sex differences requires a closer attention to detail and subtlety of meaning than many readers might tend to give *In a Different Voice*. Gilligan illustrates her argument on behalf of an ethic of care with interesting pieces of many individual lives, which she draws not only from her research, but also from literature and films; she has a conversational style that is unburdened by psychological jargon; and she has a chipper, fresh-air voice that is easy to read. I doubt, however, that either interpretation of the book is dependent on close rather than casual attention to the question of whether sex differences are inherent. Far away as well as up close there is ambiguity in the book on this question. Thus, a reader's interpretation of the book can be a function of what she wants to find rather than what the book definitively says.

Defining Differences

The conservative view that the gender differences Gilligan discusses can be universalized entails a fixed definition of those differences that is quite at odds with the relational definition a progressive reader ascribes to such words as "caretaking." This subsection addresses the conflicting evidence within *In a Different Voice* regarding this definitional dispute. In the preceding subsection, I tried to present evidence in support of the conservative and progressive interpretations even-handedly, a goal reflecting my view that *In a Different Voice* contains conflicting evidence regarding the essential character of sex differences. As I will soon reveal, my view that the conservative definition of the sex differences Gilligan describes is wrong prevents me from maintaining this balance here. I will, however, try to account for the conservative (mis)reading.

The conservative view that *In a Different Voice* validates gender differences is substantially fueled by the sympathy and enthusiasm Gilligan displays in her book for women, for the ethic of care so closely associated with women, and for the traits of groundedness, caretaking, and connectedness which are linked to the ethic of care as a model of moral development. Gilligan's book-length commitment to legitimating the ethic of care constitutes the most significant evidence for the conservative position that the feminine traits implicated by the model should be promoted in other contexts.

However, the conservative move to sever these traits from moral development discourse depends upon a static definition of the traits, a definition which does not take into account the role the traits play as concepts in the ethic of care as a model of moral development. In contrast, the progressive view that the book's sex differences are context-bound depends upon a strategic definition of these traits; that is, a definition of each trait which subtly but constantly changes depending on the particular person and circumstance being described.

The progressive definition of sex differences as flexible, rather than static, can be illustrated by considering the meaning of "caretaking" in the context of Gilligan's ethic of care. Gilligan describes this model of moral development as a sequence of three stages that occur over time in the life of an individual. During the first stage an individual is primarily focused "on caring for the self," a stage which is described in retrospect, by the one who has left it, as "selfish."[64] The second (and probably most familiar) stage is the "feminine" stage, in which "good is equated with caring for others."[65] During this stage an individual is often unable to "sort out the confusion between self-sacrifice and care inherent in the conventions of feminine goodness."[66] At the third stage an individual learns to care for herself as well as for others, to accept responsibility for moral choice. Gilligan describes the move to this stage as the transition from "femininity to adulthood."[67]

In the context of this complicated model of moral choice-making, caretaking has multiple meanings, some of which are disabling and unappealing while others are inspiring and attractive. Indeed, Gilligan illustrates a multiplicity of meanings for the term "caretaking" quite effectively over the course of her chapter describing the abortion research project, for the women who are quoted in this chapter are depicted in various stages of moral development.[68]

Several aspects of *In a Different Voice*, other than Gilligan's affectionate stance toward the ethic of care, may contribute to the conservative reader's static definition of sex differences. The ethic of care is misleading but attractively introduced in the second chapter, which is entitled "Images of Relationship,"[69] as a "web of connection [in which] no one is left alone."[70] By immediately contrasting the web with an image of hierarchy, Gilligan emphasizes the two-dimensionality of the web, a misleading gesture, in my view, because it flattens the ethic of care. This imagery deprives the ethic of care of the dynamic character Gilligan gives it elsewhere. The web imagery also sentimentalizes the ethic of care, in that the modifying words "of connection" euphemistically transform the sticky, trapping character of a spider's web into a more agreeable landing place. The conservative claim that "feminine" traits are fixed in meaning and good in character corresponds to an image that is like a party manners version of the ethic of care.

Because Gilligan occasionally neglects to acknowledge the dark side of the "feminine" traits when she deploys them, these omissions also contribute to the conservative assumption that sex differences have a fixed meaning. Thus, for example, after Gilligan relates a child named Jeffrey's account of deciding a conflict about playing outside or staying with his mother on the basis of what is right, she then describes his resolution as "hierarchical" and "abstract."[71] In contrast, after she relates a child named Karen's account of choosing which friend to play with on the basis of "taking turns," or "who's alone," Gilligan describes Karen's resolution as "focusing on who is left out."[72] Gilligan does not acknowledge the abstract character of Karen's implicit rule system. Moreover, by characterizing Jeffrey's decision-making as "hierarchical" she emphasizes its (his?) inherent violence, but she does not admit the potential for violence in Karen's decision. This omission is inconsistent with Gilligan's acknowledgments elsewhere of the harm moral responsibility sometimes entails.[73] It is an incident that romanticizes the female child, in contrast to the male, and it may encourage the conservative tendency to romanticize and generalize feminine traits.

Staking a Claim: What's at Stake

In this section I return to Susannah Sherry's conservative reading of *In a Different Voice.* My purpose in describing and assessing the consequences of her work for issues that concern women is to discuss an example of what can be at stake in the choice legal activists make regarding the interpretation and use of Gilligan in their work. It probably comes as no surprise that I think feminist legal politics are at stake in this choice. Indeed, Sherry's piece seems a particularly appropriate selection as an example of a conservative interpretation of Gilligan because of her explicit disavowal of feminist politics in her article. "[My piece is] not limit[ed] to a feminist perspective," she states. "Feminists have a particular political agenda that may or may not be shared by all women (and is shared by some men). Rather this is an analysis of a feminine perspective that encompasses aspects of personality and relationship to the world that have nothing to do with one's political preferences."[74] Since I believe that any use of gender is likely to have consequences for the position of women in some way, one of the questions one might ask of Sherry's article is what her politics turned out to be.

Relying on Gilligan, but also other feminist scholars who have critiqued dominant theories, Sherry decontextualizes two sets of traits Gilligan identifies as related to the ethic of care and the ethic of rights, and abstracts them into generalized descriptions of female and male worldviews. Thus, she claims that women have a connected, contextual and responsibility-oriented worldview, whereas men have an autonomous, abstract, and rights-oriented perspective.[75] Sherry then uses these dichotomized pairs of traits to genderize two competing but hierarchically related political theories, liberal individualism and civic republicanism. She asserts that civic republicanism, or communitarian jurisprudence, is feminine, whereas liberal individualism is masculine.[76]

Having identified civic republicanism as feminine, Sherry also argues that a feminine perspective or civic republicanism can be identified in Sandra Day O'Connor's Supreme Court opinions. This leads to an exposition of O'Connor's opinions and a largely uncritical appraisal of a number of decisions in which O'Connor participated. Despite Sherry's claims about O'Connor's feminine jurisprudence, she acknowledges that O'Connor is "solidly in the conservative camp on most issues," and that were she replaced by a "male ideological soul mate of Justice Rehnquist" it wouldn't make much difference.[77] The claim for O'Connor's feminine perspective is supported by an analysis of several cases in which she asserts that O'Connor is particularly protective of rights that protect individuals against exclusion from community membership or that prevent individuals from being condemned to outsider status, and that this illustrates her femininity.

What is Sherry up to in this article? Why does she invoke gender differences to critique liberal individualism and to analyze the particular role of Sandra Day O'Connor on the Court? Does Sandra Day O'Connor have "a different voice"? And what's the difference between feminism and femininity?

Sherry claims, invoking Gilligan, that by describing civic republicanism as feminine she hopes to correct the historical masculine distortion of law in which liberalism triumphed over republicanism.

I am dubious that identifying civic republicanism with women is going to do much for it as a political theory, although I could be wrong. With respect to her focus on Justice O'Connor, Sherry hypothesizes that recognizing that O'Connor "draws her jurisprudence from her femininity rather than her politics . . . might change the outcome of some cases."[78] Well, that would be desirable. Indeed, the American Law Professors' brief submitted in *Webster* included an argument that government regulation of abortion should be rejected because it prevented women from making their reproductive decisions in conjunction with their communities—a direct pitch to O'Connor's feminine/civic republicanism, although it is unclear from her opinion in *Webster* that she caught it. This objective, like Sherry's plans for civic republicanism, also seems like a long shot. Her particular take on O'Connor's feminine jurisprudence does not seem to me predictive of how O'Connor decides particular cases.

If, for example, O'Connor is concerned about excluding individuals from community, how can we explain her vote in *Hardwick*,[79] which excluded homosexuals from the community of those who can legally practice sexual intimacy? How can we explain her vote in *Croson*,[80] which overrode a community's decision with respect to the distribution of job opportunities among its citizens? Moreover, I am suspicious that the voice Sherry sought when she studied O'Connor's opinions was not *a* different voice, but *the* different voice, the model woman conservatives see in Gilligan's book. I am less interested in O'Connor as caretaker and connector than I am in her experience of discrimination at an elite law school, her life in a western state court system, her relationships on the Court, her treatment for cancer. Sherry's distinction between feminism and femininity is disingenuous, I think, for her characterization of O'Connor's feminine jurisprudence is an exercise of power. Her interpretation imposes a stereotypically feminine image of womanliness on O'Connor's opinions.

The question then becomes: What's at stake in my critique of Sherry's conservative reading of Gilligan? I have speculated that I don't think much will come of the gender-related aspects of her project, as she describes it, although I certainly hope I'm wrong with respect to influencing Justice O'Connor. But is there any harm in Sherry's approach? Is it the concern of feminist legal activists—that the strategy of difference is accompanied by a danger that gender will be strengthened as a form of social control through such efforts?

One specific danger I see in Sherry's conservative reading of Gilligan is that her description of O'Connor as a feminine communitarian affords a womanist defense for O'Connor's judicial, political conservatism, for her unprogressive votes in a wide range of cases. I do not think she should be screened from responsibility for those positions because she is a woman.

A second danger I see in Sherry's use of Gilligan, and other conservative interpretations which abstract Gilligan's discussion of traits relating to the ethic of care in order to plant them in foreign soil, is that this treatment of caretaking or connectedness artificially valorizes domestic roles traditionally assumed by white middle-class women. It sentimentalizes and romanticizes self-sacrifice, and inadequately acknowledges the costs and problems of this attitude. Although Sherry's treatment of these traits may not have serious material consequences, other such treatment could. This was the case, as I have already pointed out, with Rosalind Rosenberg's testimony in *Sears*,[81] in which she claimed that because women were relationship-focused they were unlikely to want the commission sales jobs the EEOC was suing Sears to extend to them.[82]

Although Sherry's piece does not raise this issue directly, a third problem with reading Gilligan conservatively is that such a reading can narrow the feminist political agenda to issues involving the work/family conflict. If women are limited, as the conservative interpretation suggests, to caretaking and relationally-focused issues, then many other concerns women have which these concepts do not address or which they misrepresent will be overlooked as we plan the next campaign.

Finally, the most significant problem—not particularly in Sherry's piece but generally—with reading Gilligan conservatively is that a static interpretation of gender stereotypes drawn from Gilligan's book excludes alternative stances and postures of women who do not conform to the conservative reading of Gilligan's book. Those excluded are likely to be different from the subjects of Gilligan's research projects, which means they are likely to be women of color, non-middle-class, lesbian, non-Western, or aged. There is harm caused to these women by neglecting their interests, and there is harm caused to all women by privileging differences between the sexes, as the conservative interpretation does, to differences within the sexes.

Under a progressive reading of Gilligan, sex-linked differences in discourse function as a clue, as a "logic of identification" to the location of silenced, marginalized, or subordinated groups for whom legal assistance may be helpful. This use of sex-linked differences is cautious, nondualistic, partial, contingent, and sensitive to many constituencies of women. These characteristics make it a decided improvement over a conservative use of *In a Different Voice*. Nevertheless, to the extent sex differences are deployed at all, they are likely to have some effect on the construction and protection of gender. And a progressive reading does not avoid the danger of the difference strategy. But I am unable to imagine how we can advance the position of women in law without thinking of what the position of women is. The best we can do, I think, is rephrase what I have just said: we must try to think of what the positions of women are.

Re-reading Contracts: A Feminist Analysis of a Contracts Casebook

4

A Feminist Analysis of a Casebook? An Introductory Explanation

Like many other contracts instructors, I presently teach my course from Dawson, Harvey, and Henderson's contracts casebook.[1] The next three chapters are a feminist examination of that casebook. My objective is critical in character, for I believe a feminist analysis should change one's consciousness. However, I do not intend to deliver a diatribe against the casebook or its editors. Rather, I am writing this for the readers of other casebooks, as well as for readers of *Dawson, Harvey, and Henderson*, in the hope of accomplishing two goals. First, I want to demonstrate that readers' views about gender affect their understanding of a law casebook. Second, I want to demonstrate that gendered aspects of a casebook affect readers' understanding of the law and of themselves. If these endeavors are successful, I hope that casebook readers will be liberated from some of their opinions about gender, opinions that casebooks foster and sustain. Indeed, this book is designed to contribute to the feminist effort to diminish the power that ideas about gender exercise over our lives. I also hope, somewhat paradoxically, that exposing and examining gender in a casebook will liberate and vitalize qualities within readers, as well as approaches to contract doctrine, that are currently linked with women.

My plan is to use this chapter to discuss the nature and value of a feminist analysis of a contracts casebook. I will also describe a variety of possible casebook readers in order to create a shared sense of readers and their attitudes toward gender. In the next chapter, I will undertake an overview of *Dawson, Harvey, and Henderson*, examining both how women are treated in the casebook and the "maleness" of the casebook. Finally, in chapter 6, I will combine and elaborate some of the approaches used in the overview section by considering two individual cases.

The analysis of *Dawson, Harvey, and Henderson* which follows is primarily concerned with the power of gender in the casebook. It is this focus on gender that makes me claim my analysis is feminist. I use "gender" to mean the reductive, dualistic classification of a wide array of social and psychological characteristics according to biological sex. Gender has power because we use it as a category to explain differences among individuals; it is an idea that organizes and colors many of our responses to others—what we expect of them, what we hope for them. It also affects what we desire for ourselves and how others view us. I believe that gender is a significant constraint on the lives of most women and men. It affects how I present myself (my voice, in this book), who my friends are, which students seek me out, which ones I will care for, and what my work is—which courses I teach and which scholarly projects I choose. Indeed, because the explanatory force of gender can be so convincing, gender often functions as a kind of emotional and rational shortcut. Our reliance on it, as on any theory,[2] can save us effort. But it can also induce us to avoid thinking, listening, or responding very carefully. Thus, despite the fact that we could understand our differences in other ways, and often do, our ideas about gender have a profound impact on our lives: they divide us from one another and from ourselves.[3]

I also claim my analysis of this casebook is feminist because of my oppositional stance toward gender. Some individuals who explore and analyze gender characteristics implicitly subscribe to that aspect of gendered thinking that privileges "male" traits over those generally thought to be female.[4] I maintain, however, that a gender-focused analysis is feminist only when its analyst is consciously oppositional, when the analyst seeks to change the impact of gender categories either to improve the position of women[5] or to liberate both sexes from gender constraints.[6] This oppositional aspect of feminism has important implications for my book. Because I believe that the social and psychological differences between men and women are constructed and mutable, rather than biologically determined and immutable,[7] I believe that the act of focusing on gender should be oppositional; it should change the effect of gender on a writer and her readers by unsettling those ideas in their consciousnesses.[8]

I have identified my work as a feminist analysis with some reservations. I recognize that the feminist label may seem uninviting to certain readers, and I do not want to lose those readers peremptorily. Moreover, I believe that the creativity, flexibility, and subordinated opposition that women's life experiences often demand and cultivate are important to the constitution of feminism.[9] I do not want a "feminist" label for this project to jeopardize claims that differing analyses are also feminist.[10] Nevertheless, calling my analysis "feminist" seems desirable as a way to distinguish my project from the task of eliminating overt sexism in a book. I fear that "eliminating overt sexism" could seem limited to rooting out instances of pejorative, demeaning treatment of women in casebooks, and that would not accurately describe my essay. While I believe eliminating that kind of sexism in books is an important and challenging enterprise,[11] I concede at the outset that *Dawson, Harvey, and Henderson* seems cleansed of any gratuitously negative comments about women. But I believe editors could conscientiously eliminate all instances of female degradation in their casebooks and still produce books that would affect readers' views about gender and that would be subject to multiple interpretations because of readers' gender attitudes. A "feminist" casebook analysis will be useful, therefore, as long as the concept of gender has any meaningful content.[12]

Thus far I have discussed the significance that the power of gender has for my work. However, since my subject is the relationship between gender and a casebook, my analysis of *Dawson, Harvey, and Henderson* also depends on several assumptions about casebooks which I should state. I do not believe that a casebook is simply a neutral reflection of what students need to know to practice law, to pass the bar, to think like lawyers, or to become law teachers. I maintain that, even within the constraints of professional necessity,[13] editors have a wide range of choice in their case selections, their comments, their notes, their problems, and their questions, and the choices they make are not inevitable. The choices could be different and, indeed, choices about content do differ among casebooks within particular subject areas. I also believe that a casebook is a powerful document. The editorial choices within a casebook determine how many readers think about the law of a doctrinal area, about lawyering in that field, about clients, and about legal reasoning. (Indeed, since *Dawson, Harvey, and Henderson* may be one of only five books a first-year student reads in a given year, its influence over students' views may extend beyond the "professional" concerns just listed.) Because a casebook has such power, and because its contents are subject to editorial choice, analyzing the biases of a particular casebook could challenge the effect of the casebook on its readers.

Despite my position that casebook editors are responsible for creating works of significant power over readers, I do not believe that casebooks are frozen artifacts. I believe, with Stanley Fish, that "linguistic and textual facts, rather than being the *objects* of interpretations are its *products.*"[14] Readers cannot fully screen themselves out of their reading and interpretation, just as they are unable to ignore the social and institutional setting in which a casebook is read. Think, for example, of how differently one might interpret *Dawson, Harvey, and Henderson* by reading it along with Patrick Atiyah's *Rise and Fall of Freedom of Contract*[15] rather than with *Legalines*.[16] Since I believe readers have a significant role in creating the meaning of a casebook, I want at this point to introduce my impressions of a group of typical casebook readers. I hope that by drawing portraits of a variety of individuals who read casebooks I can convince my readers that singular interpretations of *Dawson, Harvey, and Henderson* are unlikely. My portraits of casebook readers concentrate almost entirely on the readers' attitudes toward gender, in order to broaden and deepen our shared views about the content of gender. By using these portraits later in the book I hope to convince you that I am not the only reader of *Dawson, Harvey, and Henderson* with a gendered perspective, and I also hope these portraits will remind you of your own ideas about gender.[17]

The readers I have created are fictional; indeed, they may not avoid seeming stereotyped. Nevertheless, I believe they resemble students and colleagues I have known in twelve years of law teaching, and, while you may not see yourself as any one reader, you may see parts of yourself in more than one. Because I will refer to these examples of readers later in the book, I am giving them taglines for names.

The Feminist

Whether this reader is male or female, he or she is a self-identified feminist. If this reader is female, she is proud to be a woman; if male, he is admiring of women's achievements. These readers are interested in the historical, social, and psychological discrimination against women in our society; they oppose such discrimination; and they are informed about the ways in which such mistreatment has been resisted. They also believe that the construction of gender has locked many men into sex roles that uncomfortably restrict them. Gender is on this reader's mind; she notices how many women are in a room, how many speak, and who listens when they do. She has special knowledge about women and their concerns, the way some people know a lot about the Civil War, about jazz, or the history of baseball. This reader might chide me for making such comparisons, however, for The Feminist can be quite single-minded and somewhat humorless about feminist issues. They mean a lot to her.

The Woman-Centered Reader

A modified version of the Feminist is the woman whose experience as a wife and mother has altered her career. She is acutely conscious that the majority of male students and faculty members have not had to modify substantially their work lives for the sake of their spouses or their children. Having needed other women's help in her family work, where carpooling, child care exchange, and nursery school cooperatives require a high degree of cooperation, reliability and trust, she tends to see women students and faculty members as friends and allies. She may not identify herself as a feminist, in part because she fears that might alienate her from her family and her old friends, but because she continues to take care of other people as an additional, time-consuming occupation, she has learned to live a divided life, with some attention on her casebooks (and single-minded instructors), some on her family's demands and some attention reserved for her natural law school allies, who are often The Feminist Readers.

The Reader with a Chip on the Shoulder

The female version of this reader is angry at men, perhaps because of some mistreatment she has suffered, or perhaps because of her empathy for other women who have suffered mistreatment on account of sex. Because anger is often repellent, one may attribute a paranoid personality style to this reader. She seems to be constantly looking for clues that women will be denied justice in law school, as they have been elsewhere. If this reader is a student, she is vigilantly examining her instructors or the casebooks they have chosen for any indication she can find of prejudice against women. As a faculty member she is likely to have her colleagues and her casebooks under steady surveillance for sexist offenses. This reader may not, however, make herself known to individuals whom she considers unsympathetic. She can be very isolated in the law school setting.

The male version of this reader is angry at women. For many reasons he resents the women in law school, whether they are students or teachers; he sees them as threats to a system of male dominance that he supports. Faculty members of this type are clever about masking their anger, at least around self-described feminists, but students, who sometimes act as if faculty members can't see them (or perhaps don't care if they do), reveal themselves by snorting if they hear the name of Geraldine Ferraro—but not, say, Mario Cuomo, or by a tease of a hiss if too many classroom hypotheticals involve *female* judges, lawyers, or parties. This reader may be searching his classes or his casebooks for evidence that patriarchy lives, despite the aberrational presence of the women who surround him. Or, like the female version of this reader, he may be looking for clues to justify his anger.

The Innocent Gentleman

This casebook reader also sees law school women as a challenge to his view of a male dominated world, but he is more bewildered than angry about their presence. He may never have seen his father drink a glass of water his mother didn't pour, and he does not understand how to treat women as colleagues and authority figures. Must he, or can he, compete with them? What about sexual relationships; how can he understand such people other than as sexual objects? He may be searching his classes and his casebooks for evidence about the truth of a worldview where women have more restricted roles than they have in the law school setting.

The Reader Who Is Undressed for Success

Whether these casebook readers are male or female, their primary characteristic regarding gender is insecurity about their ability to conform to a popular image of "lawyers," which they understand as masculine, not feminine. They fear that successful lawyers are analytical, rather than emotional; adversarial, rather than cooperative; certain, not tentative; ambitious, not flexible. They do not identify with Paul Newman in *The Verdict*, Professor Kingsfield in *The Paper Chase*, or even the elegantly tough Katharine Hepburn in *Adam's Rib*, and they have grave doubts that their (purportedly) masculine traits are sufficiently dominant to allow them to succeed in law school, as students or faculty members. Whether they read the casebook to find evidence to confirm their fears, or to dispel them, they are very sensitive about gender questions in their casebooks.

The Individualist

These readers are assertive, conscientious students and faculty members who have modelled themselves after men and women who have succeeded in the public world. Because they have seldom met an obstacle they have not been able to overcome, they are suspicious of claims that membership in a group can handicap a person, regardless of individual merit. Some of these readers conduct their lives quite self-consciously and high-mindedly according to the tenets of sex neutrality; others harbor traces or even wide stains of misogyny. As men, they want to continue rising to the top or revolving on the fast track unimpeded by a group of women who seek to change the rules of the game. As women, they do not want consciousness-raising to spoil their victories. These readers try to be unconscious about the sex or the gender of people in the casebook or elsewhere.

The Civil Libertarian

Because of their general political stance as individuals who favor civil liberties and rights for the oppressed, these readers are likely to oppose invidious discrimination against women. Indeed, some of these readers may have been interested in feminism at some time, particularly during the late sixties and the early seventies. However, these readers are currently committed to other causes, such as opposition to racism, the elimination of hunger, and the antinuclear movement. Whether they genuinely believe that the oppression of women is less significant than it used to be, or whether they simply believe that other oppression deserves a superior claim to their attention, they prefer to avoid noticing gender in the casebook.

The Undeserving Male or Female Reader

Like the Reader Who Is Undressed for Success, these readers are also insecure about their abilities to succeed in law school, as students or faculty members. Because they have had good luck, well-placed connections, or ample money in their lives, they may fear that they do not deserve the positions and opportunities that have come their way. Unlike the Individualists, these readers are not insensitive to the effects group membership can have on an individual. Noticing gender in the casebook, however, unacceptably reminds both the Undeserving Male and Female about the backs they have walked over. The Undeserving Female, whose gender may have given her a boost she feels she was unworthy to receive, wishes to avoid hard questions, like affirmative action, which noticing gender might provoke.

Before turning to *Dawson, Harvey, and Henderson,* let me acknowledge again that casebook readers are much more complicated than I have presented them. Many people may not consciously notice gender at all, while many others may combine attitudes and personality traits which I have divided among the types I have drawn. Because the sketches are brief, and because they concentrate almost entirely on the readers' attitudes toward gender, these readers seem one dimensional and more like caricatures than I want them to. But I believe that any discussion of the choices the editors have made in creating this casebook requires a shared sense of variety of casebook readers; the character sketches are necessary, in my view, to underscore the variety of readers' attitudes concerning gender.

5

An Overview of the Contracts Casebook: Dis-covering the Gender of Contract Culture

By segregating social and psychological characteristics into two categories and linking those categories to one sex or the other, our ideas about gender constrain our beliefs about what kinds of work men and women can do, what their interests are, how they can act, and how they can feel. In addition, because traits commonly identified as male are generally more highly valued than characteristics associated with women, our ideas about gender have a constituting effect on the continuing imbalance of power between men and women. For example, because "men's" work is considered more important than "women's" work, and "male" analytical skills are more valued than "female" intuition, women who choose a conventional woman's job and exhibit common feminine attributes are likely to have less respect (from women as well as men),[1] less power, and less money[2] than women who are more masculine in manner and occupation. I believe that *Dawson, Harvey, and Henderson* strongly supports this ideology of gender, and my primary objective in this chapter is to expose how the casebook functions to sustain and further these gender-related ideas.

I have chosen to begin with an overview of the casebook because, for many of my readers, the casebook's relationship to ideas about gender may seem apparent only after a cumulative description of the gendered aspects of many different facets of the book. This will be particularly true, I think, for readers who are unaccustomed to noticing gender-related ideas, readers who identify with casebook readers like the Individualists and the Civil Libertarians.[3]

In providing an overview of the book, I pursue two different kinds of discussion. In the first part, my analysis proceeds from concrete questions regarding women. I look at women as "characters" in the cases, among the "authors" whose decisions or legal commentary the editors have included in the book, and in the language of the book.[4] Most appellate decisions allow one to learn something about the people who are parties in the cases, such as what their jobs are, what activities they undertake that lead to litigation, and occasionally what their characters are like. Judicial descriptions of parties do not, however, stand alone in a casebook. Just as editors are responsible for choosing the cases readers read, they also influence readers' views about the parties in the cases by the comments, elaborations, or questions they include with the decisions. Indeed, as I will show, readers can also interpret the significance of editorial silence about the parties. In addition, readers' views about people in a case will be affected by the people in neighboring cases, so that editorial organization will trigger readers' views regarding gender. Thus, I also observe the effect of the editorial arrangement of women's cases. In the first part of the chapter I shall look at men primarily as a gauge by which to evaluate the treatment of women.

In the second part of the chapter, my focus shifts to comparisons between abstract characteristics which we commonly attribute to men and characteristics of the casebook. I shall concentrate, in other words, on the analytical, autonomous, abstract, and neutral qualities of the book. Because the book does not exhibit many characteristics commonly characterized as feminine (such as sentimentality, earthiness, and compassion), I use women in this part primarily as a way of understanding what is not womanly. My aim in this second part is to reveal the gendered aspects of the book which do not directly pertain to women.[5] Although I am describing the gender-related aspects of the casebook in both parts of this section, I try to demonstrate the ways in which different casebook readers would interpret the materials the editors have chosen. I want to show not only how the editors' choices affect the readers' views of contract doctrine and their views of themselves, but also the different ways they understand the editors' choices.

The Casebook Treatment of Women

Women as Characters

There are substantially fewer women than men among the parties in *Dawson, Harvey, and Henderson's* cases. Only 39 of the 183 major cases in the casebook contain women.[6] Men, therefore, vastly outnumber women as "characters" in the book. Indeed, men not only monopolize the majority of the cases in which women do not appear but they also appear in most of the cases involving women.[7] Because Dawson,

Harvey, and Henderson allow male parties to outnumber female parties so significantly, readers who notice gender differences are likely to be sensitive not only to the marginal representation of women in the casebook, but also to any sex role stereotyping within the decisions. Moreover, the cumulative impression provided by similarities among the women parties could provoke readers somewhat disinclined to notice gender to observe the casebook's links between women and ideas about gender.

Women's Work

The most obvious commonality among the women parties is the narrow range of life situations in which they appear. Women, in this casebook, have legal problems arising from the limited activities typically associated with their sex, and the jobs they have are the most stereotypical forms of women's work. Their disputes involve contract problems arising from some experience in a family relationship—as wife,[8] as mother-in-law,[9] sister-in-law,[10] or niece.[11] Outside family relationships, one can see a woman in this casebook having contract issues that arise only from such limited stereotypically female roles as home purchaser,[12] home seller,[13] nurse,[14] fashion designer,[15] charitable benefactress,[16] entertainer,[17] mental incompetent,[18] and welfare recipient.[19] Men in *Dawson, Harvey, and Henderson* also have legal problems arising from family relationships,[20] as well as from positions such as home purchaser,[21] home seller,[22] mental incompetent,[23] and nurse.[24] But men's legal problems in *Dawson, Harvey, and Henderson* also stem from much broader, more diverse situations, such as their work as a doctor,[25] contractor,[26] farmer,[27] miller,[28] coal dealer,[29] town commissioner,[30] lumberman,[31] deputy sheriff,[32] sportscaster,[33] prize fighter,[34] engineer,[35] manager[36]—there's even a man in one case who is a lawbook writer with a drinking problem.[37]

One might object to the critical implications of the preceding observations on the grounds that "life is, or has been, like that for women; the cases which have been selected accurately reflect differences between men and women in the real world." One might think that Dawson, Harvey, and Henderson's inclusion of a few cases in which women are successful entrepreneurs, such as the fashion designer and the entertainer cases,[38] fully vindicates their choices of cases involving women. The entrepreneurial cases not only complement the cases in which women are engaged in stereotypical activities, but the diminutive number of such cases proportionately reflects the actual participation of women in the predominately male world of business. Indeed, one might claim, including more cases in which women do untraditional things would deceive students about the actual status of women outside the casebook milieu.

This argument strikes me as an ironic diversion. In fact, my impression is that casebook editors generally fail and seldom make much effort to select cases and materials on the basis of how accurately they depict the "real world."[39] Moreover, the issue is not, I think, whether Dawson, Harvey, and Henderson could defend the cases they have chosen. Perhaps they could.[40] What is important to me is the effect that their choices have on readers' views regarding gender. Read together, the cases in this book confirm, rather than challenge, the generalization that women and men mostly do different things, and that women's opportunities are drastically more limited than men's. Most women who read the casebook do so to prepare for a career that historically has been predominantly male, and they may be concerned about the effect gender will have on their legal careers. Because almost all the women in the *Dawson, Harvey, and Henderson* cases do traditional "women's work," the casebook is likely to reinforce readers' fears (or fantasies) that, because gender has been a factor linked to career choice and success in the past, it may inhibit their options in the future.

In addition to perpetuating readers' views about occupational distinctions between women and men, cases in which women do traditional women's work can pose pedagogical problems for casebook readers. Although women's work has not been highly regarded or fairly compensated historically,[41] relying on these views regarding women's work in a decision may inadequately inform readers how to use the case in other situations. *Fitzpatrick v. Michael*[42] is an example of a case in *Dawson, Harvey, and Henderson* in which a court's failure to appreciate women's work obscures the reasoning of the opinion.

Fitzpatrick involves the claim of a practical nurse for specific performance of her employer's agreement to employ her until he died and to leave her a substantial interest in his estate. In exchange, she was to remain with him until he died and provide such services as giving him company, managing his house, driving his car, and nursing him when he was sick. The court declined to grant relief specifically enforcing the contract or negatively preventing Mr. Michael from hiring anyone else, in part because the court was unconvinced that Ms. Fitzpatrick's services were sufficiently "rare and unusual" to warrant these extraordinary remedies:

> [Her services] were varied, it is true, but they required no extraordinary or unusual skill, experience, or capacity. Under the employment, the appellant acted as a nurse, chauffeur, companion, gardener, and housekeeper, and, while it may be difficult to appraise in monetary terms the value of services so varied, nevertheless they involved no more than doing such things as a housewife often does as a part of the ordinary routine of life.[43]

The court in *Fitzpatrick* dramatically devalued the kind of "woman's work" Ms. Fitzpatrick performed for Mr. Michael in concluding that, because her services involved "no more" than things a "housewife often does," her work was not "rare and unusual." This judgment ignored the social significance of the kind of work women have traditionally done, thereby indicating that "women's" work is inferior to "men's." In addition to nourishing this idea about gender, however, the court's distorted treatment of "women's" work functions as an analytical shortcut in the opinion: by analogizing Ms. Fitzpatrick's work to a "housewife's" work, the court avoids explaining why her services for Mr. Michael were not "rare and unusual." This avoidance is likely to prevent some readers from mastering the rules regarding specific enforcement of personal services. For example, Woman-Centered Readers, as well as the Feminist Readers and the female Readers with Chips on Their Shoulders, may be so offended by the court's dismissive attitude toward work they and other women have done that their feelings of rejection or their anger may interfere with their ability to understand the court's refusal to grant Ms. Fitzpatrick specific relief.

The *Fitzpatrick* opinion also pedagogically disserves readers who are undisposed to favor women. Readers who share the court's opinion that women's work is unimportant may be unwisely lulled by this opinion into believing that the law, like the labor market, generally devalues such services.[44] Moreover, Dawson, Harvey, and Henderson make sure that at least some of these readers will be as unlikely to understand the rules regarding specific enforcement of personal services as the readers who support women's concerns. Although the court in *Fitzpatrick* asserts that a negative form of specific enforcement is unavailable if personal services are "part of the ordinary routine of life," the editors place a note case immediately after *Fitzpatrick* involving a contract for personal services that is negatively enforced.[45] In this decision an appellate court temporarily enjoined a football player from playing for any team other than the Dallas Cowboys, pending the completion of a new trial on the plaintiffs' claim against the player for breach of an agreement to play football exclusively for their assignor. By combining *Fitzpatrick* with *Dallas Cowboys*, the editors present without apparent embarrassment two opinions involving the "ordinary routine[s] of [American] life" in which judges assert that while nursing, housekeeping, and companionship are not unique services, playing football . . . ah, well, that's another matter.

Because of its failure to appreciate the uniqueness of "women's" work, the *Fitzpatrick* opinion fails to clearly explain the prohibition against specific enforcement of personal services contracts. The prohibition could be clarified, however, by an interpretation of the decision that might occur to the Feminist, the Woman-Centered Reader, or the Reader with a Chip on Her Shoulder. These readers might wonder how the court could have overlooked the possibility that from the perspective of the parties the services Ms. Fitzpatrick rendered to Mr. Michael may have been uniquely valuable and uncommon. They might think, for example, of how a patient can feel about the care given by a favored nurse, how a parent can feel about the services a valued babysitter performs for her children, and then how an individual like Mr. Michael might have felt about the work a capable housekeeper did for him. When services are personal they can be intensely unusual; no one else can do them quite the same way. Their rareness will depend on the relationship of the individuals involved and the way they evaluate the quality of the work. Only by separating such services from the relationships in which they occur and by dismissing their personal and social significance can their uniqueness be denied. Had the *Fitzpatrick* court been less influenced by traditional ideas about women and more sensitive to the value of personal services such as Ms. Fitzpatrick's, its refusal to award specific performance could actually have been more persuasive.

Dawson, Harvey, and Henderson apparently rely on students or instructors to "save" *Fitzpatrick*. The editors run the risk, however, by placing *Dallas Cowboys* next to *Fitzpatrick* and by failing to comment on the sexism in the *Fitzpatrick* opinion, that the *Fitzpatrick* decision may only be effective in this casebook to perpetuate gender stereotypes about "women's" work.

Women's Character

Moving from observations of what women in the casebook do and how their work is valued to what their characters are like, readers who notice gender issues will find women described in stereotypical and unflattering ways in *Dawson, Harvey, and Henderson.* Although the two major case studies included in the next chapter are designed to illustrate the effect of such treatment in greater depth,[46] I will briefly offer here the examples of two cases in which the characterization of the women could affect how readers view themselves and, in one instance, how they understand the law.

In *Wood v. Lucy, Lady Duff-Gordon,*[47] Judge Cardozo describes a dispute between a man and a woman who agreed to allow him the exclusive right to promote her fashion designs. The designer broke the agreement with the promoter by selling her products elsewhere, in an apparent attempt to make more money by double-dipping.

Lady Duff-Gordon is one of the few women in *Dawson, Harvey, and Henderson* who appears to have had an unconventional, successful career, and she is one of only four parties whose photograph is included in the casebook.[48] Her character, therefore, has more significance than if she were one of many businesswomen, some good, some bad, some in between. Her unique position in the casebook casts her character into prominence, particularly for those readers who are conscious of gender, and from several viewpoints Lady Duff-Gordon's character is disappointing.

Readers who have observed the phenomenal jeans-to-shampoo expansion of designer designated products must wonder how a woman in the early twentieth century could have earned money from dress manufacturers for "a certificate of her approval." The caption under her photograph, reproduced in the casebook from *Good Housekeeping Magazine*, intriguingly states that Lady Duff-Gordon "employ[ed] psychology in designing clothes for women,"[49] but Cardozo and the editors do not describe whatever talent, energy, or imagination this woman may have had.[50] Moreover, the decision's treatment of her legal defense does not redeem the greedy fickleness that her breach of contract suggests. Instead, her claim that the contract lacked mutuality of assent seems like a technical attempt to dodge responsibility in Cardozo's skillful exposition of the reasons for his decision against her. Thus, readers who are inclined to look to Lady Duff-Gordon as a role model are likely to observe that as a successful woman she seems undeserving and unethical. This is not a promising message for those readers who seek to abandon conventional women's roles, although it will be reassuring to the Gentleman Reader and the Reader with a Chip on His Shoulder who hope women will be inhibited in their efforts to break away from gender restrictions.

Other readers, who could be among the Feminist Readers or the female Readers with Chips on Their Shoulders, might be offended that in one of the rare instances in this casebook in which a woman has a nondependent, untraditional career her work involves commercializing the personal appearance of women. These readers believe the fashion industry exploits and degrades women, and they may feel belittled, angered, or disappointed that a woman with Lady Duff-Gordon's prominence in the casebook is engaged in work they cannot respect.

Jackson v. Seymour,[51] a case involving a woman's contract with her brother for the sale of land, illustrates the casebook characterization of women who, unlike Lady Duff-Gordon, do not have successful careers outside the home.[52] I find *Jackson* significant not only because the imagery of the case conveys a restrictive message to readers about what women are like, but also because the imagery is critical to the readers' understanding of the law of the case. Moreover, like Lady Duff-Gordon, Mrs. Jackson's image is particularly meaningful because her case is rare; her case is the only case in *Dawson, Harvey, and Henderson's* unit on consideration in which a contract with inadequate consideration is set aside.

In *Jackson*, Lucy Jackson, having sued her brother because he paid her considerably less for her land than it in fact was worth,[53] manages to have the transaction set aside because of the parties' "confidential relationship." "The parties were brother and sister," the court explains. "He was a successful business man and she a widow in need of money."[54] Because the court in *Jackson* does not elaborate its discussion of the parties' confidential relationship, and because it is unlikely that the decision rests solely on the biological relationship between the parties, the reader who seeks to understand the resolution of the case needs to develop the relationship between Mrs. Jackson and her brother more fully than the court has done.

Connecting the language of the case with typical, gendered ideas about what women and men were generally like in the 1950s, and before, a reader might construe Mrs. Jackson's confidential relationship with her brother in the following manner. Most women need to depend on one man or another in order to get along, and the court's description of Mrs. Jackson as a "widow," along with indications of her poverty, and in contrast to her brother's economic success, suggest that Mrs. Jackson was shrouded with the entailments of emotional bereavement, vulnerability, and economic dependency. All of these characteristics, if they accurately described her situation, could have cast her into a relationship of dependence, trust, and confidence with her brother, in which she was weak and needy and he was strong and providing. This interpretation of Mrs. Jackson as victim simplifies the doctrinal issue in the case: a court will more closely scrutinize the terms of a contract on the grounds that it is based on a confidential relationship when one of the parties can be designated a weakling.

In contrast, if one shuns or does not recognize the stereotypically gendered idea that poor widows have usually been victims, the doctrinal issue in the case is harder to resolve. Suppose, for example, that Mrs. Jackson was an emotionally vigorous woman whose widowhood was of so many years standing that she had long overcome the vulnerability she experienced when her husband died. Or suppose that she was never so emotionally dependent on her husband that his death could affect her relationship with her brother. If neither party in

Jackson is obviously a weakling, the standards the court used to intervene in the parties' contract are harder to understand. We can conceive of a confidential relationship based on deep intimacy and shifting dependencies, particularly between a brother and sister. We can imagine a relationship in which Mrs. Jackson sustained her brother through the trials and tribulations of his business affairs while he offered her economic assistance and emotional support when she needed help. However, overturning a contract based on this sort of confidential relationship would require more blatant judicial judgment calls than the objective theory of contract interpretation usually contemplates.[55] It is not surprising, therefore, that the court in *Jackson* appears to depend on our not thinking of Mrs. Jackson as a vigorous widow and vigilant sister. Rather, the court and the casebook editors (through their silence) count on our complicity in the more typically gendered view of the widow as victim.

I do not mean to suggest that emotional dependency, poverty, or bereaved feelings are unnatural or odious; indeed I believe a court should intervene to protect men and women when their vulnerabilities prevent them from making contract judgments in their best interests.[56] My point about the *Jackson* case is that the brevity of the court's reasoning and the words that the court uses to describe the parties encourage readers to think of Mrs. Jackson in the gender stereotype of the pitiful widow. However innocently, the opinion reinforces a restrictive view that men are strong and women are weak, and it uses that limiting idea as an analytical shortcut to avoid a challenging doctrinal problem.

Readers may wonder, reading this case, whether men who are weak can also obtain this kind of protection, or whether women who are strong cannot count on assistance of this sort. Indeed, readers could easily conclude from reading this case, along with Lady Duff-Gordon's, that women who remain in conventional sex roles are rewarded, while those who break away are not. Moreover, because the decision in *Jackson* implicitly relies on a restrictive way of thinking about what women are like, it particularly discourages readers from broadening their views about the possible ways men and women can act and feel. Instead, *Jackson* teaches readers that gendered thinking will contribute to their success as lawyers.

I hope that the *Lady Duff-Gordon* and *Jackson* discussions suggest how women are stereotypically and unflatteringly depicted in the cases Dawson, Harvey, and Henderson have selected for their casebook.[57] I do not mean to imply here that men should monopolize the villainous roles in a casebook. However, by disproportionately limiting the number of cases involving women in their casebook, and by selecting cases in which women are given stereotypically "feminine" personality traits, Dawson, Harvey, and Henderson offer readers a casebook that furthers gendered ideas that women are not as significant as men and that women are limited to "female" personalities.

Women's Silence

In addition to choosing cases in which women have limited occupations and constricted characterizations, Dawson, Harvey, and Henderson foster confining ideas about women and men by their silence about matters that are important to women. By omitting material which is traditionally more closely linked to women and their experiences than to men, the editors perpetuate that aspect of gendered thinking which privileges "male" concerns. I will briefly discuss one case which illustrates two forms of editorial silence regarding "women's" interests.

Crenshaw v. Williams,[58] the fourth case in the casebook, is an example of a case in which both the opinion writer and the editors omit historical information, relevant to the case, that is of special significance to women. *Crenshaw* would be the first major case in the casebook in which a woman is a party, if the case had not been decided in Kentucky in 1921, before the 1942 amendments to that state's Married Women's Property Act.[59] Although the case involved a contract for the sale of land that Mrs. Williams inherited from her father, her husband—rather than she—was the party in the case, because she was not allowed to convey her land without her husband's consent at the time of the events giving rise to the lawsuit.[60]

Nothing in the casebook explains the problem of incapacity that state law imposed on Mrs. Williams, and other women, at the time of the lawsuit. This silence about the impact of common-law restraints on married women has two effects. First, it leaves Mrs. Williams, who might have been the first principal female "character" in the casebook, standing helplessly in the wings of her own lawsuit, completely dependent on and subordinate to her husband. This stereotypical image of a woman may misrepresent Mrs. Williams' actual relationship with her husband, and it definitely imparts a first impression about women parties for readers that encourages restrictive rather than expansive notions of how women can be.[61]

The editors' failure to mention the status of Kentucky's Married Women's Property Act at the time of the decision in *Crenshaw* is also significant because readers who are familiar with women's history are likely to notice this omission. Because the casebook contains notes about other historical events long overridden by change,[62] these readers may question the editors' avoidance of an appropriate and obvious opportunity to mention a major historical issue affecting women in the field of contract law. Female readers who are aware of past restrictions on married women may be angry at the editors for failing to discuss the problem of married women's legally restricted capacity. Or they may feel belittled by the casebook's silence on this subject—if women's history is unimportant, how important can we ourselves be? Do we have significance only insofar as we are like men, and take men's history for our own? For readers who are unaware of the historical disabilities women endured under the common law, the casebook's silence permits them to remain ignorant and, perhaps, insensitive to the continuing implications of these problems. The editors' silence on this issue nourishes the Individualist and the Civil Libertarian Readers' opinions that women's issues are unrelated to legal concerns.

Crenshaw also symbolically illustrates the silence that the casebook generally evidences regarding legal problems of current significance to women by suggesting one of the "women's" subjects which the casebook omits.[63] The lawsuit in *Crenshaw* arose when the Williamses could not convey clear title to Mrs. Williams' property—a disability which occurred because "[t]hough Mrs. Williams had reached an age at which in the ordinary course of nature she would bear no children, the Kentucky Court of Appeals had earlier held that the possibility remained of her having another child, who, under the will of Mrs. Williams' father, would inherit the property after her death."[64] Thus, a woman's sexuality and reproduction, a subject of enormous historical, current, theoretical, and practical interest to women, lies at the heart of the contract problem in *Crenshaw*.[65]

Although the line I have quoted from the *Crenshaw* decision is the only material in the casebook on the subject of reproduction and sexuality, contractual arrangements have been utilized by women and men availing themselves of recent developments in reproductive technology, and cases involving these issues could be utilized in a contracts course. Thus, for example, a woman who seeks to become pregnant through artificial insemination by a donor other than her husband is required in many states to obtain her husband's written consent if she wants him to be legally responsible for the support of the child she conceives;[66] sperm donors in some states may use contracts to accept or relinquish their rights and responsibilities in children who are conceived with their sperm;[67] and men who wish to sire and father children in marriages in which their wives are infertile have attempted to use contracts as a way to structure arrangements with other women to bear children for them.[68]

The disputes involving reproductive technology generally arise in the context of support or paternity cases, and yet they raise very traditional, basic contract issues, such as problems of consideration, assent, and the interplay between private ordering and social control.[69] Moreover, these disputes can only be understood and successfully argued with contract doctrine and discourse,[70] a discourse which fully dominates the decisions.[71] Because the issues are often cast in a complicated configuration that would be pedagogically stimulating, and because the cases contain subject matter such as human reproduction, the organization of the family, and the legal protection of personhood which could be very meaningful to students, including these materials in this casebook would be a plausible way to break the silence it otherwise imposes on legal problems which currently have particular significance for many women.

Contracts casebook editors might object to using reproductive technology materials, or other materials thought to be of special interest to women, such as cohabitation and separation agreement disputes, on the grounds that they should not be expected to satisfy special interest groups in their case selections. I agree that legal content, not interest group satisfaction, should be the appropriate standard for including material. However, even when "women's" materials like the reproductive technology cases satisfy other pedagogical requirements, editors generally exclude such material from contracts casebooks, presumably because it is "customary" to omit material from casebooks that is considered basic subject matter in other courses.[72] Omitting "women's" issues in contracts, therefore, is purportedly justified as a neutral curricular decision to defer such issues to more appropriate courses, which usually means the domestic relations or sex discrimination courses.

This deferral is not neutral. By confining issues that particularly concern women to domestic relations or sex discrimination courses, casebooks combine with standard law school curriculums to perpetuate the idea that women's interests are personal, concerning only themselves or their families. Men, in contrast, are concerned with the rest of life. Introducing reproductive technology materials into a contracts casebook would integrate a "woman's" issue into a commercial course, thereby loosening a traditional curricular link between subject matter and the sexes. This change would challenge the gendered message curriculums usually imply regarding the separate interests of men and women.

There may, however, be reasons other than course jurisdiction for excluding women's issues like reproductive technology from *Dawson, Harvey, and Henderson*. In this casebook, the editors use predominantly commercial issues to illustrate the complicated doctrines of mutuality of assent, while more personal issues are used to illustrate the counterprinciples of reliance and promissory estoppel.[73] This commercial and personal dichotomy between the cases invites readers to analogize the stereotypical gender differences between the sexes to the differences between groups of conflicting rules. That is, readers could assume that, because men as a group customarily dominate women, the rules of assent, which are illustrated with cases involving the commercial side of life, where men dominate, must be more significant than the rules of reliance, which are largely illustrated with cases involving the more personal side of life, where women have traditionally been consigned. Excluding "women's" issues from this casebook, therefore, permits the content of the cases to work doctrinally to further gender stereotypes. Because readers interpret gendered clues in cases, the editors' selection and organization of cases subtly communicate a message that estoppel doctrine is subordinate to assent doctrine. Although Dawson, Harvey, and Henderson do not editorially address the relationship between the doctrines, the editors implicitly suggest their views to readers.

Including the reproductive technology materials in this casebook would decrease the power that its gendered messages exercise over readers' views of themselves. But including these materials would also loosen the relationship between gender and the editors' presentation of legal doctrine. Thus, because these materials seem solicitous and protective of male donors and male spouses,[74] the materials would challenge readers impressions from cases like *Jackson v. Seymour*[75] that contract doctrine can only be used altruistically for women. Similarly, because these decisions involve obviously personal issues, including them in the casebook would disrupt the commercial/personal dichotomy that presently prevails in the mutual assent and promissory estoppel sections. This would not only break the implicit link the casebook now makes between the sexes and "hard" rules like assent and "soft" rules like reliance;[76] it would also force Dawson, Harvey, and Henderson to confront their position regarding the relationship of the assent and estoppel rules more straightforwardly. Just as gender provided an analytical shortcut to the courts in *Fitzpatrick* and in *Jackson*, so gender has permitted Dawson, Harvey, and Henderson to skirt their views about the relationships within legal doctrine in their casebook. Breaking the book's silence on women's issues, therefore, would challenge the power of gender over the casebook editors themselves.

Women as Authors and in the Language of the Casebook

In addition to their significance as "characters" in the casebook, the way women appear as authors and in the casebook language also influences readers' ideas about gender. Thus, some readers who see the judges and legal commentators whose work editors select for reproduction in a casebook as professional role models are interested in how many women are among those selected. Readers today are also sensitive to whether editors recognize women in the language of a casebook, both as characters in a book's questions and problems and through the use of feminine pronouns when authors or editors write about the generic person.[77] Readers who examine *Dawson, Harvey, and Henderson* closely to evaluate the appearance of women as authors or in the language will find, however, that women are virtually invisible in these aspects of the casebook.[78]

Beginning with the language of the book, readers will find that the editors and their authors use masculine pronouns consistently throughout the cases and the materials to refer to the generic person. A provision of the U.C.C., which the editors include in the casebook, forthrightly claims that "words of the masculine gender [should be understood to] include the feminine and the neuter."[79] The practice extends, however, substantially past the U.C.C. in *Dawson, Harvey, and Henderson* to reach even cases involving women, where judges use masculine pronouns to phrase the rule statements that apply to female parties.[80]

Historical custom might explain the exclusive use of masculine pronouns in the U.C.C. and the older decisions, but it will not eliminate the impact that the casebook's lack of feminine pronouns has on most readers. And yet the casebook editors never take corrective measures through their editing prerogatives to assure readers that the particularity of women is recognized. Thus, for example, the editors leave undisturbed law review excerpts in which influential commentators write as if parties to contracts are exclusively male,[81] or in which distinguished scholars speak directly and specifically to readers as men.[82]

Dawson, Harvey, and Henderson also fail to modify their own language to include feminine pronouns. Of the nine problems which the editors have created for the casebook, almost all contain neutral, nongendered names such as "*s*" and "*b*," "*a*" and "*b*," "trustee" or "vendee."[83] But in those instances where the editors do not describe the figures in the problem neutrally, they refer to them by male pronouns,[84] with the sole exception of one question (out of six, in the fourth problem), in which the editors refer to a shopper interested in purchasing an alligator handbag as "she."[85] Using a feminine pronoun once, and then only in conjunction with the stereotypically woman's role of mindless consumer, hardly compensates for the many instances in the casebook where women were not recognized because of historical custom. Instead, a reader's overwhelming impression is that the casebook is not addressed to, nor does it contemplate, women.

In addition to blocking women out of the language, the casebook conveys the mistaken impression that legal authors are exclusively male. One cannot tell from reading the cases whether the judges who wrote the decisions are men or women. In other materials that introduce readers to some of the heroes of the law and their ideas,[86] however, the editors leave many clues that men monopolize legal authorship in contracts.[87] Unlike their sex-blind treatment of case authors, the editors often indicate the sex of legal commentators in the book, either by including their first names when their names are used[88] or by using masculine pronouns to refer to them in editorial material.[89] Indeed, by including their portraits or photographs among the illustrations in the book the editors remind readers that Holmes, Mansfield, Corbin, Llewellyn, Cardozo, and Hand were not women.[90]

Well, *of course* they weren't, the Individualist Reader might object here. Surely Dawson, Harvey, and Henderson should not be asked to distort history, nor should they be blamed for the historical discrimination against women in the legal profession. No, they shouldn't; and yet I think they are responsible for the way their casebook influences readers' views regarding women's current opportunities in the legal profession. I think the invisibility of women as legal authors and in the casebook language may be a significant omission to readers. Readers may well understand that for pedagogical reasons the casebook must rely heavily on materials produced when women were not recognized in common language usage—when they could not practice law, teach, or write decisions—indeed, when they had little opportunity to generate problems amenable to legal solutions. Some readers may also fully realize that circumstances have changed dramatically for women, that this casebook need not be understood to reflect current opportunities and attitudes. Because the casebook is one of the few sources from which many readers draw their sense of current legal culture, however, they may interpret the absence of women in the casebook language and among its authors in a way Dawson, Harvey, and Henderson did not intend.

If, for example, the Feminist Reader or the Reader with a Chip on Her Shoulder, uses the presence of women among the authors and in the language of the casebook to test the editors' stance toward women, the editors will fail to win her confidence. The casebook might then become a less effective learning device for such a reader. Alternatively, if the Feminist Reader, the Reader with a Chip on Her Shoulder, or Readers Who Are Undressed for Success look for women among the authors and in the casebook language because they need and seek some assurance that women or womanly people are not excluded from the profession, they will find nothing in this casebook to reassure them. Because the authors of the law in Dawson, Harvey, and Henderson all seem to be men, because legal scholars address men exclusively in their writing, and because the editors and judges do not refer to women in their rule statements or their questions, these readers will not know from this book that they can listen when legal authors speak, or that they might some day join their ranks.

In contrast with readers who are angered or hurt by the invisibility of women, the Gentleman Reader and the Reader with a Chip on His Shoulder will be relieved that these aspects of the casebook confirm their view that women are as unimportant in the legal world as they are (or should be) elsewhere. Insofar as the self-confidence of these readers is related to their feelings that they are better than women, the casebook supports their particular form of self-esteem.[91]

The Placement of Women's Cases: Gender and the Implications of Casebook Organization

We have now examined women as "characters" in the cases, among the "authors" of the casebook, and in the casebook language. My claim in the preceding discussion has been that in the course of learning contract doctrine from these casebook materials, readers receive messages about gender that perpetuate their ideas about the divisions between the sexes. In some instances, the gendered messages also affect their view of doctrine, either because of an idea which a particular case conveys or because the organization of cases involving women or subjects generally associated with them suggests a gendered message to readers.[92] My final observations regarding the treatment of women in this overview of the casebook elaborate my claims regarding the significance of the casebook's organization of cases involving women.

The position that case organization affects readers' views of legal doctrine and legal theory is undoubtedly familiar. Editors can affect the way readers interpret the content of doctrine or the way they think about legal reasoning by rearranging the customary order of subjects within a casebook,[93] or by placing decisions with similar facts but different outcomes side by side. If women were more represented and less stereotyped in the casebook, readers might be unlikely to take gender into account in considering the doctrinal or theoretical significance of the relationships among cases. The limited number of cases involving women in *Dawson, Harvey, and Henderson,* however, renders the presence of women a factor readers can interpret when they consider the significance of casebook organization.

Because readers hold multiple and conflicting ideas regarding the distinctions between the sexes, readers might attribute a number of different meanings to the organizational significance of cases involving women. The two illustrations I discuss below involve only *one* of the many organizational issues one could explore and only *one* gender message. I focus on the use of women in two variations of the case/countercase organizational technique, a technique often used in casebooks.[94] And I concentrate on the message of subordination, which I believe readers can construe from cases involving women. Because the subordinate status of women in society is so commonly acknowledged, I think readers will be most inclined to think of that message when they consider the relationship between conflicting cases where only one of the cases involves a woman.

The case/countercase scheme typically encourages readers to dispute the formalistic reasoning of cases that are paired together. On a theoretical level, readers can interpret this scheme to imply that rules are ruthlessly indeterminate, that legal doctrine fails to provide a predictable way to determine a certain result in particular situations. More conservatively, readers can interpret the case/countercase scheme to imply that the rule of one case is an exception to the rule of the other case. This rule/exception interpretation is based on an assumption that one of the cases has less authority than the other, while the indeterminate interpretation is based on a belief that the cases could have equal authority. I believe that pairing a case involving a woman with a conflicting case involving male parties invites readers to adopt the rule/exception interpretation of the case/countercase scheme rather than the indeterminate or rule/counterrule interpretation. The two examples I have chosen from the casebook not only contextualize this assertion but also suggest how gender strongly tempts readers to choose the more conservative interpretation of the case/countercase scheme.

Dawson, Harvey, and Henderson were unable to resist beginning their casebook with the decision of *Hawkins v. McGee,*[95] the well-known case a patient initiated against his doctor after plastic surgery left the patient with a hairy hand instead of the perfect hand the doctor had promised. As the introduction to contract remedies, the decision in *Hawkins* utilizes the expectation measure of contract damages.[96] The ludicrous results that the standard promises to yield in the

Hawkins case may prejudice the reader's respect for the expectation measure, however.[97] The law review comment on reliance damages that follows the case,[98] and a note case, also involving plastic surgery, in which the reliance measure of damages provides more reasonable compensation to the injured party,[99] undoubtedly assist this result. Thus, most readers would agree that the expectation measure does not work well in situations like *Hawkins*.

Dawson, Harvey, and Henderson, however, obviously believe that the expectation measure is the primary standard by which contract remedies are gauged, for expectation dominates the first three sections of their book. If one holds this attitude toward the expectation measure, then one would not want readers to confuse their criticism of the effectiveness of the expectation measure in Hawkins with their appreciation of the importance the measure generally has in other remedial situations. In my judgment, the editors' choice of *Sullivan v. O'Connor*[100] as the note case following *Hawkins* signals readers that the reliance damage measure is an exception to the primary standard of the expectation measure. The plaintiff in *Sullivan* is a woman, "a professional entertainer," who sought plastic surgery on her nose to "enhance" her beauty and improve her appearance. These facts will surely remind many readers of the stereotypical image of woman as princess (or beauty queen)—vain, self-absorbed, and decidedly inferior not only to men but to worthier women as well.[101] Connecting this image of inferiority to the reliance measure of damages utilized in the case will encourage readers to believe that, however fairly the decision in *Sullivan* seems to come out, the reliance standard it utilizes is inferior to the basic principle set forth in *Hawkins*.

The *Hawkins* and *Sullivan* case/countercase example concerns a relationship between a major case and a note case. My second example of the way the subordinate status of women affects the interpretation of casebook organization involves a relationship between sections within a chapter. (This is a section/countersection variation on the case/countercase scheme.) The editors have organized the four sections of the contracts remedies chapter so that the first two sections are primarily concerned with the expectation standard for measuring damages. The expectation standard also dominates the third section, which deals with reliance and restitution damages, because the editors present these alternative damage remedies in terms of their relationship to the expectation measure. The expectation measure, therefore, commands considerable authority by the time the reader turns to the fourth section of the chapter, which is on equitable remedies. The preceding sections of the chapter have demonstrated that money damages often fail to secure an injured party her expectation interest.

Upon learning that an equitable remedy requires the breaching party to do exactly what she agreed to do, readers might assume that equitable remedies promise to achieve the goals of the expectation standard more satisfactorily than money damages. Indeed, the reader approaching the casebook section on equitable remedies is likely to wonder whether it contains the ultimate form of expectation damages—this unit might be the capstone of the chapter.

The concentration of cases involving women in the equitable remedies section, however, is likely to signal readers that equitable remedies are subordinated to money damages as the common method of effectuating the expectation standard. Of the eighteen major cases that precede the equitable remedies section in the chapter, a reader may have noticed only one woman among the parties.[102] In contrast to the low number and proportion of cases involving women in the preceding cases, three of the five cases in the equitable remedies section involve women as parties.[103] Since women dominate this unit of cases, some readers will use this fact as a clue to the relative value of equitable remedies. By comparing the inferior status of women to the relationship between the "women's" unit on damages (the equitable remedies section) and the "men's" unit (the money damages sections), these readers would assume that money damages are dominant. Under this interpretation, which comports with the position of the Restatement,[104] the equitable remedies section is not the capstone of the contract damages chapter; instead it demonstrates that some aspects of law—like some aspects of society—are subordinate to others.

Because the organization of cases involving women in both of the preceding examples reinforces a doctrinal message that is in accord with substantial authority,[105] it might be tempting to assume that readers will benefit from the gendered messages they gleaned from the organizational significance of these women's cases. As I will demonstrate in the two major case studies presented in Chapter 6, however, there are times when certain readers will misinterpret the organizational significance of women's cases, which will hinder their ability to learn particular doctrinal messages. In addition, I believe that readers are personally harmed when the relationship between casebook structure and doctrine depends on gender. Utilizing the subordinate status of women as part of doctrinal analysis reinforces the division between the sexes. It reminds men and women of the different historical treatment of the sexes, it revitalizes the nefarious contention of gender-related thinking that men are superior to women, and, as in the examples discussed here, it sometimes rewards readers for extending these ideas to legal analysis. Readers who think about the subordinate status of women understand the casebook better than those who don't.

Readers are harmed when the relationship between casebook structure and doctrine depends on gender, because this kind of organizational message analysis is implicitly based on the manipulation of women. Although cases involving men are organized so that their position in the book also conveys doctrinal messages, these messages are not sex-linked. Cases involving women are the cases that carry the extra organizational punch. Admittedly, the casebook organization manipulates *cases* involving women, rather than women themselves, but this form of organizational interpretation nevertheless symbolically conveys the message to readers that men and women can be treated differently. By utilizing the idea of different treatment in the placement of women's cases, the casebook furthers the constraints of gender, nourishing a reader's consciousness that the sexes are divided by more than their biological differences.

The Maleness of the Casebook

Although the preceding part of the casebook examination focused on the treatment of women, the casebook treatment of men was an integral, if submerged, part of that discussion. Thus, we not only saw that the masculine pronoun overwhelmingly dominates the feminine when the book utilizes gendered pronouns, but that the language of the book specifically and exclusively addresses readers as men.[106] Moreover, the authors of the opinions and of the supplementary material included in the book all seem to be male;[107] (indeed, the editors themselves are all men). Finally, men—and only men—are generously represented as parties in the casebook, in many different occupations and roles.[108]

I did not include in the preceding part of this chapter any discussion of the manner in which the cases characterize men. Although the imagery of the cases may reinforce readers' opinions about the limitations of male personality traits, there are so many men in the casebook that, by dint of sheer numbers, the male "characters" exhibit a much broader range of human behavior than the women do. There may be no nurturing parent or tempestuous sex object among the male parties in the casebook, but Lady Duff-Gordon's fickle greed[109] can be matched by the cheap callousness of the father in *Mills v. Wyman*,[110] who failed to honor his promise to repay the innkeeper for nursing his adult son through his final illness. Similarly, Mrs. Jackson's pitiful dependency[111] can be matched by the exploited pathos of the hired hand in *Britton v. Turner*,[112] whose employer attempted to fleece him out of his salary for ten months' work. There is perseverance in the nephew who gave up drinking, smoking, swearing, and gambling for six years,[113] and there is extravagant self-confidence in the entrepreneur whose self-serving testimony became the basis for his whopping damages award.[114] There's a dogged loser,[115] a loyal son,[116] an antagonistic son-in-law,[117] a public-spirited citizen,[118] a contrary farmer,[119] and a self-sacrificing employee.[120] Indeed, there is so much variety in the male parties' behavior that determining the confines of male character, based on the representation of men in the casebook, would be a daunting task.

My claim about the maleness of the casebook does not rest, however, on how many men there are in the casebook or the wide range of behavior they exhibit. I believe that, even if the editors transformed the casebook by equalizing the number of cases involving men and women and by editorially defusing stereotyped characterizations within all the cases, the casebook would still seem male. My objective in this part is to demonstrate why this is so.

The assumption underlying my claim that a casebook can be male is my belief that, because ideas about gender are deeply rooted in our culture, casebook readers are accustomed, if not reconciled, to categorizing characteristics according to the masculine/feminine paradigm. Many casebook readers may not share the opinion that women and men differ in ways that far exceed the biological distinctions between them; they may believe that gender differences are not required by the inherent, unalterable, biological differences between women and men.[121] Indeed, for many readers (and I include myself among them), gender distinctions do not accurately describe our friends, our colleagues, our children, or ourselves as women and men. Nevertheless, dividing our ideas by sex is sufficiently familiar that we could agree in a rough way which characteristics "most people" attribute to men and which to women. My analysis of the maleness of *Dawson, Harvey, and Henderson* proceeds on the assumption that casebook readers generally share my views that analytical intellect, detachment, autonomy, and control seem masculine, whereas emotional intellect, attachment, compassion, and spontaneity seem feminine. I do not claim that these qualities are essential to either sex. In fact, I would argue that they aren't. I only claim to have described my impressions of the way many people understand the content of gender.[122]

Because we can also use the traits that we attribute to men and women to describe things (such as boats, machines, and buildings), objects which are described by characteristics predominantly related to one sex can be directly identified by gender.[123] Although any cultural artifact can seem gendered, books are especially susceptible to seeming male or female because one can use their contents, as well as their form and function, to determine their character. For me, considering the style as well as the contents of *Dawson, Harvey, and Henderson*, the casebook's most salient characteristics are its analytical, abstract character and its authoritarian neutrality. I believe that these characteristics are commonly understood as masculine and, therefore, that the casebook itself seems male. In the remaining pages of this chapter, I will demonstrate why the characteristics I have mentioned accurately describe *Dawson, Harvey, and Henderson*; I will also describe the effect of the casebook's maleness on readers.

The Analytical, Abstract Character of the Casebook

The analytical and abstract character of *Dawson, Harvey, and Henderson* stems in part from the organizational structure the editors have chosen. The editors have used several organizational techniques that not only are abstract or analytical in themselves but that also encourage abstract analysis in casebook readers. The editorial decision to open the book with a substantial unit on contract remedies illustrates this kind of technique.[124] This opening distinguishes *Dawson, Harvey, and Henderson* from most other contracts books.[125] The idea of beginning a contracts casebook with remedies was originally introduced as a way to use the organization of the contracts casebook to challenge formalistic legal analysis,[126] and even today this way of organizing a book seems counterintuitive. Students expect that they should learn about contract formation and breach before they study remedies.[127] The analytical challenge of the casebook's organization tends to dominate readers' responses to the casebook. The remedies beginning encourages readers to focus, from the very outset of the book, on an enormously complicated rule structure that they find hard to connect with their own experience. The opening of the casebook thus initiates and facilitates an abstract and analytical response to the casebook.

After the opening chapter on remedies, the editors continue to organize the casebook according to doctrinal categories that are divorced from the chronological or relational contexts of contract transactions.[128] This organization also encourages readers to focus on rules in the abstract. Because the structure separates the rules from the more concrete and personalized aspects of the casebook—the case settings, the parties, and even the judges who authored the decisions—the casebook encourages an approach to contracts which can seem exceedingly impersonal.[129]

The extensive use of the case/countercase organizational technique also illustrates the book's analytical and abstract character. This technique could produce concrete rather than abstract readings of conflicting cases if readers could evaluate the factual differences between decisions. The factual distinctions do not speak for themselves, however, and the casebook does not provide any guidance about how to evaluate them. If readers of *Dawson, Harvey, and Henderson*, therefore, use the case/countercase technique to focus on factual comparisons between conflicting cases, this analysis is likely to produce an abstract discussion. Moreover, as I have stated earlier,[130] the case/countercase technique typically invites readers to use the doctrinal relationship between specific contract rules as a way of thinking about the theoretical implications of contract doctrine. This too produces an abstract analysis of the materials.

Although the organizational factors discussed above contribute to the analytical, abstract characteristic that makes this casebook seem male, this characteristic stems primarily from the contents of the casebook. Like the majority of law casebooks, this casebook mostly contains appellate decisions that concentrate on doctrinal analysis. Just as casebook editors like Dawson, Harvey, and Henderson adopt strategies that encourage readers to separate rules from contexts, so appellate courts commonly subordinate discussion of the contexts of disputes in order to focus on rule analysis. Thus, a major reason that *Dawson, Harvey, and Henderson* seems male is because it contains so many appellate decisions.

My claim that *Dawson, Harvey, and Henderson* seems male because it utilizes organizational techniques and subject matter that are routinely used in legal education may seem fanatical. Using appellate opinions or organizing materials by doctrinal categories shouldn't be considered "male," the Individualist or Civil Libertarian Reader might object: using these things is simply normal. However "normal" the character of this casebook may seem to some readers, its abstract, analytical traits will make it seem male to other readers. One of the problems with the ideology of gender is that men's dominance over women permits the eclipse of traits that are associated with women. Male traits seem standard only because female traits are suppressed from observation and consideration.

In any event, it is disingenuous to claim that this casebook is so "normal" that its analytical and abstract character should not be considered male. Other editors in recent years have departed from the organizational forms and case-conservative content that Dawson, Harvey, and Henderson have chosen. Casebooks that are organized around problems particularly challenge the assertion that this casebook is a standardized, nongendered document, because the problem technique renders casebooks substantially more "feminine" than *Dawson, Harvey, and Henderson*.[131] Problems permit readers to personalize casebooks. Problems require students to undertake tasks that involve their interaction with the materials, that allow them to observe contexts which include settings, characters or issues that often mirror their lives. Casebooks utilizing the problem technique dispute the claim to "normalcy" of a casebook like *Dawson, Harvey, and Henderson*, and the contrasting level of abstraction between the two types of books emphasizes the "maleness" of *Dawson, Harvey, and Henderson*.

In addition to the appellate decisions that dominate the content of *Dawson, Harvey, and Henderson*, I believe that the illustrations the editors have included in the casebook also demonstrate the casebook's abstract and analytical character. I consider the illustrations part of this casebook's appeal for readers; students are unaccustomed to charming felicities in legal reading matter. The *idea* of using illustrations in a law casebook suggests an editorial compassion for weary readers and a somewhat impish desire to surprise: the *idea* seems, in a word, "feminine." As it turns out, however, the illustrations in this casebook emphasize the abstract, depersonalized quality of the book as a whole, partially because when one comes upon them the illustrations seem so odd, in contrast to the other material, and partially because the editors fail to connect the illustrations to the content of the book. Although none of the illustrations included in the casebook can literally be labeled abstract, because they each represent a concrete object or person, they seem abstract because, with two exceptions they have only a tenuous relationship to the substance of the book.[132] The illustrations are interesting but only in themselves; they are sometimes funny (one is surprised in seeing them), but they do not help readers understand the cases or the legal doctrine they are studying.[133]

Because the form and content of this casebook together make its analytical and abstract character so predominant, the casebook encourages readers, by example, to cultivate the analytical portions of their intellect, and to separate themselves from their work. Readers do not receive positive reinforcement to nourish their emotional sensibilities or to empathize with clients and their problems as part of legal problem solving. Insofar as the activities that the casebook neglects to nurture are commonly understood as feminine, the casebook subtly warns readers, as future lawyers, to repress the feminine characteristics within themselves.

The Authoritarian Neutrality Characteristic

Like many law casebooks, *Dawson, Harvey, and Henderson* seems neutral both in style and content. The editors have not visibly injected themselves or their opinions into the casebook, so that there seems to be no editorial presence in the casebook. Moreover, the editors have selected uncontroversial material to accompany the appellate decisions in the casebook, so that the contents of the casebook are quite unlikely to provoke emotional responses from readers. Although the editors have chosen to evade personal involvement and commitment in their casebook, they never acknowledge that the book's neutrality is deliberately contrived; they do not admit that their casebook has a point of view. Thus, the editors are authoritarian about the casebook's neutrality; they offer readers no information about what is left unsaid in their casebook. Because most readers associate detachment and control with men, the authoritarian neutrality of this book seems male. Several examples demonstrate this characteristic.

I have already examined the impersonal style of the casebook in my earlier discussion of the editors' use of neutral names and neutered pronouns in the casebook's problems and questions.[134] The neutrality of that language is consistent with other ways in which the editors maintain a distance between themselves and their casebook. The casebook lacks, for example, any significant discussion regarding the theoretical implications of beginning the casebook with materials on remedies.[135] Similarly, there is no editorial explanation or discussion of the authors' use of the case/countercase organizational technique.[136] In addition, the editors usually do not express their own views regarding the justice of the decisions, the complexity of cases, or the ethical conduct of lawyers and parties. Disembodied hands seem to have dropped the cases into doctrinal categories.

The kinds of questions the editors pose following cases illustrate the uncommitted and uncontroversial aspect of the book's neutrality. These questions are typically composed by modestly changing one or more facts of the preceding case, or by asking how the Uniform Commercial Code would affect an outcome.[137] While readers undoubtedly can benefit from addressing these kinds of questions, they would also benefit from addressing more provocative and controversial questions, such as those that would challenge the fairness or the coherence of decisions or which would ask about the assumptions underlying judicial attitudes. But these questions have been neglected in this casebook.

The casebook's dry, narrow, and unprovocative editorial commentary also illustrates the uncontroversial aspect of the book's neutrality. For example, the legal history materials in *Dawson, Harvey, and Henderson* predominantly relate to the development of legal procedures, such as the changing forms of legal actions,[138] the merger of law and equity,[139] and the shifting roles of juries and judges.[140] Some of this material helps readers understand portions of decisions that otherwise would seem mystifying,[141] while some of it undoubtedly evokes a "yeah, so?" response.[142] The material as a whole suggests that legal history is technical rather than lively, and that legal history does not offer contract doctrine any larger perspective. If the editors had included several other kinds of legal history in the book, readers would have a much more engaged response to the materials.

For example, despite the contributions of one of the casebook editors to legal realism,[143] the editors do not include any intellectual legal history in the casebook.[144] Readers, therefore, do not have access in the casebook to the relationship between the way the courts decided cases in the book and the changing perspectives in legal thought that both influenced the decisions and that the cases themselves represent.[145] Similarly, because the editors do not include economic and social history relating to the periods in which the cases were decided,[146] the casebook gives readers no assistance in considering the effect of this material on the courts' decisions.[147] When the editors do depart from procedural history to include history of substantive legal doctrine in the casebook, the material tends to describe the legislative or practical resolution of a contract issue.[148] The editors do not present material focusing on current, heated disputes about contract doctrine. Thus, for example, although there are several cases in the book involving employees' claims of unfair discharge,[149] the editors scatter these cases throughout the book and do not refer to the uncertain status of these claims or the stimulating doctrinal debate they have engendered.[150]

The primary effect of the authoritarian neutrality I have described thus far is to mislead readers about the kind of questions one can ask about cases and about the kind of legal history that might be relevant to consider in studying contracts. This casebook, like many others, discourages readers from developing ethical, social, and moral opinions on legal issues. Insofar as these questions and opinions seem feminine, because they involve attachment, compassion, and emotion, repressing these questions encourages readers to repress the feminine characteristics within themselves. This promotes a narrow concept of professional conduct, and it also devalues authentic self-development.

Although the editorial style and noncase material that the editors have written or selected for the book are enough, in my judgment, to give this casebook the authoritarian neutrality that makes it seem male, the Feminist Reader or the Reader with a Chip on Her Shoulder might also argue that by omitting legal issues of current interest to women the editors have selected cases that contribute to the casebook's "maleness." The Individualist or the Civil Libertarian Readers would staunchly contest this position. They would claim that the cases in this casebook are not gendered. Not only do the editors include "women's" issues in the casebook (there are cases involving contractual transactions within families), but the wide range of commercial contract problems they have included should be of concern to both sexes. Regardless of what's left out of the casebook, these readers would argue, what's in the book is neutral.

Although it seems obvious to me that cases can be as gendered as the editorial material I have been discussing,[151] this observation deeply challenges the claim of impartiality that is a traditional aspect of legal rhetoric. I have tried to show, however, in this overview of the casebook, that Dawson, Harvey, and Henderson's casebook is a gendered document. The editors' treatment of women and the "maleness" of the book's style and contents support and nourish gendered thinking within casebook readers. By reinforcing the restrictions that gender-related ideas impose on readers, the editors encourage readers to understand themselves partially, as men or women. One of the dangers casebook editors risk by linking their books with gender is that gender-related ideas may spread. If the casebook and its editors are closely linked with ideas about gender, it should not be surprising that some readers should believe that gender infects not only the casebook and its editors, but the law itself.

6
Re-reading Cases: Challenging the Gender of Two Contract Decisions

This chapter will focus on an extended discussion of two cases in *Dawson, Harvey, and Henderson*. While the previous chapter concentrated on the impact that the gendered aspects of the casebook have on readers, this chapter will emphasize the impact that readers' ideas regarding gender have on their understanding of legal doctrine. By analyzing each case from feminist and nonfeminist perspectives, I want to demonstrate that gender-related ideas can be embedded in nonfeminist as well as feminist case readings. My goal in this chapter is to expose and question the gender constraints that often affect case interpretations, and yet, I also hope this chapter will arouse interest and respect for gender-related readings that draw on attitudes and concerns commonly linked with women. Specifically, I want the feminist attitudes toward the social history that I describe in conjunction with the first case to change readers' views of that case, and I want the feminist oppositional stance that I adopt in analyzing the second case to lead readers to resist the standard doctrinal synthesis of that material.

Shirley MacLaine and the Mitigation of Damages Rule: Re-Uniting Language and Experience in Legal Doctrine

Parker v. Twentieth Century Fox Film Corp.[1] involves a breach of contract claim against a motion picture studio by a "well-known" actress, whom the editors identify as Shirley MacLaine.[2] Just before production was to begin on a musical entitled *Bloomer Girl*, the studio cancelled its contract to pay MacLaine $750,000 to star in the film, offering her instead the role of leading actress in a "western type" movie, *Big Country, Big Man*. MacLaine did not accept the offer. The studio opposed her motion for summary judgment on the grounds that her claim for lost wages in *Bloomer Girl* should be reduced by the wages she could have earned in *Big Country, Big Man*. This defense is based on the general rule of mitigation of damages, elaborated for casebook readers in the preceding major case: a party injured by breach of contract cannot recover compensation for any damages she could have avoided (or mitigated).[3] The doctrinal issue in *Parker* involves an employee's obligation to avoid damages after her employer has breached their employment agreement: Was Shirley MacLaine's claim for compensation foreclosed because of the opportunity, which she refused, to avoid her loss by working in *Big Country, Big Man*?

In deciding the case for Shirley MacLaine, the court in *Parker* relied on the fact that, under the mitigation rule, an employee need not avoid damages by accepting "employment of a different or inferior kind."[4] The majority concluded that the " 'Big Country' lead was . . . both different and inferior":

> The mere circumstance that "Bloomer Girl" was to be a musical review calling upon plaintiff's talents as a dancer as well as an actress, and was to be produced in the City of Los Angeles, whereas "Big Country" was a straight dramatic role in a "Western Type" story taking place in an opal mine in Australia, demonstrates the difference in kind between the two employments; the female lead as a dramatic actress in a western style motion picture can by no stretch of imagination be considered the equivalent of or substantially similar to the lead in a song and dance production.
>
> Additionally, the substitute "Big Country" offer proposed to eliminate or impair the director and screenplay approvals accorded to plaintiff under the original "Bloomer Girl" contract[5] . . . and thus constituted an offer of inferior employment. No expertise or judicial notice is required in order to hold that the deprivation or infringement of an employee's rights held under an original employment contract converts the available "other employment" relied upon by the employer to mitigate damages, into inferior employment which the employee need not seek or accept.[6]

The dissenting judge, however, charged that the majority relied on a "superficial listing of differences" between the films, asserting that

> It is not intuitively obvious . . . that the leading female role in a dramatic motion picture is a radically different endeavor from the leading female role in a musical comedy film. Nor is it plain to me that the rather qualified rights of director and screenplay approval contained in the first contract are highly significant matters either in the entertainment industry in general or to this plaintiff in particular. Certainly, none of the declarations introduced by the plaintiff in support of her motion shed any light on these issues. Nor do they

attempt to explain why she declined the offer of starring in "Big Country, Big Man."[7]

By calling attention to the majority opinion's conclusory application of the "different or inferior" qualification, the dissenting opinion encourages the casebook reader to feel uncertain about how to use the mitigation rule in the employment context. It will seem unjust, to some readers, that Shirley MacLaine is apparently going to get $750,000, after this decision, for doing nothing. The mitigation rule seems to lose all of its muscle as a result of this "different or inferior" qualification. Would MacLaine have been entitled to damages if she had refused the lead in *Annie Hall*, because that extremely successful film is not a musical? Would she have been denied damages if she had turned down *Springtime for Hitler*?[8] How can you tell?

I believe the Feminist Reader and the Reader with a Chip on Her Shoulder (as well as other readers who are familiar with feminist social history) might find the majority's application of the "different or inferior" standard much less mysterious than other readers. Their views would be based on their acquaintance either with Amelia Bloomer, a mid-nineteenth-century feminist, suffragist, and abolitionist, or with "bloomers," the loose trousers that some women wore under a short skirt, without hoops, multiple petticoats, or restricting underwear, in the early 1850s. (Bloomer, whose magazine, *The Lily*, was the first American magazine published by and for women, publicized and stirred enthusiasm among some women for the trousers, or pantelettes, as they were sometimes known, and they came to be called after her.)[9] These readers might have the intuition, as I did in reading the *Parker* case, that a film entitled *Bloomer Girl* was related in some way to the radical effort feminists in the last century made to achieve more freedom of movement and control over what they wore by reforming their dress. Moreover, simply because Shirley MacLaine is a woman, these readers might assume that the role in *Bloomer Girl* had personal significance for the actress;[10] even if the film treated women's issues in the light-hearted fashion typical of musical comedy, it would still link the actress with events that are historically significant to other women.[11] *Bloomer Girl* would seem different, from this perspective, not only from a western but from other musical comedies, because of its political overtones.

In contrast with their favorable attitudes toward *Bloomer Girl*, the Feminist Reader as well as the Reader with a Chip on Her Shoulder would probably assume that a movie entitled *Big Country, Big Man* would offer a leading actress the inferior kind of leading role westerns have typically offered women. Like Miss Kitty in *Gunsmoke*, a woman in a western is usually very much subordinated to the main focus of such films—the cowboy-hero. Because feminist readers oppose the subordination of women, they are likely to believe that, assuming *Big Man* portrayed women as men's sidekicks, it would be "inferior" to *Bloomer Girl*, where women were probably shown leading their sisters to fight for control over their own bodies. Thus, the readers' gender-related presumptions regarding the political overtones of *Big Country, Big Man* would affect their opinion of why the film would seem "different or inferior" to *Bloomer Girl*.

Although these readers might not know whether *Bloomer Girl* had feminist themes[12] or whether *Big Country, Big Man* portrayed women according to the usual demeaning western stereotype,[13] because of their skepticism about women's roles in westerns and their intuitions regarding *Bloomer Girl*'s feminist themes, they might understand MacLaine's rejection of the *Big Country, Big Man* role in terms of their own efforts to reconcile their politics with their careers. These readers would be able to ground the language of the "different or inferior" qualification in their own lives.[14] They might assume that MacLaine not only sought to refuse a role that would be demeaning to her as a woman, but that she also wanted to avoid contributing to the oppressed images of women in popular culture. Rather than thinking that Shirley MacLaine is being paid to do nothing in *Parker*, and that the "different or inferior" qualification to the mitigation rule was unfairly applied, their attitude toward the two films could enable them to infer an ascertainable but complicated standard for determining when the "different or inferior" qualification should be applied in employment cases. That is, they would assume that *Parker* demonstrates that an employee's serious and recognized personal goals should be respected and protected when they are connected to a concern that is respected and acknowledged by others. Under this interpretation, some degree of mitigation can be required (mitigation does not lose all of its muscle in *Parker*), and yet a wrongly discharged employee would not have to take just any substitute employment. Money would not be the only test for determining whether jobs are comparable, and yet other employment objectives would require social as well as personal significance in order to be protected under the "different or inferior" qualification.

The interpretation of *Parker* generated by feminist attitudes and information about the social history related to the case offer readers useful guidance in applying the "different or inferior" qualification to other situations. This interpretation also allows readers who identify with Shirley MacLaine (because she is a woman) to attribute dignity to her conduct. However, readers of *Dawson, Harvey, and Henderson* will have to struggle to interpret *Parker* in the manner I have described. Inexplicably, the editors omit material that would confirm readers' intuitions that the social context and political significance of the films might explain the application of the "different or inferior" qualification in *Parker*.[15] Dawson, Harvey, and Henderson thus subtly deter readers who are familiar with nineteenth-century feminist activists and their work from utilizing their personal connections with the case to understand *Parker*; these readers may even be led to believe that social context and politics are not legitimate interpretive tools. Although readers' intuitions about the Parker case may in fact explain the otherwise baffling result of this decision, the casebook does not encourage them to draw on those intuitions. It discourages—in the context of these opinions—the sensitivity to what is influential but not said, a sensitivity that women have often found to be a source of strength.[16]

The negative pedagogical effect of omitting information about the feminist themes in *Bloomer Girl* extends to other readers too. Most casebook readers are unlikely to know about Amelia Bloomer or the nineteenth-century feminist dress reform effort. Had Dawson, Harvey, and Henderson included the information about *Bloomer Girl*, which Charles Knapp provides in his casebook, then feminist attitudes toward the subordination of women in westerns and the importance of dress reform could have been tapped in other readers to develop the complicated, contextualized interpretation of mitigation suggested above. By failing to describe the social context of this case, the editors probably deprive many readers of an interpretation of *Parker* that would advance their understanding of mitigation doctrine.

Although the Feminist Reader or the Reader with a Chip on Her Shoulder may pursue her intuitions about *Parker* despite the editors' silence, the editors include a photograph of the actress in the casebook which could distract many of these readers from such an understanding of the majority's result in *Parker*. MacLaine is pictured, pouting, in a fringed, lowcut cocktail dress. Her legs are crossed, a knee is bared, she's wearing open-toe, sling-back high heels, and her cheek is resting on her hand. She might look to some readers like a "sex kitten," an image which is subtly reinforced by the stuffed rabbit tucked under her arm. Her picture, on page forty-seven, is the third illustration in the casebook, following a magisterial full-page portrait of Holmes, in judicial robes, on page thirty-one,[17] and then a picture of a bridge, on page forty-three. (The bridge was built by the injured party in the preceding case after he failed to mitigate his damages; it is the object he produced as he piled up his damages.)

Some feminists might relish the contrast between the images of Holmes and MacLaine in that each is wearing a costume that emphasizes the nature of its subject's power—for Holmes, the judicial robes; for MacLaine, the sexy dress and shoes. The conjunction of these illustrations could remind such readers that sexuality has been a considerable source of power for some women. Regarding MacLaine's illustration as a statement that her sex appeal is linked to her exceedingly successful acting career, these readers would believe that their interpretation of the *Parker* case was sound; MacLaine is exactly the kind of female actress who might have had the courage to stand up to the studio and turn down *Big Country, Big Man*.

Many feminist readers, however, might find a different message in these illustrations. Comparing Holmes with MacLaine might remind them of the substantial disparities between the public achievements of men and women. Comparing the picture of the bridge with the picture of MacLaine, these readers might assume they are being shown two "objects" in the mitigation section of the casebook—a bridge and a woman. Because treating women as if they were nothing more than objects for sexual pleasure is a significant feminist concern, these two illustrations could remind feminists that sexuality has often been a form of oppression in women's lives. Thus, MacLaine's photograph could prevent many readers from believing that her refusal to accept the *Big Country, Big Man* role was motivated by her political integrity. Instead, MacLaine's photograph might deter them from considering Amelia Bloomer's significance to the case. How could Shirley MacLaine have stood up to the studio for feminist reasons, they might think; she's not a feminist but a "sex object."[18]

Without any clues in this casebook regarding the feminist themes of *Bloomer Girl*, most *Dawson, Harvey, and Henderson* readers will have to find other ways to cope with their uncertainty about the meaning of the "different or inferior" qualification of the mitigation rule. In the remaining pages of this section I shall elaborate interpretations of *Parker* that do not depend on social context or feminist attitudes in order to demonstrate how assumptions regarding gender can also be implicated in interpretations that are not overtly linked with feminism.

The breach of an individual's employment contract sharply presents a basic conflict underlying all mitigation issues. We earnestly want to protect the contract objectives of individual employees against employer breach (they should be compensated for their losses under the contract), and yet we also abhor the idea that such employees should be excused from the communal work ethic by getting paid for doing nothing. The general rule of mitigation of damages favors the communal pole of this conflict (one cannot recover compensation for damages that can be avoided),[19] while the qualification to the general rule, that one need not avoid damages by accepting work of a "different or inferior" kind, favors the individualist pole. Without the qualification, the mitigation rule would swallow an employee's contractual freedom—her employer could fire her with little risk of fiscal responsibility. Thus, *Parker*, like all mitigation cases, presents the question of how to resolve in a particular situation a fundamental conflict between the individual and communal claims mediated by the mitigation rule and the "different or inferior" qualification.

To some readers, the conclusory application of the "different or inferior" qualification by the majority in *Parker* will seem like appropriate, if unreasoned, deference to individualism. Searching for some rational explanation of the majority's decision, they will conclude that the directorial rights MacLaine would have lost in *Big Country, Big Man*, in conjunction with the lost opportunity to advance her musical comedy expertise, would justify the application of the "different or inferior" qualification in this case. These readers will agree that MacLaine's autonomy deserved more protection than the general social good that would have come from not letting her off the working hook the rest of us are on.

This interpretation of the case will seem gendered to some readers because the individualism/community duality I have described is generally understood to be gendered. Individualism and autonomy are commonly associated with men while altruism and community are generally linked with women, just as, more concretely, men are usually expected to pursue their individualistic careers single-mindedly while women are expected to subordinate other career objectives to care for their families or to participate in community activities.[20] Readers who justify the majority's decision on the basis of an autonomy rationale are also likely to be influenced in this reading by gender-related ideas about MacLaine and what her objectives were regarding *Bloomer Girl*. Thus, some of these readers may approve of MacLaine's efforts to stand up to the studio—to "act like a man"—and the studio be damned, while others may approve of the decision because MacLaine was seeking to protect directorial and approval privileges which these readers understand as participatory and "feminine."

Whatever the particular rationale underlying an interpretation of *Parker* which justifies the majority's decision, it offers readers very little guidance for arguing future employment cases involving a mitigation issue. The majority's conclusory opinion provides readers almost no guidance in how to make an individualist or "masculine" argument. As Judge Sullivan points out in his dissenting opinion, "there will always be differences" between two jobs, and "a superficial listing of differences with no attempt to assess their significance may subvert a valuable legal doctrine."[21]

Because this preceding reading is so unsatisfactory, I believe most readers will be inclined to assume that the majority opinion in the *Parker* decision is an irrational capitulation to individualism. Gender-related ideas may also contribute to this conclusion. As I have stated in an earlier discussion, one way the insignificance of a decision can be suggested to readers is through the organization of the casebook.[22] Because the editors pair *Parker* (the first case in the book in which a woman is a party) with a case setting forth the general obligation of mitigation, readers who link the traditionally inferior status of women to the countercase position of the *Parker* decision will be encouraged to consider the *Parker* rule subordinate to the principal mitigation obligation.

MacLaine's photograph will encourage other readers to treat the *Parker* case skeptically. Because the photograph plays on gender-related ideas about female sexuality, these readers will be reminded that men have historically been able to manage and control the power such a picture suggests in its subject.[23] These readers will be encouraged to believe that the *Parker* rule can be managed and controlled, just as women have been.

Finally, still other readers will be encouraged to dismiss *Parker's* significance because of the customary disposition in our culture to devalue any kind of women's work. These readers may be dubious at the outset of the opinion about whether acting is *real* work, and MacLaine's sex[24] will foster their belief that *real* employees doing real work will not be treated like MacLaine.[25]

Each of these gender-related ideas legitimates a reader's conclusion that *Parker* is incorrectly decided, or insignificant, but the ideas would not help such a reader elaborate altruistic arguments for a different result. Thus, like the earlier interpretation supporting the majority's decision, the dismissive reading of *Parker* disserves readers pedagogically. It fails to offer them guidance for arguing and resolving a mitigation conflict. In addition, because *Parker* is the first major case in the book in which a woman is one of the parties, the dismissive reading is likely to affect the way gender-conscious readers feel about women.

The dismissive reading of the case tempts instructors and students to ridicule MacLaine, to imagine her as an indulged starlet lying around eating chocolates, while the defendants, hard-working studio types, struggle to manage their business efficiently despite her arbitrary whims. Some readers may be proud that MacLaine is a woman who manages to "beat the system" by getting paid for doing nothing, but other readers may internalize any disrespect that they think the opinion generates for MacLaine. If these readers believe that women are morally superior to men (and some readers will hold this opinion), they will be shamed if MacLaine, as a woman plaintiff, seems success- ful because she cleverly manipulated the legal system. In contrast, the misogynist feelings of readers who are undisposed to favor women will be intensified by any derogation of MacLaine; women are just as bad as these readers have always supposed. A distinct advantage of the *Parker* reading based on feminist attitudes toward the social history implicated by the case is that this interpretation will challenge the effect dismissive readings would have on readers; it will encourage feminist as well as nonfeminist readers to rethink their ideas about women.

I am not immune to the diversion *Parker* offers from standard com- mercial contracts reading. It's fun to talk about the movies. My objec- tive has not been to spoil the fun, but to illuminate some of its dark- ness. Indeed, *Parker* would be a good case with which to introduce feminist themes into the classroom: as I have argued, feminist atti- tudes improve its pedagogical usefulness. An interpretation of *Parker* that acknowledges and utilizes feminist attitudes is valuable because it challenges the lessons readers learn from cases such as *Jackson v. Seymour*[26] and *Fitzpatrick v. Michael*[27] that gender-related ideas are only helpful to legal interpretations when they draw on negative images of women.

Understanding MacLaine as a powerful actress whose feminist poli- tics are respected by the California Supreme Court could also stimu- late readers to draw connections between social contexts and legal decisions, between the experiences of parties in a case and the experi- ences of readers themselves. Although these interactions are not unique to feminism, they are similar to the skills of "deep reading" many women claim as part of their gendered heritage. Recognizing the value of such skills will affirm, for some readers, an attribute they identify as feminine. Because "women's" attributes are so often less valued than "men's," affirming a "feminine" attribute through an analysis of *Parker* will contribute to the release of gender-related re- strictions on our lives.

Allied Van Lines, Inc.: Exposing the Power Issue in Standard Form Contract Doctrine

Allied Van Lines, Inc. v. Bratton,[28] introduces *Dawson, Harvey, and Henderson's* five case unit on standard form contract doctrine.[29] The decision involves companion cases brought against a national moving company by two householders—both women—after their household goods were destroyed in transit. Both women sought relief from provisions in standardized agreements that limited their carrier's liability for loss and damage. Mrs. Bratton and Mrs. McKnab argued that these provisions should not be enforced against them because, although they had signed the carrier's forms, they had not actually read or agreed to the terms. The court in *Allied* rejected Mrs. Bratton's argument; it disregarded her ignorance of the restrictive terms in the carrier's bill of lading and held that her signature was sufficient to bind her to the agreement. In contrast, the court held that Mrs. McKnab's signature did not bind her. The carrier's agent had advised Mrs. McKnab incorrectly that the agreement gave her no choice regarding the amount of insurance coverage available to her. This misstatement, the court held, relieved Mrs. McKnab of the presumption of assent that her signature on the agreement would otherwise have warranted. By granting relief to Mrs. McKnab, *Allied* indicates to readers that standardized agreements need not always be binding. In denying relief to Mrs. Bratton, however, the court in *Allied* demonstrates that standardized agreements are often enforceable.

Allied is the only case in this unit in which a court enforces a standardized agreement against a party.[30] Therefore, as a result of its introductory position in the unit and its unique support of a standard form contract, *Allied* has a substantial impact on readers' views about standard form contract doctrine. I believe that because readers' ideas regarding gender affect their interpretation of *Allied*, these ideas influence their subsequent approach to standardized contract interpretation. In this section, I will discuss two different interpretations of *Allied* that demonstrate these claims about the significance of gender. The first interpretation, which I call a traditional reading of the case, is an elaboration of the rationale the court presents in support of its decision. Readers who interpret *Allied* in the traditional manner are unlikely to acknowledge that gender-related ideas are a factor in their reading of the case. Yet, as I will show, gender-related ideas are implicated in this interpretation. I label the second interpretation a feminist reading, because gender-related ideas are overtly recognized in this interpretation. In addition, this reading is characterized by its opposition to *Allied* and to the traditional interpretation of the decision.

The traditional interpretation of *Allied* leads to a conclusion that, by and large, standardized contracts are legitimate, fair, and benign. Several aspects of the decision invite this favorable view. Thus, for example, the court frames the question of standardized contract enforceability as an issue of whether the individual householders agreed to the standardized terms.[31] By discussing the legitimacy of the agreements in the language of assent, the court implies that individual householders have the ability to avoid the severity of the terms of standardized contracts if they simply adequately assert themselves. Mrs. Bratton "realized that she was signing a contract,"[32] the decision reports. Moreover, the carrier's agent did not "prevent" her from reading the document.[33] She "simply did not read . . . or even ask questions about the Bill of Lading."[34] The court indicates that, because Mrs. Bratton deliberately chose both to sign the documents and not to read them, she voluntarily relinquished her right to judicial protection against the harshness of the standardized form. She, not the carrier or the court, is responsible for her inability to obtain relief from the onerous terms in the standardized agreement.

The particular form of standardized agreement at issue in the case contributes to the view that Mrs. Bratton should be held responsible for her own loss. Unlike many standardized contracts (including those in the cases following *Allied* in the casebook), the standardized documents Mrs. Bratton failed to read actually offered her the choice of more insurance if she wanted it.[35] Mrs. Bratton was not stuck with a form document that offered her only one set of terms. Traditional readers are more likely, therefore, to feel critical of Mrs. Bratton's conduct than to feel critical of standardized agreements.

The contrast between the court's treatment of Mrs. McKnab and Mrs. Bratton also conveys the benign nature of standardized agreements to traditional readers. The rationale that locked Mrs. Bratton into her agreement protected Mrs. McKnab. Although the court seemed ready to hold Mrs. McKnab responsible for her signature— she too "knew" she was "signing a contract"[36]—ultimately the court is persuaded that the conduct of the carrier's agent "prevent[ed] [her] from exercising her right to choose adequate coverage."[37] The court referred to prior conversations between Mrs. McKnab and the agent in which she had alerted him to her desires for maximum insurance coverage.[38] Readers can infer from this that the agent's misstatement to Mrs. McKnab was deliberately deceptive. The agent's statement seems like a concrete obstacle which he placed between Mrs. McKnab and the bill of lading; his words seem to have wrested control of the situation from Mrs. McKnab. Because the court relieved Mrs. McKnab of liability for her signature on the grounds that the agent prevented her from assenting freely to the standardized form, the *Allied* decision assures readers that the law of standardized agreements can be flexible and particularized. It will protect someone like Mrs. McKnab who actively seeks to protect herself, but it will not protect someone who is negligently passive, like Mrs. Bratton. Unlike Mrs. McKnab, Mrs.

Bratton did nothing concrete to indicate to her agent that his silence about the agreement would deceive her. An active/passive distinction between the conduct of both the two women and the two agents, therefore, provides readers an explanation for the different treatment the women receive. More importantly, Mrs. McKnab's situation indicates that in discreet, predictable, and exceptional circumstances, courts will not enforce standardized agreements.

The form of legal analysis that the court utilized in *Allied* also legitimates, for traditional readers, the legal doctrine dealing with standardized agreements. Because the court judged the enforceability of Mrs. Bratton's agreement by her signature, rather than by an examination of her actual knowledge of the contents of the standard form, the *Allied* court seems scrupulously neutral and objective. Unlike later cases in the standardized agreement unit, the court in *Allied* did not inquire into inequality of bargaining power to determine the enforceability of the standardized agreements.[39] Nor did it consider the justice of permitting a national moving company to limit its liability for loss of an individual householder's belongings. By avoiding these approaches, the court in *Allied* also avoided the troublesome question of whether setting aside standardized agreements violates the principle of judicial neutrality regarding the substance of contracts. Its silence on these issues enhances the apparent defensibility of its decision.

All of the justifications for the *Allied* decision advanced so far are reinforced by gender-related ideas. Readers can convince themselves that Mrs. Bratton could have avoided the limited liability of which she complained by attributing a restrictive notion of self to her that is customarily linked with men.[40] The court in *Allied* protects Mrs. McKnab's "masculine" attempt to be autonomous, aggressive, and self-reliant, and the court denies Mrs. Bratton relief because she didn't try to conduct her affairs in a similarly "masculine" way. If traditional readers implicitly recognize Mrs. McKnab's conduct as masculine and Mrs. Bratton's conduct as feminine, accepting *Allied* will be as natural as the superiority of "male" traits sometimes seems. Indeed, the gendered view of self implied in the opinion tends to prevent readers from being troubled by the complicated issue the case poses about the power of standardized contracts.

Dawson, Harvey, and Henderson's overall use of cases involving women is another gender-related factor that encourages *Allied*'s traditional readers to believe that standardized contracts are fair and benign. The editors have not only selected *Allied*, a case with two women plaintiffs, to introduce their materials on standardized contracts, but four of the five cases in this unit involve women plaintiffs.[41]

The unusually high number of women connected with standardized contract cases[42] invites readers to analogize the status of these cases to the status of women in society. Women are victimized by standardized agreements in these cases, just as they are socially and economically subordinated to men and their concerns. But they are also protected and cared for by the application of standardized contract doctrine in the cases following *Allied*. Because the traditional reader may believe that standardized contract doctrine protects women more than people are generally protected in most aspects of life, this decision will have set this reader up to treat standardized contracts as a normal, acceptable part of modern commercial life. He may discount the extent to which such contracts can lead individuals who use them to treat one another as if they are as standardized as their documents. Although all of the cases succeeding *Allied* refuse to enforce standardized contract terms, these cases will be unlikely to change this reader's view that standardized contracts should, in a man's world, be generally enforceable—for the reasons explained in *Allied*.

The feminist reading of *Allied* leads to a conclusion that standardized contracts can be oppressive and unfair—not just to women but to men as well. The same gender-related ideas that supported the traditional interpretation of the case will encourage feminist readers to oppose the benign reading of the decision. Thus, the exclusive presence of women as plaintiffs in *Allied*,[43] and the disproportionate number of women in the standardized contract materials, will encourage these readers to criticize the effect of gender on the law of standardized contracts.[44] Because standardized contracts appear to oppress mainly women, these readers will doubt whether the law adequately protects women.

The gender-related insight regarding the "male" notion of self underlying the *Allied* rationale will provide feminist readers with a basis for developing a critique of the traditional analysis. Mrs. Bratton's idea of self apparently did not conform to the view, commonly linked with men, that individuals should allow the assertive, self-centered aspects of their personality to dominate their conduct. The self-reliant view of personhood underlying *Allied* permitted the court to believe that Mrs. Bratton was free to choose whether or not to agree to the carrier's form, that her agent did not "prevent" her from reading the bill of lading before she signed it. But footnotes to the opinion reveal that Mrs. Bratton testified at trial that she did not read the document because "the house was really cold; and the men were tired. They were in a hurry to get out."[45] Although some people might feel free in such a situation to ignore the workers' discomfort in order to pause to study carefully the moving company's documents, it is not surprising that Mrs. Bratton could not. Women are socialized to consider and value others' feelings above their own, and Mrs. Bratton simply acted like a woman in this situation. Because feminist readers are sympathetic to characteristics commonly associated with women, the court's refusal to evaluate the substantive content of Mrs. Bratton's standardized contract will not seem like a neutral judgment to these readers but a preference for male rather than female personality traits. Rather than feeling critical of Mrs. Bratton, feminist readers are likely to feel critical of the standardized documents and of standardized contract doctrine that fails to protect and value "feminine" personality traits.

As the feminist reading of *Allied* implies, the court's analysis in *Allied* might have been different if the court had valued feminine as well as masculine personality traits. The court could have considered whether Mrs. Bratton's agent should have extended more sensitivity and compassion to her by understanding her sympathy for him and his men, by informing her about the insurance option, and by preventing her from signing without indicating the liability coverage she wanted. The court could have considered whether the agent should have been as solicitous of Mrs. Bratton as she was of him.

Just as the traditional reader's interpretation of *Allied* could lead him to overlook the critique of standardized contract doctrine, the feminist reader's desire to criticize *Allied* may lead her to exaggerate the doctrinal significance of the succeeding cases. Because she believes that the decision affecting Mrs. Bratton was wrong, the feminist reader will look for ways to overturn standardized agreements in the cases following *Allied*. Her lack of confidence in the *Allied* rationale may prevent her from believing that standardized contracts are generally enforceable; she may believe that standardized contract doctrine is much more indeterminate and uncertain than it is.[46] She is likely to undervalue the *Allied* opinion as a useful source of persuasive arguments in favor of enforcing standardized agreements.

Although both the traditional and the feminist readers will be disadvantaged in their later reading of the standardized contract material if they are not exposed to alternative readings of *Allied*, the feminist reading is less likely to receive attention. It is, therefore, particularly important to emphasize how this reading will benefit traditional readers. A feminist reading will help these readers see the legal issue in standardized contract situations not as a question of assent but as a question of power.[47] The court in *Allied* utilized individual consent as the exclusive standard by which to evaluate contract enforceability. The court assumed, in justifying this standard, that individuals could make informed judgments about the wisdom of contracts, that they could obtain full access to all the knowledge they need to exercise their consent wisely. Indeed, the Restatement section on standardized agreements, which Dawson, Harvey, and Henderson reproduce at the conclusion of the standardized agreement unit, emphasizes the knowledge of the parties as the critical factor for determining when such agreements should be enforced.[48]

The feminist reader of *Allied*, who is sensitive to the subordinate status of women, would challenge this single-minded focus on a consumer's obligation to inform herself about her contracts as misleading. The focus on knowledge masks the power exercised in contractual dealings. Mrs. Bratton's agent exercised power over her through his physical control over her bill of lading and through his familiarity, derived from prior experience, with its contents. But because he was a man, the agent also had power over Mrs. Bratton that she, as a woman, was socialized to acknowledge. By requiring Mrs. Bratton to assume full responsibility for informing herself about her bill of lading, the *Allied* court not only required her to challenge the agent's control over what she needed to know about the bill of lading, but also to challenge the control he as a man had over her as a woman.

A feminist reading of *Allied* exposes these forms of power.[49] Moreover, it reveals that traditional contract doctrine, by treating the parties as if they had an adversarial relationship, implicitly rejects the more cooperative way in which many women have traditionally experienced power and knowledge. The major form of power available to most women, given the kind of work they have done, has been the power to nurture and share. Women primarily occupied with family responsibilities have learned to live in the context of relationships that are trusting and interdependent. In this sphere, many women do not respect or adhere to the traditional male view of power as force, authority, and domination. Given the concern she stated she felt for the workers, Mrs. Bratton earned her own self-respect by recognizing the workers' discomfort and doing what she did to ease their situation. Had she been in the agent's position at that point, she would have spoken to the householder about the insurance option; she would have recognized the householder's need to know and would have helped her.

By analyzing Mrs. Bratton's claim as a question of whether she *agreed* to the challenged terms, the *Allied* court sought to have Mrs. Bratton act unauthentically—to reject her own sense of self and be "more like a man." The court's assent analysis does more than simply deny the extent of the agent's power over Mrs. Bratton; it also prevents her from being able to exercise power in her own way. Thus, the act of framing the *Allied* issue in terms of assent is itself a form of power over Mrs. Bratton and others like her. Mrs. Bratton cannot adequately defend herself as long as the standardized contract issue is discussed as it is in *Allied*. Feminist readers, because of their sympathy—indeed, their empathy—for Mrs. Bratton and because of their opposition to the outcome of her case, will recognize that the court's rhetoric of freedom of choice in *Allied* is simply another way of exercising power.[50]

A feminist reading of the decision reveals the aspects of the *Allied* opinion that foster traditional ideas about gender—aspects that in turn constrain readers' lives. Moreover, it exposes and stands in opposition to the domination of traditional legal doctrine. If readers understand that utilizing assent doctrine is a form of power over Mrs. Bratton's situation, they will be empowered to question and challenge the use of that doctrine. Indeed, by suggesting a way to oppose an outcome that would otherwise seem unassailable, the oppositional stance of feminist analysis becomes a source of power for the willing reader.

My aim in the casebook overview was to demonstrate the influence of gender-related ideas within the casebook. I emphasized the effect the casebook has on readers' attitudes toward themselves, although I also discussed the impact of gender on readers' understanding of legal doctrine. My discussion of *Parker* and *Allied* has reversed this emphasis. Although I asserted that the gender-related ideas that I identified in readers were stimulated by the two cases and their presentation in the casebook, my major goal in both discussions was to advance alternative interpretations of the cases that an oppositional focus on gender illuminated. I do not claim that the untraditional interpretations presented here are only available by the feminist route that led me to them. But insofar as the interpretations are useful the feminist approach to their development enables readers to struggle against the constraints of gender which casebooks foster.

Concluding Discussion

I hope that my rereading of *Dawson, Harvey, and Henderson* has raised two questions for readers. I hope, first, that readers wonder how a feminist analysis of this casebook should affect the use of *Dawson, Harvey, and Henderson* in the classroom. I also hope that readers wonder whether my analysis of *Dawson, Harvey, and Henderson* can be extended to other casebooks. Because both of these questions are related to my goals of challenging the influence of gender in reading and writing casebooks, I address these questions in this conclusion. Focusing on these questions also allows me to reexamine the objectives and methodology of the preceding sections and to discuss the implications of these chapters for further efforts to loosen the constraints of gender on our lives.

Because other casebooks, as I have implied, could be subject to the analysis I have applied to *Dawson, Harvey, and Henderson,* I think it would be unrealistic and unfair to advocate abandoning this casebook on the grounds of my discussion. I would like instructors and casebook editors to undertake major efforts to modify the importance gender plays in classroom materials, but I recognize that for many reasons most of us do not want to junk the bulk of the traditional materials we presently use in teaching. The question most of us face, therefore, is what changes my rereading of *Dawson, Harvey, and Henderson* suggests we make in our classroom use of this or similar books.

My aim in the preceding chapters has been to indicate the power and authority that law casebooks have over their readers. At the same time, I have suggested that because of the wide variety of attitudes and ideas that casebook readers have about gender, readers interpret casebook material (and casebooks affect readers) differently and with varying intensity. The dialectical nature of the relationship between the casebook and readers is replicated in the relationship between students and an instructor who seeks to introduce a feminist casebook analysis into the classroom. Let me illustrate the student aspect of this relationship by considering a class discussion concerning the significance of Shirley MacLaine's photograph.[51]

Students will come to class with different attitudes toward this photograph. Some readers, such as The Feminist, the Woman-Centered Reader, or the Reader with a Chip on Her Shoulder, may be offended by the editors' use of a picture they think is denigrating to Shirley MacLaine in her role as a woman plaintiff. Other readers, who may also be Feminist readers and female Readers with Chips on Their Shoulders, may be elated by the bravura of MacLaine's photograph. Here's a woman, they may think, who can use her sexual power effectively. Readers Who Are Undressed for Success may come to class feeling concerned that being a woman, or having "feminine" characteristics, is a disadvantage professionally. They are likely to believe that Dawson, Harvey, and Henderson exploited MacLaine by using her photograph in their book. Still other readers, like male Readers with Chips on Their Shoulders, may be pleased to think the editors share their views that women are primarily sex objects. Because students vary so dramatically in their views about gender, an instructor's discussion of the photograph may validate the attitudes of one group of students toward gender at the same time that the discussion creates pedagogical problems for others. Consider the impact of two interpretations an instructor might put forward regarding the MacLaine illustration.

If an instructor believes that the editors' use of MacLaine's photograph is degrading to women, she may seek to mitigate the effect of the photography by criticizing the editors in class for including the illustration in their book. Her criticism would probably offend readers who believe the photograph communicates a positive image about women, and it might embarrass other readers who resent having their need for reassurance that sexism is unacceptable recognized. There is also a danger that the anger of Readers with Chips on Their Shoulders might erupt during such a discussion and interfere with the instructor's control over the assuring, defusing message she seeks to convey.

The instructor would fare no better if she used the photograph, as I did in the *Parker* case analysis, to discuss the effect of gender on one's interpretation of the *Parker* decision. Many students, like the Individualist or the Civil Libertarian readers, do not acknowledge the power of gender over their ideas. They would come to class without any position at all about MacLaine's photograph. Failing to mention the problems of gender would leave the arrogance or the isolation of these readers undisturbed, permitting them either to embrace the gendered messages of the photograph or to remain ignorant of other readers' distress. However, a serious discussion of the photograph might cause these students to see their instructor as a zealot; the discussion might reduce their confidence in her as a reliable teacher. "She has no sense of proportion," they might say. "She gets off the track." Thus, the different attitudes students have regarding gender will affect the treatment a feminist analysis of casebook materials receives in class.

Ideas relating to gender will also affect the way in which instructors determine how a feminist analysis should affect their treatment of *Dawson, Harvey, and Henderson* in class. In my contracts course, for example, I am willing to introduce those parts of my analysis that relate to the relationship between gender and how students understand cases, but I seem reluctant to discuss how the casebook affects students' views of themselves and of gender roles.[52] I thus subordinate the deep pleasure and appreciation many students would derive from having their intuitive responses to the casebook legitimated to my concerns about the negative reactions of other students. I succumb to the position I have disputed that doctrinal instruction can be isolated from students' views of themselves.

My reluctance to pursue fully this book's ideas in my classroom is a gendered reaction. Like many women law teachers, I am suspicious of the authority and power that students are accustomed to extending to instructors.[53] Because students expect me and I expect myself to be more conciliatory, more deferential, and more understanding than male teachers, I am reluctant to exploit my power in the classroom by introducing some of this controversial material into class.

I am also reluctant to incorporate completely a feminist casebook analysis in class because the analysis is not only radically different from traditional classroom discussion but also closely related to my identity as a woman. Having been educated exclusively by men in the law schools I attended and having taught on predominantly male faculties, I link traditional classroom discussion with men. In order to pursue feminist material in class, I must struggle against the customary deference I have been socialized to extend to men. Challenging the restrictions my own ideas about gender impose on me is an effort I cannot always make.

Because one's own attitudes about gender affect what one believes is acceptable in the classroom, and because one's views of what is acceptable in the classroom affect one's attitudes toward gender, any decisions regarding the classroom implications of this book must be personal and contextualized, as my own decision has been. Faithfully replicating the analysis set forth in this book is unlikely to be a useful way for anyone, even me, to challenge the influence of gender in class discussions of *Dawson, Harvey, and Henderson.* The variety of student—as well as instructor—attitudes needs to be considered. I hope, however, that I have convincingly demonstrated that current classroom conduct is already molding students' views about themselves as men and women and about the relationship between gender and the law. Although the question of how one's treatment of *Dawson, Harvey, and Henderson* should change because of my re-reading cannot be given a uniform answer, there is no way to *avoid* the issue of gender in the classroom. Each of us must address this issue, but for him or herself.

My discussion of the classroom implications of this book suggests that I am unlikely to claim that one can simply "apply" my analysis to other casebooks. Indeed, I want to caution readers not to freeze this analysis into a rigid, prescriptive, analytical formula for eradicating gender. At the same time, however, I believe that these chapters provide an approach for evaluating other casebooks. By using editors' case selections, editorial comments, and silences, one can examine their treatment of the work women do. One can analyze the way they permit women to be characterized in their casebooks, and the sensitivity they exhibit to information and legal issues of special interest to women. One can evaluate editorial use of language and the selection and presentation of authors, seeking in both these instances to determine whether the editors have granted recognition to the particularlity of women. By analyzing the organization of cases involving women, one can determine whether and how these cases are used to convey gendered messages about legal doctrine. In short, one can examine the gendered characteristics of casebooks, determining through this effort the potential a casebook has to foster some traits within readers at the expense of others. Using the techniques described above, I determined in the casebook overview and case analyses sections that *Dawson, Harvey, and Henderson* favors masculine interests and masculine characteristics. This stance not only divides and limits readers' views about people, but it also divides and limits readers' views about the law. I believe these conclusions are significant and should prove illuminating to readers of this casebook.

But the method I have used to reach these conclusions poses problems for extending my analysis to other casebooks. As I acknowledged earlier,[54] challenging gender constraints requires using the gender-related ideas that a project such as this is designed to undermine. For example, I found significance in the stereotyped characterizations of the limited number of women among the casebook "characters" because, like the Reader with a Chip on Her Shoulder or the Feminist, I read the casebook with gender on my mind. Although I attempted to dilute the singularity of my own reading by suggesting other readers' views of material, these descriptions were also affected by my particular consciousness as a describer.

I believe the gendered stance of my own reading in the casebook overview section was essential to my ability to demonstrate the influence of gender in the casebook. Describing examples of gender constraints enabled me to portray concretely how readers connect their sex and their views of law and how the casebook affects readers' views of themselves. However, literally applying my analysis of the gender-related aspects of *Dawson, Harvey, and Henderson* to every legal text one reads would foster rather than challenge the constraints gender ideas have over our lives. It may be accurate at this particular point in time to state that a casebook inhibits readers' views about what men and women can do by containing a large number of cases in which women are described as widows or dependent wives. Similarly, it may be accurate to say that a casebook that is analytical and abstract seems male. Continuing to assert over a long period of time that dependency and abstractions are gender-related characteristics, however, could strengthen rather than loosen the connection between those characteristics and the sexes. Some aspects of my analysis may need to be extended to other legal texts in order to break the hold of gender constraints on our consciousnesses, but other aspects should be transformed in order to achieve the same objective.

A feminist analysis of *Dawson, Harvey, and Henderson* can be successful not by being "applied" to other legal writing but by generating other re-readings. Although we need to use gender-related ideas in order to challenge gender constraints, we will only be able to accomplish that objective by constantly re-examining the ideas we are using. Ultimately, in order to challenge gender constraints effectively, our use of gender-related ideas must change with our shifting cultural context and the changes within ourselves. Only by continually rethinking who we are and why we are making the choices we make can we free ourselves from the belief that our selves are constructed by our sexual identities.

A Postmodern Feminist
Legal Manifesto

7

Rescuing Impossibility Doctrine: A Postmodern Feminist Analysis of Contract Law

In this chapter, I seek to enrich contract doctrine by using feminist strategies as a means of contesting and restructuring conventional and stalemated understandings. At the same time, I hope to contribute to feminist theory by exposing, on the somewhat unlikely terrain of the common law, how conventional analytical devices are deeply implicated in the construction of our current gender system. In the pursuit of these objectives, I am going to be particularly concerned with three "texts." The "texts" are law review articles written by male legal scholars for a law readership.

I originally chose the doctrinal problem I am going to discuss for a research project as a result of political happenstance. In 1988, a contracts scholar, who was then serving as chair of the Contracts Section of the Association of American Law Schools, declined a proposal for a joint Association program with feminists. In a publicly circulated letter, the chair explained his decision by elaborating his view that the topic of the relationship between feminist theory and contract law was not "developed . . . to a point where it is ready for such a sponsorship," that it does not yet have "a respectable basis."[1] "In contrast," he wrote, the topic upon which the Contracts Section would focus its program, "excuse of performance, adjustment of contract and limitation of remedy on account of unexpected events," "has been thoroughly developed in the literature."[2] Feminist theory, he concluded, was unlikely (ever) to contribute significantly to contract law because "the male bias of our society . . . has not had important consequences for contract law."[3]

Since debates regarding different ways of handling doctrinal problems are a staple component of legal scholarship, I immediately decided to challenge his prediction by writing, as a feminist, about whatever doctrinal issue his group was discussing at the time. In a coincidence that may arouse your interest as it did mine, the contract doctrine I blindly assigned myself uncannily resonates with a postmodern stance toward the female subject. "It is *impossible* to dissociate the questions of art, style and truth from the question of the woman," Derrida writes in *Spurs*.[4]

> Nevertheless the question "what is woman?" is itself suspended by the simple formulation of their common problematic. One can no longer seek her, no more than one could search for woman's femininity or female sexuality. And she is certainly not to be found in any of the familiar modes of concept or knowledge. Yet [he concludes] it is *impossible* to resist looking for her.[5]

"Impossible to dissociate . . ." and "impossible to resist looking. . . ." The contract doctrine which is the subject of the "texts" I will discuss is the doctrine of impossibility.

Introduction

The "texts" involving impossibility doctrine that I am going to discuss are an essay by Richard Posner and Andrew Rosenfield in the 1977 *Journal of Legal Studies;*[6] Robert Hillman's 1983 *Cornell Law Review* essay;[7] and a second Hillman piece which is in the 1987 *Duke Law Journal*.[8] These articles are important because they capture the conflict of the academic dispute about the application of impossibility doctrine. I am going to argue that the rhetoric and analytical characteristics of the Posner/Rosenfield position on impossibility doctrine are helpfully understood as stereotypically masculine, both in their strengths and in their weaknesses. In contrast, the Hillman article is helpfully understood as offering a feminine alternative version of the doctrine, with the strengths and weaknesses associated with that stereotypical position.

As Fran Olsen has written in her article, "The Sex of Law," it is often the case when opposing discourses develop, in law but also elsewhere, that the relationship between the dichotomies in the opposing discourses is likely to mirror cultural stereotypes of women and men.[9] Identifying the gendered character of the discourses can therefore be a feminist strategy for challenging the extensive and complicated network of social and cultural practices which legitimate the subordination of women. The assumption underlying this strategy is that language is a mechanism of power, that there is always more at stake in the relationship of gender and language than "just" a question of literary style—indeed, that style itself can constitute a powerful socializing apparatus.

There are at least three forms which such a feminist strategy can take. One form, which I will not pursue in this chapter, focuses on the specific gender of individuals noted in a text, analyzing the ways in which male and female characters and even their pronouns are deployed. This practice is illustrated by some of my argument in reviewing Dawson, Harvey, and Henderson's fourth edition,[10] such as the assertion that the disproportionate number of male parties in the cases reproduced in that text is likely to foster sexist attitudes in readers regarding the position of women or womanly persons in the law.

A second form of feminist discourse practice is to examine the relationship between the dichotomies in a particular discourse and cultural stereotypes of women and men. Such dichotomies are often unconsciously but sometimes consciously molded by their authors to resonate with stereotypical sex differences. In this chapter I am going to argue that the academic literature on impossibility doctrine can be arranged along such a masculine/feminine axis—indeed, that it is hard to avoid the sense that this work involves unconscious self-stereotyping around gender categories.

A third form of feminist discourse analysis is to show the way meaning can acquire gendered overtones through the use of rhetoric which a reader consciously or unconsciously registers as sexual double entendre. Thus, I am going to argue that the Posner/Rosenfield and the Hillman articles contain rhetoric which is repeatedly suggestive of stereotypical male and female "sex talk."

Before turning to a discussion of the articles themselves, let me state in a generalized way some of the reasons why I believe that analyzing the gender of legal discourse is useful.

First, to the extent that there is a cultural compulsion to maintain the gendered integrity of texts, pursuing the gendered character of a particular text is likely to facilitate a reader's understanding of that text. For example, having identified the Posner/Rosenfield piece as stereotypically masculine, my appreciation of the authors' technical argument about impossibility doctrine is likely to be enhanced by using my understanding of masculinity as a stereotyped role, persona, or mask as a guide to its meaning.

Second, because of the relational character of gendered identities, a reader's understanding of opposing discourses can be furthered by using a gendered trait within one discourse to predict, to understand, or to critique the other. In addition, the hierarchical dimension of gender relations can illuminate the positioning of opposing discourses. In legal debates about doctrinal problems it is almost always the case that one line of thought is understood as the standard or dominant approach, and the second line of thought is treated as exceptional or subordinate to the first. Identifying the gender mask an author assumes not only helps predict which hierarchical position a text will occupy but may also help one understand its entrenchment in that position.

Finally, and perhaps most significantly, the gendered character of discourse can expose weaknesses in legal argument. The cultural compulsion to maintain the gendered identity of one's text involves one—inevitably, perhaps—in the vices of one's virtues. Finding ruptures in a text where its gendered character falters is likely to indicate a problem in the line of thought the text is developing.

One last point of introduction might also be useful—a brief definition of two phrases I have already used in this article, "feminist theory" and "impossibility doctrine."

I am usually reluctant to define feminist theory separately from the broader, more politically charged category of "feminism" on the grounds that this division can lead to a falsely abstracted and misleading unification of feminist projects. Nevertheless, it seems fair to acknowledge that, like other political movements, feminism has a discourse of explanation which can reasonably be called "theory." I am not sure that much feminism will be excluded by my definition of theory as work which seeks to *account for* the condition of women as well as to illustrate it or oppose it, but this definition has the important virtue of being supple enough to include multiple and even inconsistent categories of explanation.

Although categories within feminist theory are imprecise and overlap, the treatment of impossibility doctrine I will offer here is primarily informed by postmodern feminism, the particular blend of psychoanalysis, linguistics, and philosophy which is concerned with sexual difference and which is associated with the writing of French feminists such as Luce Irigaray and Julia Kristeva, and American feminists such as Barbara Johnson and Jane Gallop.[11] In acknowledging the influence of postmodern feminist scholarship, I do not mean to imply that I am conforming to an orthodox methodology or line. I doubt that I am. What does link this paper programmatically with postmodern feminism is a shared intention to disrupt cultural dichotomies—especially, and controversially, the dichotomy of male/female.

Other feminist theories, such as socialist feminism, cultural feminism, lesbian feminism, and the feminism of women of color might also inform and affect a doctrinal analysis of impossibility, although they also might not. For the purposes of this chapter I have quite deliberately overlooked the diversity of feminist theory and the conflict within feminist theories, concentrating instead on the assistance which postmodern feminism has been able to offer my undertaking.

The term "impossibility doctrine" has generally been used to refer to a particular subcategory of law relating to cases in which contractual parties seek to escape their contractual responsibilities on account of "extraordinary," "unanticipated," or "disruptive" circumstances. Other subcategories are the doctrines of mistake, frustration of purpose, commercial impracticability, and failure of presupposed conditions. Like others currently writing about these subcategories, I think the commonalities among the doctrines are more usefully examined than the distinctions.[12] Although elsewhere these doctrines have been referred to collectively as excuse, discharge, or cessation law, I am going to use the term "impossibility" as a unifying name. I have chosen this name to indicate a deliberate break with the gendered character of current scholarship. In order for feminist theory to rescue (re-skew) excuse doctrine from (within) the respectable debate in which it is currently stuck, I intend to argue, descending only for the moment into postmodern jargon, that excuse doctrine is "impossible," that impossibility doctrine is the *différance* of contract law.[13]

The Posner/Rosenfield and Hillman Articles

The Gendered Character of Impossibility Scholarship

I begin with the gendered character of the position Posner and Rosenfield take on impossibility doctrine. Summarily dismissing prior attempts to predict when performance will be excused—"The foreseeability test . . . is non-operational"[14]—the authors articulate a new standard for deciding when contract performance should be excused. "[D]ischarge should be allowed," they propose, whenever "the promisee is the superior risk bearer."[15] This standard is applied through a three-step analysis, in which a decision maker determines (a) which party can estimate the probability of loss; (b) which party can estimate the magnitude of the loss; and (c) which party is better situated to insure against the loss.[16] Posner and Rosenfield confidently claim that the "superior risk bearer" standard can explain "the typical outcomes in the major classes of cases."[17] To the extent that decided cases are inconsistent with the standard, the authors are unperturbed. "It is not our purpose to explain or even identify every inconsistent outcome."[18] To the extent that the application of the test points in opposite directions, the authors' confidence in their standard is undiminished; they assert that "empirical studies" will resolve such conflicts.[19]

Like a phallus, this conceptual proposal is singular, daunting, rigid, and cocksure. The purpose of the "superior risk bearer" standard, as they see it, is to permit courts to decide impossibility cases as if the singular legitimate decisional objective is to facilitate efficient contract planning.[20] (In other words, the only purpose of the legal impossibility standard is to guide parties in future cases so that they can minimize drafting time and effort; the standard is unconcerned with parties already in contractual relationships who desire to know what their responsibilities might be should performance begin to seem "impossible.") In pursuit of future contract planning, Posner and Rosenfield treat all contracts as if they fit a particular, abstract model of contractual relations, in which the relationship between the parties is highly delineated and quite historically discrete.[21] Finally, the authors rely on and defend a sharply and cleanly dichotomized system of contractual remedies, according to which contractual obligations must either be performed in full or discharged.[22] Because the proposal is focused on a single goal, because it is confidently predicated on an abstract model of contractual relations, and because of its clearly decisive, on or off remedial implications, the characteristics of the Posner/Rosenfield impossibility standard correspond to stereotypical male virtues.

Hillman's article presents a sharply contrasting approach to impossibility doctrine along all the dimensions I have just mentioned. His approach actually rejects all three characteristics of the "risk bearer" standard. Thus, Hillman proposes that courts apply impossibility doctrine to serve a number of goals besides the facilitation of future contract planning. These goals, which Hillman calls "fairness norms," include favoring the party with greater equities, rewarding efforts to avoid harm to the other party, rewarding reasonable conduct, and achieving reciprocity in a deal.[23] Hillman explicitly grounds his proposal, following Ian Macneil,[24] in a pluralistic, context-sensitive model of contract relations, emphasizing that in the real world many contracts are based on long-term relationships in which the parties rely on good faith, forbearance, and sharing, rather than insisting on a literal interpretation of their contract texts. Finally, Hillman, like Richard Speidel,[25] seeks to modify the rigid dichotomy of performance or discharge, arguing for an examination of the actual harm being caused to a party and urging that a duty of adjustment should be judicially inferred in some situations.[26] Because Hillman's impossibility proposal is characterized by a concern for multiple objectives, by an appreciation of contextualized relationships, and by a desire to

achieve flexibility and sharing in the administration of contract remedies, his proposal neatly fits the popular interpretation of Carol Gilligan's depiction of the virtuous feminine attitudes toward justice.[27]

The gendered opposition between the Posner/Rosenfield article and
Hillman's articles accentuates Hillman's sometimes explicit but often
implicit criticism of the masculine impossibility position. Simply by
concretizing and disaggregating an abstract model of contractual
relations and by pointing out the merit of expanding conventional
remedial options, Hillman's articles offer a critique of the male model
which is both powerful and also reminiscent of typical feminine criticisms of masculinity. That is, Hillman's equitable approach suggests
the element of *arbitrariness* in imposing the "superior risk bearer"
standard in situations where it might have little to do with what
the parties actually intended. The gendered opposition between the
Posner/Rosenfield article and the Hillman articles also suggests the
incomplete and partial character of each position.

I turn now to the sexual double entendre of the rhetoric in these
articles. The tone of the Posner/Rosenfield article strikes me as mark-
edly masculine. The article bristles with such cockiness that some of
the authors' relatively commonplace law review language takes on
the overtones of locker-room swagger as I read it. For example, the
authors observe that conventional legal categories in this area of
law are "empty,"[28] and they comment that even the most promising
branch of scholastic commentary is "sterile."[29] In their promise to do
something about this situation, they boast that they will "give content" to an economic analysis of the doctrine.[30]

These observations undoubtedly contribute to the suggestive significance I find in the authors' disregard of the phrase "impossibility
doctrine" throughout the body of their article. Despite having used the
phrase in their title and in subtitles, elsewhere they almost exclusively
describe their subject in terms of "discharge," "discharge cases," and
"discharge law." In my judgment, the depth of the authors' substantive bias in favor of contract performance and against discharge is
emphasized by the contrast between the word performance and its
association with completed, conventional heterosexual intercourse,
and the association between the word discharge and its overtones
of coitus interruptus, nocturnal emissions, and masturbation. The
rhetorical impression of maleness this article conveys is partly derived
from the sense that these two contrasting categories of sexual activities define the authors' limited, stereotypically masculine erotic uni-
verse.

In contrast to the Posner/Rosenfield article, the structure, tone, and
language of the Hillman articles have feminine overtones. Hillman's

tone is unintimidating, accommodating, and unassuming, not cock-sure. His position on impossibility is set forth in *two* articles and developed through *four* fairness norms; it has multiple parts. In contrast to the daunting Posnerian tone, Hillman modestly describes his impossibility standard as "supplement[al]" to the principle of "freedom of contract";[31] he deferentially places his standard regarding excuse of performance after a discussion of the express and implied desires of contract parties.[32] Read in comparison with the Posnerian rhetoric, Hillman's tropes, the figurative language he uses, evoke a stereotypically female description of sexual relations. Hillman's unifying name for impossibility doctrine is "cessation" rather than "discharge," and rather than promising to "give content" to an analysis or erect a "framework" he uses the language of display: he promises to "present," to "demonstrate" his thesis.[33] His frequently stated and principal concern is the application of impossibility law where parties have left "gaps" in their contracts.[34]

Disrupting the Gendered Opposition of Impossibility Scholarship

Like other postmodern theorists, postmodern feminists use deconstructive analytical strategies to expose contradictory and repressed elements embedded within and supporting the deceptively coherent message on the surface of a text. The strategy I will use here—a strategy inspired by Jane Gallop's most recent book, *Thinking Through the Body*[35]—consists of identifying what I call a critical rupture in a passage; a rupture which, in Barbara Johnson's words, "encounters and propagates the surprise of otherness" or difference.[36] In each of the texts I examine, the critical rupture is a point where analytical cogency is sacrificed to the gendered integrity of the authors' positions.

A critical rupture in the Posner/Rosenfield article occurs at the moment two-thirds of the way into the article when the authors briefly discuss "doubtful cases."[37] "Doubtful cases" are defined as those in which the "superior risk bearer" test "will fail to yield a definite answer."[38] In singling out "doubtful cases" for separate treatment Posner and Rosenfield seem about to face a critique of their own proposal. They seem about to stray from the firm and confident masculinity that has characterized their argument. Doctrinally the authors could have chosen one of at least three solutions for cases which the risk bearer standard does not explain. They could have recommended discharge; they could have recommended, as they did, that parties be required to perform; or they could have recommended that "doubtful cases" be subject to an equitable approach, such as the one Hillman proposed. That is, they could have chosen a solution that would have broken the absolutism of the "superior risk bearer" standard by taking into account the situation of the parties after the contract had been formed.

The authors reject a Hillman-like solution. Their solution is decisive but largely unexplained. "Pending definitive empirical study," they say that the appropriate resolution of doubtful cases is to reject the application of impossibility doctrine and reaffirm the principle of strict liability in contract.[39]

By rejecting an equitable approach, with its attendant uncertainty, Posner and Rosenfield refuse an open solution that would have been inconsistent with the closure they seek. An equitable approach, as Hillman himself points out, is subject to criticism because it pursues fairness at the cost of certainty.[40] By rejecting discharge and requiring parties to perform, Posner and Rosenfield choose an authoritarian rather than a permissive solution for "doubtful cases." Confronting a threat to the logic of their argument (confronting, one might also say, difference, or woman), their response exhibits the weaknesses stereotypically associated with masculinity: they are arbitrary, rigid, and authoritarian. They are unable to claim what Keats called "Negative Capability"—the capacity "of being in uncertainties, Mysteries, doubts, without any irritable reaching after fact & reason."[41]

Although there is much to admire in Hillman's impossibility proposal, analyzing the feminization of his work similarly helps reveal the problems that adhere to his approach. A critical rupture in Hillman's proposal occurs in a short section where he concludes his presentation of the "fairness norms." Although he has earlier claimed that the "fairness norms" can "explain" impossibility decisions[42] and has minimized the Posnerian standard as "only of limited help,"[43] here he acknowledges the significance of the Posnerian proposal, admitting that "Courts sometimes justify cessation decisions . . . on the economic and social policies of avoiding economic waste and promoting the economy through contract formation."[44] Hillman seems about to analyze the relationship between his standard and the "superior risk bearer" principle; he seems about to confront a masculine challenge to the feminine virtues of his proposal.

This moment in Hillman's piece, the point when a tough question is raised in the text, parallels the Posner/Rosenfield examination of "doubtful cases." But unlike their decisive, if arbitrary, resolution, Hillman is contradictory and conciliatory. Stating at first that he must avoid the question, because the relationship between the two standards is "complex" and "beyond the scope of this paper,"[45] he immediately reverses this decision, allowing himself "some brief observations."[46] Among these observations is the disingenuous claim that the two standards "generally dictate the same result" since the two standards "correspond."[47] Hillman introduces this latter claim with a conventional feminine disclaimer. "*Intuitively*," he begins. "*Intuitively*, waste-avoidance and preserving the benefits of contracting through 'keeping the deal together' correspond with protecting the substantial reliance interest of a party on harm-avoidance grounds."[48]

The Posnerian and Hillman standards are concerned with different kinds of unexpected losses. The Posnerian standard implements the allocation of estimated losses behind the veil of history. It seeks to determine what the parties should have decided about allocation before the unexpected event occurred. In contrast, Hillman's standard is concerned with the distribution of actual losses. There is no reason to believe the standards would yield the same outcomes. To reconcile his standard with the Posnerian version Hillman *misstates* the efficiency standard by linking it with *his* goal of "keeping the deal together." The feminine virtue of Hillman's article thereby ruptures in this passage: confronting the threat of difference between his argument and another's, Hillman's response exhibits the stereotypical weaknesses associated with femininity. He appeals to intuition to cover a slight misrepresentation, using misrepresentation as it is commonly deployed to mitigate the feminine terror of confrontation, argument, and autonomy.

Although the texts I have been discussing seek to provide a useful legal standard by which to determine how impossibility doctrine is applied, they therefore fail in their objectives. Just as Hillman's legal argument fails when the gendered persona of his text falters and is reasserted, so Posner and Rosenfield's attempt to develop a legal standard for impossibility fails at a point of crisis in the gender role of their text. By asserting that "doubtful cases" should not be excused, they avoid discharge and call on the parties for performance. Masculine cockiness thus identifies the point at which Posner and Rosenfield abruptly abandon the project of delineating a legal standard for impossibility doctrine and arbitrarily reinstate the principle of strict liability in its place.

The Gendered Context of Impossibility Doctrine

Thus far my analysis of current impossibility literature has used reading strategies inspired by postmodern feminism in order to expose shortcomings in current approaches to the problem of impossibility. Let me now indicate briefly how feminist theory might yield constructive insights regarding the generation of persuasive doctrinal argument in impossibility cases.

One idea is to explore the striking parallels between impossibility doctrine and the character and development of divorce and annulment law. Like impossibility doctrine, the function of annulment and divorce is specifically to excuse performance of obligations imposed by the contractual relations of the parties.[49] But the analogies between these fields have historically been foreclosed to contract disputes because of the segregation of the legal subject areas. Because of women's historical links to and dependence on the domestic sphere, the segregation of these areas has a decidedly sex-based character. This sex-segregated character seems particularly pronounced in the context of the nineteenth century, when impossibility doctrine was purportedly "formed."[50] At that time the contracting activity of married women was largely confined to their marriage contracts. Until the reforms begun in the mid-nineteenth century by the Married Women's Property Acts, the law relating to the contracts most *women* entered was separated from the law of other contracts.[51]

I think it would be useful for feminists to elaborate the historically gendered roots of current impossibility doctrine, seeking to determine the effect on impossibility doctrine of placing it in a broader context.[52] One could, for example, track the parallels of the changing remedial consequences of divorce and impossibility over time, seeking—with some caution—to determine the significance of the historical separation between these two similar doctrinal areas. Like impossibility doctrine of the same period, the law of divorce in mid-nineteenth century American legal history offered parties narrower opportunities for excuse of contract performance than is true today. Unlike the consequences of impossibility doctrine, however, the use of divorce did not always fully discharge marital contracts, in that alimony awards functioned in many cases to extend a husband's duties of marital support after divorce had terminated his marital status.[53]

In this century, Ian Macneil and others have argued that contract doctrine ought to take into account, rather than suppress, the interest which contract parties may have in preserving their relationship beyond the event giving rise to an impossibility dispute.[54] Indeed, Macneil is often cited by those, like Hillman and Speidel, who seek to encourage a duty of adjustment in certain impossibility situations. There is a remarkable similarity between Macneil's description of "relational" contract law and its remedial consequences, and the typical descriptions of marriage and divorce law which preceded the divorce reforms of the early 1970s. Despite the warm reception that Macneil's proposals have received among some contract scholars, there is a remarkable silence regarding his work among others, including, not surprisingly, Posner and Rosenfield.

Another potentially fruitful comparison between the law of divorce and impossibility doctrine in the mid-nineteenth century is likely to be the acknowledged interest of the state in divorce suits. In the classical treatment of impossibility issues, the public interest was so decisively banished from explicit consideration that courts often heavily and unsubtly deployed the device of an invented "implied condition" to determine whether excuse was warranted, a device subjected to increasing criticism after the turn of the century.[55] In contrast, a marriage and divorce treatise writer of the mid-nineteenth century describes the public interest in divorce litigation as the "one great controlling principle running through all matrimonial suits, and bringing into subserviency all other law on the subject."[56] Indeed, in at least two states a public prosecuting officer was required to participate in divorce proceedings along with the parties.[57]

Although the public interest in divorce continues to hover over even the most liberal no-fault divorce jurisdictions,[58] the public interest in such proceedings is considerably more subtly manifested than it was in the last century; parties enjoy the appearance of more individualized control over divorce. In contrast, the public interest in impossibility disputes is more overt than it was in the last century, in part because impossibility disputes seem to arise more frequently today as a result of governmental regulatory changes than seems to have been the case in the past. The task here will be to analyze, again exercising caution, the significance of the changing roles of public interest in the separated yet analogous areas involving claims to excuse contract performance.

Rescuing (Re-skewing) Impossibility Doctrine

The gendered integrity that I have argued Posner/Rosenfield and Hillman tenaciously preserve in their essays is incompatible with the approach I attribute to postmodern feminists regarding sexual difference. There is, in fact, an illuminating parallel between the postmodern feminist desire to challenge the borders that define us as men and women and a re-skewed, cogent impossibility doctrine which is neither masculine, nor feminine, nor some confused, androgynous mixture.

Although lesbian feminists and women of color have begun to unravel the imperialistic claims many feminists make regarding women,[59] postmodern feminists have theorized these challenges. They

maintain that replacing male values with female values simply reallo-
cates power between the poles of an axis; it does not challenge the
confining structure of the (gendered) axis.[60] Maleness and femaleness
therefore persevere as confining and restraining consequences of biological data because of the oppositional framework in which we locate
them.

Postmodern feminists seek to alter this oppositional structure by
grounding their analyses of sexual difference on the structuralist insight that meaning depends on nonmeaning. Maleness is not just the
opposite of femaleness. Instead, maleness depends on femaleness.
Unlike Posner, Rosenfield, and Hillman, postmodern feminists are
willing to confront the differences *within* maleness or femaleness.[61] At
the same time, despite current claims to the contrary,[62] postmodern
feminists also *accept* sexual difference.[63] Postmodern feminists are
thus able to treat women as historically situated individuals with
commonalities *at the same time* that they are challenging the link
between femininity and biological femaleness.

Transposing their paradoxical approach toward sexual difference
to impossibility doctrine, the postmodern feminists' observation
would be that the meaning of strict liability or performance depends
on the concept of what nonperformance or excuse of performance
would mean. Contract law is constituted by the idea that parties can
count on allocating today the risks of tomorrow. By claiming that
some unexpected circumstances are *not* allocated by contract, the
doctrine of impossibility affirms the ability of contract to protect
against those risks that *are* allocated. Impossibility doctrine is thus
located at the margins of strict liability, where it constantly threatens
to disrupt expectations of performance—just as postmodern feminists
both acknowledge and challenge the borders that define us as men
and women. Indeed it is because of this location at the margins that
impossibility doctrine can perform its constituting and liberating
function within contract doctrine.

In their efforts to subject the problem of unexpected contract conditions to predictable standards, Posner, Rosenfield, and Hillman segre-
gate impossibility from strict liability. This instinct toward segregation is understandable, but oppositional relationships tend to produce
undesirable hierarchies. The value of impossibility doctrine to contracting parties would be jeopardized if the doctrine were subordinated to strict liability, just as the value of contracting would be
drastically undermined if the principle of strict liability were subordinated to the doctrine of impossibility. As we have seen, however, these
authors' segregating efforts devolve into yet another oppositional

structure, the genderization of impossibility, and this genderization defeats the project of articulating a predictable standard of impossibility doctrine application.

I think that the quest for a predictable standard is misguided—that impossibility doctrine must be articulated in relationship to but not in opposition to the principle of strict liability. This obligation makes the doctrine of impossibility doctrine "impossible." But I do not believe that claiming the impossibility of impossibility doctrine requires the doctrine to be consigned to the realm of the subjective, the irrational, the nihilistic, or the non-legal. My suggested feminist approach to impossibility adopts the approach postmodern feminists have used in confronting the problem of sexual difference. Postmodern feminists do not seek to help women be more like men or to replace male values with female values, or to achieve an androgynous reconstruction and unification of male and female. Postmodern feminists attempt to overcome the male/female opposition by accepting it and at the same time disrupting it.

Can feminist critical scholars claim a different voice in analyzing contract law doctrine? I hope I have conveyed that we can, insofar as the use of gender stereotypes is useful in legal analysis. I also hope I have indicated that we cannot.

"Who are we" is a penetrating question to turn on my discussion here. The feminine text I analyzed was written by a man. The stereotypes I associated with gender may not be every woman's or every feminist's. The negative stereotypes associated with Hillman's text distinguish his "voice" and mine from the upbeat version of femininity popularly attributed to Gilligan's book.[64] Indeed, I am willing to admit that the particular traits I associate with masculine and feminine stereotypes are undoubtedly a product of my cultural position as a white woman, a midwesterner, a heterosexual daughter of the fifties, a law professor who entered the profession when patriarchy was virtually unchallenged. Like Hillman, I speak in sexual drag. If "we" can claim "a different voice" it must be understood, like impossibility doctrine, to lack a coherent essence.

8

A Postmodern Feminist
Legal Manifesto

Preliminaries

I am worried about the title of this chapter.

Postmodernism may already be passé, for some readers. Like a shooting star or last night's popovers, its genius was the surprise of its appearance. Once that initial moment has passed, there's not much value in what's left over.

For other readers, postmodernism may refer to such an elaborate and demanding genre—within linguistics, psychoanalysis, literary theory, and philosophy—that claiming an affinity to "it" will quite properly invoke a flood of criticism regarding the omissions, misrepresentations, and mistakes that one paper will inevitably make.

The manifesto part may also be troublesome. The dictionary describes a manifesto as a statement of principles or intentions, while I have in mind a rather informal presentation. More of a discussion, say, in which the "principles" are somewhat contradictory and the "intentions" are loosely formulated goals that are qualified by an admission that they might not work. MacKinnon, of course, launched feminism into social theory orbit by drawing on Marxism to present her biting analysis.[1] Referring to one word in a Karl Marx title may represent an acknowledgment of her work, an unconscious, copyKat gesture; but I don't want to get carried away. I am in favor of localized disruptions; I am against totalizing theory.

Sometimes the "PM"s that label my notes remind me of female troubles—of premenstrual and postmenopausal blues. Maybe I am destined to do exactly what my title prescribes; just note the discomfort and keep going.

One "Principle"

The liberal equality doctrine is often understood as an engine of liberation with respect to sex-specific rules. This imagery suggests the repressive function of law, a function that feminists have inventively sought to appropriate and exploit, through critical scholarship, litigation, and legislative campaigns. Examples of these efforts include work seeking to strengthen domestic violence statutes, to enact a model anti-pornography ordinance, and to expand sexual harassment doctrine.

The postmodern position locating human experience as inescapably within language suggests that feminists should not overlook the constructive function of legal language as a critical frontier for feminist reforms. To put this "principle" more bluntly, legal discourse should be recognized as a site of political struggle over sex differences.

This is not a proposal that we try to promote a benevolent and fixed meaning for sex differences. (See the "principle" below.) Rather, the argument is that continuous interpretive struggles over the meaning of sex differences can have an impact on patriarchal legal power.

Another "Principle"

In their most vulgar, bootlegged versions, both radical and cultural legal feminisms depict male and female sexual identities as anatomically determined and psychologically predictable. This is inconsistent with the semiotic character of sex differences and the impact that historical specificity has on any individual identity. In postmodern jargon, this treatment of sexual identity is inconsistent with a decentered, polymorphous, contingent understanding of the subject.

Because sex differences are semiotic—that is, constituted by a system of signs that we produce and interpret—each of us inescapably produces herself within the gender meaning system, although the meaning of gender is indeterminate or undecidable. The dilemma of difference, which the liberal equality guarantee seeks to avoid through neutrality, is unavoidable.

On Style

Style is important in postmodern work. The medium *is* the message, in some cases—although by no means all. When style is salient, it is characterized by irony and by wordplay that is often dazzlingly funny, smart and irreverent. Things aren't just what they seem.

By arguing that legal rhetoric should not be dominated by masculine pronouns or by stereotypically masculine imagery, legal feminists have conceded the significance of style. But the postmodern tone sharply contrasts with the earnestness that almost universally characterizes feminist scholarship. "The circumstances of women's lives [are] unbearable," Andrea Dworkin writes.[2] Legal feminists tend to agree. Hardly appropriate material for irony and play.

I do not underestimate the oppression of women as Andrea Dworkin describes it. I also appreciate what a hard time women have had communicating our situation. Reports from numerous state commissions on gender bias in the courts have concluded that one of the most significant problems of women in law is their lack of credibility. Dworkin puts this point more movingly:

> The accounts of rape, wife beating, forced childbearing, medical butchering, sex-motivated murder, forced prostitution, sadistic psychological abuse, and other commonplaces of female experience that are excavated from the past or given by contemporary survivors should leave the heart seared, the mind in anguish, the conscience in upheaval. But they do not. No matter how often these stories are told, with whatever clarity or eloquence, bitterness or sorrow, they might as well have been whispered in wind or written in sand: they disappear, as if they were nothing. The tellers and the stories are ignored or ridiculed, threatened back into silence or destroyed, and the experience of female suffering is buried in cultural invisibility and contempt.[3]

Although the flip, condescending, and mocking tones that often characterize postmodernism may not capture the intensity and urgency that frequently motivate feminist legal scholarship, the postmodern style does not strike me as "politically incorrect." Indeed, the oppositional character of the style arguably coincides with the oppositional spirit of feminism. Irony, for example, is a stylistic method of acknowledging and challenging a dominant meaning, of saying something and simultaneously denying it. Figures of speech invite ideas to break out of the linear argument of a text; they challenge singular, dominant interpretations.

I confess to having considerable performance anxiety about the postmodern style myself. It may require more art, more creativity, and inspiration than I can manage. But I don't think feminist legal activists need to adopt the postmodern medium in order to exploit the postmodern message; my point about the style is simply that it doesn't require us, strategically, to dismiss postmodernism as an influence on our work.

Applying Postmodern "Principles": Law and the Female Body

Most feminists are committed to the position that however "natural" and common sex differences may seem, the differences between women and men are not biologically compelled; they are, rather, "socially constructed." Over the past two decades this conviction has fueled many efforts to change the ways in which law produces—or socially constructs—the differences and the hierarchies between the sexes. Feminists have reasoned, for example, that when women are uneducated for "men's work," or when they are sexually harassed in the men's work they do, they are not "naturally" more suited for "women's work"; they have been constructed to be that way. Although law is by no means the only factor that influences which jobs men and women prefer, how well they perform at work, or the intensity of their wage market commitment, outlawing employment discrimination can affect to some degree what women and men are "like" as workers. What law (at least in part) constructs, law reform projects can reconstruct or alter.

Regardless of how commonplace the constructed character of sex differences may be, particular differences can seem quite deeply embedded within the sexes—so much so, in fact, that the social construction thesis is undermined. When applied to differences that seem especially entrenched—differences such as masculine aggression or feminine compassion, or differences related to the erotic and reproductive aspects of women's lives—social construction seems like a clichéd, improbable, and unconvincing account of experience, an explanation for sex differences that undervalues "reality." This reaction does not necessarily provoke a return to a "natural" explanation for sex differences; but it does radically stunt the liberatory potential of the social construction thesis. One's expectations for law reform projects are reduced; law might be able to mitigate the harsh impact of these embedded traits on women's lives, but law does not seem responsible for *constructing* them.

The subject of this section is the role of law in the production of sex differences that seem "natural." One of my objectives is to explain and challenge the essentializing impulse that places particular sex differences outside the borders of legal responsibility. Another objective is to provide an analysis of the legal role in the production of gendered identity that will invigorate the liberatory potential of the social construction thesis.

I have chosen the relationship of law to the female body as my principal focus. I am convinced that law is more cunningly disguised but just as implicated in the production of apparently intractable sex-related traits as in those that seem more legally malleable. Since the anatomical distinctions between the sexes seem not only "natural" but fundamental to identity, proposing and describing the role of law in the production of the meaning of the female body seems like the most convincing subject with which to defend my case. In the following subsections, I will argue that legal rules—like other cultural mechanisms—encode the female body with meanings. Legal discourse then explains and rationalizes these meanings by an appeal to the "natural" differences between the sexes, differences that the rules themselves help to produce. The formal norm of legal neutrality conceals the way in which legal rules participate in the construction of those meanings.

The proliferation of women's legal rights during the past two decades has liberated women from some of the restraining meanings of femininity. This liberation has been enhanced by the emergence of different feminisms over the past decade. These feminisms have made possible a stance of opposition toward a singular feminine identity; they have demonstrated that women stand in a multitude of places, depending on time and geographical location, on race, age, sexual preference, health, class status, religion, and other factors. Despite these significant changes, there remains a common residue of meaning that seems affixed, as if by nature, to the female body. Law participates in creating that meaning.

I will argue that there are at least three general claims that can be made about the relationship between legal rules and legal discourse and the meaning of the female body.

1. Legal rules permit and sometimes mandate the *terrorization* of the female body. This occurs by a combination of provisions that inadequately protect women against physical abuse and that encourage women to seek refuge against insecurity. One meaning of "female body," then, is a body that is "in terror," a body that has learned to scurry, to cringe and to submit. Legal discourse supports that meaning.

2. Legal rules permit and sometimes mandate the *maternalization* of the female body. This occurs by provisions that reward women for singularly assuming responsibilities after childbirth and with those that penalize conduct—such as sexuality or labor market work—that conflicts with mothering. Maternalization also occurs through rules such as abortion restrictions that compel women to become mothers and by domestic relations rules that favor mothers over fathers as parents. Another meaning of "female body," then, is a body that is "for" maternity. Legal discourse supports that meaning.

3. Legal rules permit and sometimes mandate the *sexualization* of the female body. This occurs through provisions that criminalize

individual sexual conduct, such as rules against commercial sex (prostitution) or same-sex practices (homosexuality), and also through rules that legitimate and support institutions such as the pornography, advertising, and entertainment industries which eroticize the female body. Sexualization also occurs—paradoxically—in the application of rules such as rape and sexual harassment laws that are designed to protect women against sex-related injuries. These rules grant or deny women protection by interrogating their sexual promiscuity. The more sexually available or desiring a woman looks, the less protection these rules are likely to give her. Another meaning of "female body," then, is a body that is "for" sex with men, a body that is "desirable" and also rapable, that wants sex and wants raping. Legal discourse supports that meaning.

These groups of legal rules and discourse constitute a system that "constructs," or engenders the female body. The feminine figures the rules pose are naturalized, within legal discourse, by declaration— "women *are* (choose one) weak, nurturing, sexy"—and by a host of linguistic strategies that link women to particular images of the female body. By deploying these images, legal discourse rationalizes, explains, and renders authoritative the female body rule network. The impact of the rule network on women's reality in turn reacts back on the discourse, reinforcing the "truth" of these images.

Contractions of confidence in the thesis that sex differences are socially constructed have had a significant impact on women in law. Liberal jurists, for example, have been unwilling to extend the protection of the gender equality guarantee to anatomical distinctions between female and male bodies; these differences seem so basic to individual identity that law need not—or should not—be responsible for them. Feminist legal scholars have been unable to overcome this intransigence, partly because we ourselves sometimes find particular sex-related traits quite intransigent. Indeed, one way to understand the fracturing of law-related feminism into separate schools of thought over the past decade is by the sexual traits that are considered unsusceptible to legal transformation[4] and by the criticisms these analyses have provoked within our own ranks.[5]

The fracturing of feminist criticism has occurred partly because particular sex differences seem so powerfully fixed that feminists are as unable to resist their "naturalization" as liberal jurists. But feminists also cling to particular sex-related differences because of a strategic desire to protect the feminist legal agenda from sabotage. Many feminist critics have argued that the condition of "real" women makes it too early to be post-feminist. The social construction thesis is useful to feminists insofar as it informs and supports our efforts to improve the condition of women in law. If, or when, the social construction thesis seems about to deconstruct the basic category of woman, its usefulness to feminism is problematized; how can we build a political coalition to advance the position of women in law if the subject that drives our efforts is "indeterminate," "incoherent," or "contingent"?

I think this concern is based upon a misperception of where we are in the legal struggle against sexism. I think we are in danger of being politically immobilized by a system for the production of what sex means that makes particular sex differences seem "natural." If my assessment is right, then describing the mechanics of this system is potentially enabling rather than disempowering; it may reveal opportunities for resisting the legal role in producing the radical asymmetry between the sexes.

I also think this concern is based on a misperception about the impact of deconstruction. Skeptics tend to think, I believe, that the legal deconstruction of "woman"—in one paper or in many papers, say, written over the next decade—will entail the immediate destruction of "women" as identifiable subjects who are affected by law reform projects. Despite the healthy, self-serving respect I have for the influence of legal scholarship and for the role of law as a significant cultural factor (among many) that contributes to the production of femininity, I think "women" cannot be eliminated from our lexicon very quickly. The question this paper addresses is not whether sex differences exist—they do—or how to transcend them—we can't—but the character of their treatment in law.

Sexualization, Terrorization, and Maternalization:
The Case of Prostitution

Since most anti-prostitution rules are gender neutral, let me explain, before going any further, how I can argue that they have a particular impact on the meaning of the female body. Like other rules regulating sexual conduct, anti-prostitution rules sexualize male as well as female bodies; they indicate that sex—unlike say, laughing, sneezing, or making eye contact—is legally regulated. Regardless of whether one is male or female, the pleasures and the virtues of sex are produced, at least in part, by legal rules.[6] The gendered lopsidedness of this meaning system—which I describe below—occurs, quite simply, because most sex workers are women. Thus, even though anti-prostitution rules could, in theory, generate parallel meanings for male and female bodies, in practice they just don't. At least they don't right now.

The legal definition of prostitution as the unlawful sale of sex occurs in statutes which criminalize specific commercial sex practices and in decisional law, such as contract cases that hold that agreements for the sale of sexual services are legally unenforceable. By characterizing certain sexual practices as illegal, these rules sexualize the female body. They invite a sexual interrogation of every female body: Is it for or against prostitution?

This sexualization of the female body explains an experience many women have: an insistent concern that this outfit, this pose, this gesture may send the wrong signal—a fear of looking like a whore. Sexy talking, sexy walking, sexy dressing seem sexy, at least in part, because they are the telltale signs of a sex worker plying her trade. This sexualization also explains the shadow many women feel when having sex for unromantic reasons—to comfort themselves, to avoid a confrontation over some domestic issue, or to secure a favor—a fear of acting like a whore.[7]

This reading of the relationship between prostitution rules and the female body is aligned with but somewhat different from the radical feminist description of the relationship between prostitution and female subjectivity. Catharine MacKinnon's 1982 *Signs* piece describes the relationship this way:

> [Feminist] investigations reveal . . . [that] prostitution [is] not primarily [an abuse] of physical force, violence, authority, or economics. [It is an abuse] of sex. [It] need not and do[es] not rely for [its] coerciveness upon forms of enforcement other than the sexual. . . . If women are socially defined such that female sexuality cannot be lived or spoken or felt or even somatically sensed apart from its enforced definition, so that it *is* its own lack, then there is no such thing as a woman as such, there are only walking embodiments of men's projected needs.[8]

MacKinnon's description of the impact of prostitution on women suggests that the sexual experience of all women may be, like sex work, the experience of having sex solely at the command and for the pleasure of another. This is a more extreme interpretation of the sexualized female body than mine, and not one all women share.

> The feminist point of view? Well, I'd like to point out that they are missing a couple of things. Because, you know, I may be dressing like the typical bimbo. Whatever. But I'm in charge, you know. I'm in charge of my fantasies. I put myself in these situations with men, you know. . . . Aren't I in charge of my life?[9]

Although I believe Madonna's claim about herself, there are probably a number of people who won't. Anyone who looks as much like a sex worker as she does couldn't possibly be in charge of herself, they are likely to say; she is an example of exactly what MacKinnon means by a "walking embodiment of men's projected needs."[10] Without going further into the cottage industry of Madonna interpretation, it seems indisputable that Madonna's version of the female sexualized body is radically more autonomous and self-serving than MacKinnon's interpretation, and significantly less troubled and doubled than mine.

Because sex differences are semiotic—because the female body is produced and interpreted through a system of signs—all three of these interpretations of the sexualized female body may be accurate. The truth of any particular meaning would depend on the circumstances in which it was asserted. Thus, the sexualized female body that is produced and sustained by the legal regulation of prostitution may have multiple meanings. Moreover, the meaning of the sexualized female body for an individual woman is also affected by other feminine images which the legal regulation of prostitution produces.

Anti-prostitution rules terrorize the female body. The regulation of prostitution is accomplished not only by rules that expressly repress or prohibit commercialized sex. Prostitution regulation also occurs through a network of cultural practices that endanger sex workers' lives and make their work terrifying. These practices include the random, demeaning, and sometimes brutal character of anti-prostitution law enforcement. They also include the symbiotic relationship between the illegal drug industry and sex work, the use of prostitutes in the production of certain forms of pornography, hotel compliance with sex work, inadequate police protection for crimes against sex workers, and unregulated bias against prostitutes and their children in housing, education, the health care system, and in domestic relations law. Legal rules support and facilitate these practices.

The legal terrorization of prostitutes forces many sex workers to rely on pimps for protection and security, an arrangement which in most cases is also terrorizing. Pimps control when sex workers work, what kind of sex they do for money, and how much they make for doing it; they often use sexual seduction and physical abuse to "manage" the women who work for them. The terrorization of sex workers affects women who are not sex workers by encouraging them to do whatever they can to avoid being asked if they are "for" illegal sex. Indeed, marriage can function as one of these avoidance mechanisms, in that, conventionally, marriage signals that a woman has chosen legal sex over illegal sex.

One might argue that the terrorized female body is not that much different from the sexualized female body. Both experiences of femininity often—some might say always—entail being dominated by a man. Regardless of whether a woman is terrorized or sexualized, there are social incentives to reduce the hardships of her position, either by marrying or by aligning herself with a pimp. In both cases she typically becomes emotionally, financially, physically, and sexually dependent on and subordinate to a man.

If the terrorized and sexualized female bodies can be conflated and reduced to a dominated female body, then Madonna's claim that she's in charge, like the claims other women make that they experience sexual pleasure or autonomy in their relations with men, is suspect—perhaps, even, the product of false consciousness. But I argue that the dominated female body does not fully capture the impact of anti-prostitution rules on women. This is because anti-prostitution rules also maternalize the female body, by virtue of the interrelationship between anti-prostitution rules and legal rules that encourage women to bear and rear children. The maternalized female body triangulates the relationship between law and the meanings of the female body. It proposes a choice of roles for women.

The maternalization of the female body can be explained through the operation of the first and the second postmodern "principles." That is, because we construct our identities in language, and because the meaning of language is contextual and contingent, the relationship between anti-prostitution rules and the meaning of the female body is also affected by other legal rules and their relationship to the female body. The legal rules that criminalize prostitution are located in a legal system in which other legal rules legalize sex—rules, for example, that establish marriage as the legal site of sex and that link marital sex to reproduction by, for example, legitimating children born in marriage. As a result of this conjuncture, anti-prostitution rules maternalize the female body. They not only interrogate women with the question of whether they are for or against prostitution; they also raise the question of whether a woman is for illegal sex or whether she is for legal, maternalized sex.

The legal system maintains a shaky line between sex workers and other women. Anti-prostitution laws are erratically enforced; eager customers and obliging hotel services collaborate in the "crimes" prostitutes commit with relative impunity, and the legal, systemic devaluation of "women's work" sometimes makes prostitution more lucrative for women than legitimate wage labor. Anti-prostitution rules formally preserve the distinction between legal and illegal sexual activity. By preventing the line between sex workers and "mothers" from disappearing altogether, anti-prostitution rules reinforce the maternalized female body that other legal rules more directly support.

The legal discourse of anti-prostitution law explicitly deploys the image of maternalized femininity in order to contrast sex workers with women who are not sex workers. This can be observed in defamation cases involving women who are incorrectly identified or depicted as whores. In authorizing compensation for such women, courts typically appeal to maternal imagery to describe the woman who has been wrongly described; they justify their decisions by contrasting the images of two female bodies against each other, the virgin and the whore—madonna and bimbo. The discourse of these decisions maternalizes the female body.[11] The maternalized female body is responsible for her children. Madonna's bambino puts her in charge.

The conjunction and displacement of these alternative meanings of the female body are rationalized in legal discourse, where they are presented as both "natural" but also necessary, for reasons associated with liberalism. A Massachusetts case involving a rape prosecution,[12] and feminist controversy regarding the discriminalization of prostitution provide two examples.

Sometime after three o'clock in the morning on a December night in Malden Square, a police cruiser entered a parking lot where police officers had heard screams. "Seeing the headlights of an approaching car," Judge Liacos writes for the Supreme Judicial Court (the SJC), a woman "naked and bleeding from the mouth, jumped from the defendant's car and ran toward [the police cruiser] screaming and waving her arms."[13] She claimed that she had been raped, that the defendant had forced her to perform oral sex and to engage in intercourse twice. After the defendant was convicted on charges of rape and commission of an unnatural and lascivious act, he appealed. He claimed that he had wrongfully been denied the opportunity to inform the jury that the complainant had twice been charged with prostitution. He argued that the complainant's allegation of rape, which he denied, "may have been motivated by her desire to avoid prosecution."[14]

The trial court had prohibited the defendant from mentioning the complainant's arrests to the jury because of the Massachusetts rape-shield statute,[15] a rule that prohibits the admission of reputation or of specific instances of a victim's sexual conduct in a rape trial. The purpose of the rule is to encourage victims to report rapes, to eliminate victim harassment at trial, and to support the assumption that reputation evidence is "only marginally, if at all, probative of consent."[16] The SJC lifted the shield, reasoning that a defendant's right to argue bias "may be the last refuge of an innocent defendant."[17]

> We emphasize that we do not depart from the long held view that prostitution is not relevant to credibility. . . . Nor do we depart from

the policy of the statute in viewing prostitution or the lack of chastity as inadmissible on the issue of consent. Where, however, such facts are relevant to a showing of bias or motive to lie, the general evidentiary rule of exclusion must give way to the constitutionally based right of effective cross-examination.[18]

This interpretation of the rape-shield statute, broadly applied, denies sex workers who dare to complain of sexual violence the presumption of innocence. Because prostitution is unlawful, this ruling simultaneously terrorizes, sexualizes, and dematernalizes sex workers. This triple whammy is accomplished by an appeal to fairness:

[T]he defendant is entitled to present his own theory of the encounter to the jury. . . . The relevancy of testimony depends on whether it has a "rational tendency to prove an issue in the case." . . . Under the defendant's theory he and the complainant, previously strangers to each other, were in a car late at night parked in a vacant parking lot. Having just engaged in sexual acts, they were both naked. A police car was approaching. The defendant intended to show that the complainant, having been found in a similar situation on two prior occasions, had been arrested on each occasion and charged with prostitution. We cannot say that this evidence has no rational tendency to prove that the complainant was motivated falsely to accuse the defendant of rape by a desire to avoid further prosecution.[19]

Seems perfectly reasonable. Fair. If a guy can't explain a gal's reasons for misrepresenting a situation, that bleeding mouth might compromise *his* credibility.

It might seem obvious, at this point, that decriminalization of prostitution would be an appropriate strategy for feminist legal activists concerned about the physical security of sex workers. However, although the feminists I've read all agree that prostitution should be decriminalized, they disagree about *how* decriminalization should occur. The arguments in this dispute are another example of how legal discourse reproduces and is mired in the interpretations of the female body produced by legal rules.

Should the reform of prostitution law be restricted to the repeal of rules penalizing the sale of sex, or should other legally supported structures that create, sustain, and degrade sex work also be challenged? Feminists in favor of legalization—this is the postmodern position—argue that, unlike a narrowly defined decriminalization campaign, legalization might significantly improve the lives of sex workers. Legalization, for example, might extend unemployment insurance benefits to sex workers; it might allow sex workers to participate in the social security system; it might prohibit pimping; it might authorize advertising for their business.

Feminists who are against legalization—this is the radical position—envision a decriminalization project that would develop strategies for preventing women from participating in sex work, rather than strategies that would make prostitution a more comfortable line of work. Radical feminists, such as Kathleen Barry, are sympathetic to the plight of sex workers.[20] But their conviction that women are defined as women by their sexual subordination to men leads them to argue that sex workers are particularly victimized by patriarchy, that they should be extricated from their condition rather than supported in their work. These arguments against legalization are in the language of the terrorized female body.

Not all legal feminists believe that prostitutes are terrorized full time. Some feminists—I'll call this group the liberals—believe that at least some sex workers, occasionally, exercise sexual autonomy. But these feminists do not favor assimilating sex work into the wage market. They oppose legalization because they object to the kind of sexual autonomy legalization would support.[21] That is, although they support the right of women to do sex work—even at the cost of reinforcing male dominance—they resist the commodification of women's sexuality.

Sex workers themselves—who inspire the postmodern position as I developed it here—want legal support for sex that is severed from its reproduction function, from romance, affection and long-term relationships.[22] Because "legal" sexual autonomy is conventionally extended to women only by rules that locate sexuality in marriage, or by rules that allow women decisional autonomy regarding reproductive issues, arguments in support of law reforms that would legalize sex work conflict with the language of the maternalized female body. The arguments that sex workers are making to assimilate their work into the wage market appeal to a sexualized femininity that is something other than a choice between criminalized and maternalized sex, or a choice between terrorized and maternalized sex. This appeal to a fresh image of the female body is based on a reorganization of the three images of femininity I described earlier; it arises within the play of these three images. Its originality suggests, to me, resistance to the dominant images.

It is significant that sex workers have "found" a different voice of feminine sexuality through the process of political organizing, through efforts to speak out against and to change the conditions of their lives. For me, the promise of postmodern legal feminism lies in the juncture of feminist politics and the genealogy of the female body in law. It is in this juncture that we can simultaneously deploy the commonalities among real women, in their historically situated, material circumstances, and at the same time challenge the conventional meanings of "woman" that sustain the subordinating conditions of women's lives.

I do not think that the sex workers' claims for legalization constitute *the* postmodern feminist legal voice. I am also unsure whether I support their position on legalization. But I believe that my analysis of the decriminalization dispute in which they are participating illustrates how postmodern legal feminism can seek and claim different voices, voices which will challenge the power of the congealed meanings of the female body which legal rules and legal discourse permit and sustain.

The Maternalization of the Female Body: Family and Work

There are a number of legal rules that function to compel or encourage women to bear children and to assume disproportionately larger responsibilities for rearing children than men do. Of these rules, those that regulate biological reproduction or the structure of the family are explicitly engaged in such functions; rules that regulate the wage market or wage market subsidies maternalize the female body more indirectly.

Rules that prohibit, restrict or hinder access to abortion, and rules which prohibit or inhibit the use or distribution of birth control devices prevent women from avoiding unwanted childbirth.[23] These rules have the effect of making some women become mothers against their will. In this way these rules directly conscript the female body in the service of maternity.

Fetal protection rules,[24] decisional law that compels women to undergo unwanted caesareans, and rules that facilitate involuntary sterilization in some circumstances require conduct of pregnant or fertile women which they themselves do not desire or might not otherwise choose. Rules such as these curtail the liberty of some women in order to regulate pregnancy and protect childbirth. In this way, these rules maternalize the female body.

Once women have given birth, legal rules relating to child custody and support disputes compel or encourage women to do more child-rearing than men. Sex-specific rules only recently outlawed by the federal and state equality guarantees used to perform these functions quite directly. Pursuant to the maternal preference rule, for example, women were explicitly presumed to be better parents than men; a man could only wrest custody of his children away from their mother if he could prove she was "unfit." This rule not only allocated disproportionately more childrearing responsibilities to women in formal legal disputes; but it also signaled to men and women making "private" decisions regarding parenting responsibilities that the legal system expected women to do more parenting and to do it better than men.

Two forms of child support provisions from the not-so-distant past also ensured that women were more likely than men to become primary child-caretakers. Under civil and criminal child support rules, states formally imposed support obligations exclusively or primarily on fathers, and, under federal and state welfare benefit rules, widowed or single mothers (but not fathers) were entitled to governmental child support assistance. Both forms of child support provisions "freed" women to abandon or subordinate wage market work in order to care for children.

Although most sex-specific provisions have been formally eliminated from custody and child support rules, the neutralized rule system has not significantly reduced the gender lopsidedness of custody and support decisions; judges still impose or approve child custody and support schemes in which women undertake more physical responsibility for child care than men. Thus, the administration of domestic relations law is implicated in helping or making women "mother" their children. The law continues to signal to women and men making "private" decisions about which parent should do more or less childrearing. Mothers receive more legal support for that work than men.

Moreover, not all sex-specific provisions affecting women's parenting roles have been eliminated from domestic relations law. Procedural and substantive rules relating to the custody and support of children born to unwed parents specifically assume that unwed mothers are (or should be) the primary parents of such children. Similarly, the rules just being developed to resolve disputes over surrogate mother contracts or the custody of children conceived with technical assistance include a presumption that biological mothers have a more significant claim (or responsibility) for custody than biological fathers.

Historically, then, but also presently, child custody and support rules and enforcement practices assign more women than men the daily responsibilities for childrearing, and enforce child support duties in a way that encourages a similar allocation of child care. In this way, family law maternalizes the female body.

Legal rules that regulate the wage market compel or encourage women to bear and to rear children more indirectly than the rules described above. Nevertheless, because wage market rules undervalue the work women do in the wage market, women have much less to lose than men if they abandon, interrupt or modify their wage market work because of childbirth or childrearing. Legal rules that support women's subordinate status in the wage market thus also support (encourage or compel) women to undertake maternal responsibilities.

If employment discrimination rules actually prevented employers from treating women badly in the terms or conditions of their work, the impact of the wage market on the maternalization of the female body would be quite attenuated; it might even be eliminated. To some extent, of course, the advent of employment discrimination rules has improved women's wage work opportunities. However, the gender gap continues to exist in the wage market, partly because of gaps or omissions in the discrimination rules, partly because of the ways in which the rules have been interpreted, and partly because of the limited resources allocated to discrimination law enforcement. Consequently, the legal rules that support the wage market's undervaluation of women and the discrimination rules which don't do enough to curtail that situation support the maternalization of the female body.

Here are several examples of wage market rules that have this effect on women.

1. Although men and women are occupationally segregated into jobs that are disproportionately held by one sex or the other, and although "women's" jobs are less well compensated than "men's," legal rules validate this unequal payment system. It has been widely argued, for example, that a substantial portion of the wage disparities between sex-segregated job categories could be eliminated by requiring employers to pay wages according to the "comparable worth" of jobs. In most cases, courts have refused to hold that employment discrimination law compels employers to adjust wages in this manner.[25]

2. In most cases hazardous workplace rules that exclude pregnant or fertile women have been upheld,[26] *Johnson Controls*[27] to the contrary notwithstanding.

3. Job allocation schemes that channel disproportionately more men than women into lucrative jobs do not violate employment discrimination rules because of the narrow judicial interpretation of discrimination laws.[28]

4. An unemployment compensation scheme that denies benefits to women who leave work because of childbirth has been upheld under narrow judicial interpretation of discrimination laws.[29]

[To be worked in, maternalization and paternalization of wage market jobs (pilot/stewardess; doctor/nurse; boss/secretary; principal/ teacher)]

The Sexualization of the Female Body:
Monogamy, Heterosexuality, Passivity

This subsection describes how legal rules affect the frequency, the character, and the distribution of women's sexual practices. The argument is that by directly or indirectly penalizing conduct which does not conform to a particular set of sexual behaviors, legal rules promote a model of female sexuality; this model is characterized by monogamy, heterosexuality, and passivity. This means that legal rules favor women who marry, who have sex only with their husbands, and who defer to their husbands in determining when, how often and in what manner marital sex takes place. In contrast, legal rules discourage women from being celibate or from having sex outside marriage— with one partner, with multiple partners, or with other women; they also deter women from being more assertive than their husbands want them to be about the management of marital sex.

Although law is only one of the cultural factors that influence women's practices, if the legal rules this section describes were different, female sexuality could be different. It is hard to say whether women would have less sex than they do now, or whether they would have more; it is hard to predict how their choice of sex partners would change or how the character of their sexual experiences might be affected. Nevertheless, because the present regime of legal rules induces women to be "good girls," and imposes sanctions on "deviant" sexual conduct, it seems clear that altering the current regime would undermine the current model of female sexual behavior.

Legal rules influence female sexuality by means of three groups of rules or law enforcement practices. One group of legal rules prohibits or promotes certain forms of sex; the two other groups regulate the physical and economic conditions in which sex takes place. The remainder of this section is devoted to explaining how these rules function as a system to encourage women to conform to a monogamous, heterosexual, and passive model of female sexuality.

Legal rules promote sexual monogamy by defining marriage as a union with one other person and by punishing or indirectly penalizing sex outside of marriage. Criminal rules against bigamy prohibit marriage to more than one person at a time, while sex outside of marriage is made a criminal offense, in many states, by rules against fornication and adultery. Legal rules in most states also designate adultery as a marital "offense" that constitutes grounds for divorce. Sex outside of marriage is further discouraged by rules prohibiting prostitution, and by contract rules that make agreements between unmarried individuals who live together unenforceable to the extent that they are "based on" sex. These rules encourage women and men to be monogamous by formally restricting sex to the one person to whom they are legally married.

Because the rules against adultery and fornication are only loosely enforced, the legal impact on female sexual monogamy might not amount to much if these rules were the only legal factors affecting women's sexual practices. But this is not the case. The legal rules that regulate the economic consequences of marriage, the legal rules that maintain the inferior status of women in the wage market, and the legal rules that provide women inadequate protection against physical abuse all function to reinforce the impact of the sexual monogamy rules on women. These rules create economic and safety incentives for women to marry and to remain sexually faithful in marriage. Moreover, these rules reduce the power that married and unmarried women have in relationship to men; in this way, these rules make women more susceptible to male demands for sexual fidelity than they might be under conditions of economic equality and physical safety.

Legal rules reduce the economic power of women in relationship to men by maintaining inferior employment opportunities for women in the wage market. At the same time, legal rules make marriage a potential source of income for marital partners, by means of spousal support and property provisions that require economically dominant spouses to share what they have with their partners. In addition, alimony rules sometimes permit economically subordinate spouses to continue to receive support even after their marriages have formally ended. Government benefit rules also structure marriage as an economic enterprise, through rules that provide retirement, death, and disability benefits to the spouses of wage earners.

By structuring marriage as a significant source of financial support, legal rules make marriage a plausible substitute—or supplement—to wage market work for both sexes. However, as a result of their inferior position in the wage market—a position legal rules sustain—women are likely to be more financially dependent on marriage than men. This condition affects the responses they might otherwise have to the lax enforcement of the rules against fornication and adultery. Legal rules induce women to marry, and to stay married, for financial reasons. Even though fornication rules are not stringently enforced, wage market and marital economic benefit rules provide women financial incentives to comply with them. Moreover, married women who are economically dependent on their husbands have economic incentives to have sex only with their husbands. Despite the lax enforcement of anti-adultery rules, the wage market and marital benefit rules function to make divorce financially risky for many women; complying with anti-adultery rules enables them to avoid giving their husbands a legal reason for divorce. By inducing some women to marry and to avoid divorce for financial reasons, wage market and marital economic rules reinforce the impact on women of rules that formally restrict sex to marriage.

The legal rules that regulate social violence reduce women's power in relationship to men because they enhance the significance of the cultural convention that a woman is more likely to be verbally or physically attacked if she is alone or in the company of other women than if she is with an individual man. By ineffectively enforcing legal rules governing rape, sexual assault, and other violent crimes against the person, the social violence rule system places women in physical jeopardy. Women can sometimes mitigate the impact of these circumstances by relying on individual men for protection against violence. To the extent that these rule-enforcement practices provide women with a safety incentive to marry and to stay married, the social violence rule system reinforces anti-fornication and anti-adultery rules that penalize nonmonogamous sexual practices.

By reducing the power of women in relationship to men, the wage market rule system and the social violence rule system provide financial and safety incentives for women to defer to their sexual partners in determining the conditions of intimacy. If their partners value sexual monogamy—an ethic, as we have seen, that legal rules help form—then women are likely to comply with their partners' demands for fidelity. Legal rules make women less inclined to resist such demands than they might be in different circumstances. Legal rules also diminish the ability of women to demand fidelity of intimate partners who are unwilling to give up sexual promiscuity.

I have argued thus far that—by inducing women to marry, by discouraging them from having affairs, and by creating economic and physical conditions that help their sexual partners to impose monogamy on them if they want to—legal rules discourage women from having sex with more than one man. The legal model of female sexual monogamy also gives some women incentives to be more sexually active than they would otherwise be. Sex workers and women who want to be celibate are examples of women whom the sexual monogamy rule system induces into sexual activity.

The legal rules that devalue "women's work" in the wage market make prostitution—like marriage—a significant economic alternative or supplement to wage market labor. Moreover, the rules against prostitution, like the rules against fornication and adultery, are not stringently enforced. Legal rules thus provide de facto protection for prostitution; they enable prostitution to function as a safety valve against the constraints of sexual monogamy. Even though anti-prostitution rules are notoriously enforced more systematically against female sex workers than against male customers, legal rules induce some women to violate the criminal rules against prostitution by making sex work more lucrative than legitimate wage labor.

Legal rules also coerce some sex workers into having more sex than they might otherwise want to by inadequately protecting them from customer abuse, which can include unwanted sex. In addition, legal rules do not protect sex workers against the demands pimps may make of them for sexual activity. Since sex workers are induced to affiliate with pimps in order to defend themselves against customers and in order to broker their way through the criminal justice system when they are caught up in it, legal rules and law enforcement practices are complicit in imposing more sex on these women than they might have if their work were not illegal and if it were physically safe.

The sexuality of women who want to practice celibacy may not be affected by the rules prohibiting bigamy, fornication, adultery, and prostitution. However, by creating economic and safety incentives for women to marry, legal rules encourage some women to abandon celibacy in favor of marriage. Since legal rules in most states provide that refusal to have sex within marriage constitutes grounds for divorce, legal rules inhibit women who marry because of economic or safety incentives from practicing celibacy within marriage.

Legal rules also create economic and safety incentives for women to sacrifice celibacy in order to have sex with men to whom they are not married. In addition to encouraging women to turn to men for physical protection, legal rules reduce women's ability to pay their own way; the wage market treatment of women makes it hard for them to go "dutch treat." These physical and financial pressures encourage unmarried women to yield to the sexual demands of escorts or companions they have turned to—at least in part—for protection against abuse from other men.

Although men and women are both subject to the rules that directly penalize or specifically require sexual monogamy, I have argued that the legal rules establishing the economic and physical circumstances in which women and men have sex encourage women to be more sexually monogamous than men. This sex-based difference in the impact of legal rules on monogamous conduct also has an effect on the character of heterosexual relations. To put this point more bluntly, these rules not only encourage a "double standard" of sexual conduct for women and men; they also enable men to have greater control over the terms of heterosexual intimacy—they give men more power over women in sex. This is one of the ways that legal rules encourage passivity as a model of female sexual conduct.

Women are induced to choose men rather than women as sexual partners—to comply with heterosexuality as the model for female sexual conduct—by legal rules that prohibit sodomy and other sexual acts between individuals of the same sex. Although the criminal rules penalizing homosexual conduct—like the sexual monogamy rules— are not vigorously enforced, decisional law defines marriage as a heterosexual union. Women who might expect that sexual relationships with other women could

[to be completed by:
economic and security incentives which make a male partner more advantageous for nonsexual reasons than a same-sex partner for women.

rules and procedures establishing passivity norm, which include the marital rape exemption, economic and security incentives for doing what your guy wants, and the lax enforcement of prostitution laws, which induce economically or physically dependent women to let men have their way sexually in order to avoid losing their protectors to illegal sexual competition.]

The Politics of Postmodern Feminism: Lessons from the Anti-pornography Campaign

A particular phase of the legal anti-pornography campaign is dead in the water. The ordinance which Catharine MacKinnon and Andrea Dworkin initially authored and then vigorously promoted in Minneapolis, Indianapolis, Cambridge, and other cities would have made pornography a form of discrimination against women. It would have permitted women to bring civil actions against those who produce, make, distribute, or sell pornography, which the ordinance generally defined as "the graphic sexually explicit subordination of women, whether in pictures or in words."[30] It would have provided civil remedies for the harm that pornography causes. But the Supreme Court's summary affirmance of the Seventh Circuit's decision holding the ordinance unconstitutional has rendered continued efforts to enact this particular ordinance very problematic. The campaign to enact the MacKinnon/Dworkin ordinance may, however, offer lessons for other feminist political projects.

The ordinance campaign fascinates me. As a political event involving the community of feminist lawyers it was a dazzling success and an appalling disaster. It politicized feminist lawyers, by engaging many of us in the practicalities of a grass-roots legislative reform effort which was widely publicized and electrifyingly controversial. But it also politicized us by brutally and bitterly fracturing our community. Catharine MacKinnon, in particular, put a high price on feminist opposition to her campaign. In a chapter chillingly entitled "On Collaboration," from her book *Feminism Unmodified*, she charged, with an emotional intensity which also characterized other campaign participants, that "women who defend the pornographers are defending a source of their relatively high position among women under male supremacy, keeping all women, including them, an inferior class on the basis of sex, enforced by sexual force."[31]

"I really want you to stop your lies and misrepresentations of our position," she continued, "I want you to stop claiming that your liberalism, with its elitism, and your Freudianism, with its sexualized misogyny, has anything in common with feminism."[32]

For reasons I will soon make clear, I don't particularly regret the anti-pornography ordinance defeat. But like the architects of the ordinance I too believe in using law to oppose the oppression of women. Indeed, the apparent jeopardy of *Roe v. Wade*[33] makes me especially cognizant at this moment that retaining the legalization of abortion may soon become a pressing project requiring astute political skills among feminists forced to seek legislative reform all across the United States. I hope, therefore, that closely examining the ordinance campaign, as a salient incident in the politics of legal feminism, will advance the prospects of an abortion reform effort that the Supreme Court might thrust upon us, as well as the prospects of other future feminist legal projects.

I want to make two points about the campaign. First, I intend to challenge the somewhat familiar criticisms of the campaign by suggesting that some of the campaign's weaknesses can also be understood as political strengths, strengths which might be adapted and deployed in other efforts. That is, my claim will be that the conventional failures of the campaign also constituted the campaign's successes.

Second, I will outline what I think is a new critique of the ordinance campaign. Shamelessly relying on the advantages of hindsight, I will argue that the ordinance proponents were fatally reluctant to apply the theory underlying the campaign to their own efforts.

Having brilliantly identified the subordination of women by sex as a lynchpin of women's oppression, the ordinance proponents relentlessly perpetuated the dichotomy of gender in the style of their rhetoric, in the content of their arguments, and in the absolutism of the ordinance's structure, which would have rigidly divided pornographic material into two opposing categories—actionable or unactionable. My claim will be that the greatest strength of the anti-pornography ordinance campaign was also its greatest weakness. Having identified pornography as a cultural practice importantly implicated in the problem of women's condition, the ordinance advocates sought unsuccessfully to use law reform to destroy pornography. I now seek to turn this failure to some profit, by using an analysis of their campaign as an opportunity to deconstruct pornography. The interesting and perhaps troubling question that underlies my own position, however, is what effect this deconstruction would have had on the ordinance campaign.

A word of caution before I proceed. Each of us is likely to have a relatively concrete, relatively firm understanding of what we consider pornography, but we probably disagree about the components of a common conception. When I was twelve, pornography meant a few pages in my parents' copy of *From Here to Eternity*[34] and a few words, like "coitis," and "fornicate," thrillingly available in my own dictionary. My personal definition now is more far ranging, but I do not know how widely shared it is.

Two Meese Commission guys recently published a survey in the *Michigan Journal of Law Reform* which comically purports to describe the character of "adults only" pornography currently sold in the United States.[35] The survey classifies the cover photos of books, magazines, and films sold in "adults only" bookstores, in four cities. Because the investigation is limited to "adults only" stores, the survey does not include material which I consider part of the pornographic genre. Examples of omitted material I would include are: formula romances; science fiction and comics which feature sexually explicit material; lesbian and gay erotica which is too pretentious for "adults only" bookstores; the dark, serious literature of sex and violence characterized by books like *The Story of O*[36] and Georges Bataille's *Story of the Eye*;[37] and portions of material found in many women's glossy magazines. I am not going to try to solve the problem of confusion which the term "pornography" generates in listeners by contriving a general, abstract definition which many of you would probably dislike. I simply want to assert that what constitutes pornography is usually a charged and unexplored question in any discussion involving pornography.

Conventional Failures Reinterpreted:
The Strengths of the Ordinance Campaign

A familiar criticism of the ordinance campaign is the charge that it produced an alliance between ordinance advocates and non-feminist conservatives. Many feminists during the campaign voiced concern that conservative support for the ordinance indicated their intention to turn the ordinance against material that is offensive only because it describes or depicts "untraditional" sexuality. Because conservatives have considered the use of birth control devices and sexual activities such as cunnilingus "untraditional sexual practices," ordinance opponents feared that the ordinance campaign might lead to repressing sexual freedom rather than to preventing sexual oppression.

The conservative alliance might not have occurred had the ordinance advocates been clearer, narrower, and more consistent in their explanation of what constituted pornography. The advocates repeatedly attempted to reassure wary feminists that the ordinance did not need to function to impose an orthodox, traditional form of sexuality on anyone. However, the general definition of pornography as "the graphic sexually explicit subordination of women, whether in pictures or in words"[38] was broad enough to encourage the Vanilla-Sex Gestapo that they could get with the ordinance program.

I claim the conservative alliance was a virtue of the ordinance campaign because of its role in extending the ordinance debate beyond predictable feminist constituencies. In contrast to the typically narrow circle, for example, which has exhibited interest in radical legislative reforms related to the anti-family structure of the labor market, the ordinance campaign boldly and successfully engaged non-feminist political camps. Conservative support for the ordinance undoubtedly posed troublesome management issues for the feminists supporting the ordinance. However, a broad theater of political involvement was obviously vital to the ordinance campaign, and similarly broad coalitions will also be important to the success of other feminist law reform projects.

I acknowledge that extending feminist issues beyond familiar constituencies occurred in the ordinance campaign at the cost of feminist unity. My claim is that breaching this unity is a necessary component of feminist efforts against women's oppressions.

The broad definition of pornography adopted by the ordinance advocates radically challenged a fundamental premise of post-Freudian, Lacanian theories of self, the premise that domination and subordination are an inevitable aspect of interpersonal relations. Ordinance advocates assume that by eliminating *depictions* of sexual domination, *sexual domination* could be dealt a fatal blow. In contrast, ordinance opponents believed that domination and subordination constitute a psychological structure that does not depend on the pornography industry and that *need not* depend on gender division for its existence.

This dispute involves a profound question about the nature of the self. It is not surprising that people disagree about this issue; it is not surprising that women—indeed, that feminists—disagree about this issue. Although powerful, broad, and coherent political community is critical to feminist law reform projects, I believe it is a mistake to fear or avoid or condemn differences among feminists as we pursue these projects. Accepting and exploring our differences, in my view, is a critical component of challenging the ideology of gender difference, which includes the assumption that there is a feminine essence which unalterably unites women, binding us together under the generic category "woman."

A second criticism which has been leveled against the ordinance campaign is that it distracted feminists from other work more important to the women's movement. Ordinance advocates argued that pornography triggers massive physical violence against women; they claimed that by sexualizing domination and subordination, pornography functions to consign all women to unequal social and economic status on account of their sex; and they asserted that as an eight billion dollar industry, pornography economically exploits the women who participate in its production and drains substantial resources away from other, more significant purposes. In making their criticism that the ordinance campaign was a fruitless diversion, ordinance opponents disputed all these claims.

Opponents claimed that the data causally linking pornography to violence against women was insubstantial, unconvincing, and predicated on a simplistic and unpersuasive theory of causation. They disputed the claim that regulating pornography could have much effect on the subordination of women, arguing, as I have suggested above, that this subordination is not rooted in pornography. Indeed, some feminists claimed that pornography usefully functions in certain cases to channel and subdue troubling fantasies. The opponents were skeptical that bringing down the pornography industry would make eight billion dollars available for women's causes, and they were critical of the costs of pursuing the ordinance campaign.

In contrast to the ordinance opponents, but for different reasons, I believe that concentrating so much effort, energy, expertise, and even money on the anti-pornography issue simplified and thereby facilitated feminist political organizing, much the same way single-issue campaigning often constitutes an organizational advantage in electoral politics. Political success is predictably correlated with coordinating and consolidating efforts.

I also believe the theoretical claim that the subordination of women is rooted in sex is a message that will significantly benefit the feminist movement. This claim radically challenges the traditional focus of feminist concerns. It legitimates pornography as an appropriate field for struggle, analysis, and interpretation. It challenges the traditional feminist agenda of appropriate strategies for contesting the oppression of women. Whatever skirmishes or battles we may have lost because of the anti-pornography diversion will be worth the challenge to conventional attitudes which the theoretical innovations of the movement facilitated. I attribute the exposure and discussion that occurred about this theory to the choice of pornography as the theory's practical target. This suggests to me an important political lesson for feminists. Issue choice affects our political potential, and legislative reform efforts produce political capital beyond the passage or defeat of legislation.

The last criticism of the ordinance campaign I will mention may be less familiar, but I will raise it because of how disappointed I was when the ordinance campaign came to my town in the form of model or boiler plate legislation. By preventing feminists outside the circle of those who originally worked with MacKinnon and Dworkin from having a voice in the structure and scope of their local ordinances, the architects of the ordinance lost the organizing potential and the consciousness-raising benefits that would have inured from wider drafting participation. Moreover, broader drafting consultation, or experimenting in different cities with different ordinances, might have revealed that some of the model legislation provisions were miscalculations, mistakes that could have been corrected as the campaign moved from town to town.

Despite the criticism that using model legislation warrants, I realize that model legislation facilitates publicity and supports scholarship and efficient legal defense work, all of which strengthen local campaigns to enact feminist reform projects. Moreover, the ordinance campaign overall was remarkable for its broadly participatory character. The campaign heavily relied on indigenous, newly formed groups of concerned individuals in each of the targeted towns, and the ordinance utilized the strategy of allowing the victims of pornography to institute claims on their own behalf against pornographers. By eschewing city or state attorneys, the ordinance functioned to empower women. This strategy too could be adaptable and important in other feminist projects.

Destroying Pornography or Deconstructing It

I now turn to my claim that the ordinance campaign's greatest strength was also its greatest weakness, my claim that the advocates should have sought to deconstruct pornography rather than single-mindedly seeking to destroy it.

The ordinance campaign's most significant contribution to feminism was its pursuit of Catharine MacKinnon's theoretical insight that the oppression of women occurs through sexual subordination. The anti-pornography campaign allowed MacKinnon and others to dramatize what this theory means in practice, through its focus on a complex cultural phenomenon which is exclusively devoted to sex, a cultural practice consumed with depictions of what "the oppression of women through sexual subordination" means. In pornography, women get fucked.

Now, women get "fucked" in the workplace, too, where we do "women's work" for "women's wages," working for male bosses and working on male schedules. We get assigned to this inferior work track because we are identifiable by our sex. In addition, our past and present economic, social, and physical subordination makes us vulnerable to physical abuse at work, on the way there, and on the way back. We are raped at work or on route to work because of our sex, because we are cunts.

But the moment I say women get "fucked" in the workplace, the clarity of the relationship between women's oppression and sex is jeopardized. "Women's work" is a complicated construction; its origin and perpetuation depend on many factors in addition to misogyny. Pornography is a much cleaner site for demonstrating the practice of the theoretical insight; pornography is about women getting fucked.

I hasten to acknowledge here that pornography is also about violence against women, and that ordinance advocates sought to attack pornography in order to prevent women who participate in its production from being harmed and in order to prevent other women from being harmed by the imitative reactions of pornography users. But the ordinance campaign was not restricted to preventing these two forms of harm.

Ordinance advocates also attacked pornography in order to oppose the sexualization of hierarchy and the objectification of women. They understood the ordinance as more than a good example of the truth of feminist theory in practice. They believed that destroying pornography would lead to the end of women's oppression on account of sex. They believed that destroying this particular depiction of women's oppression would change the experience of women's oppression in its many manifestations. I believe this was a fatal miscalculation.

If women's oppression occurs through sex, then in order to end women's oppression in its many manifestations, the way people think and talk and act about sex must be changed. The ordinance campaign was not well organized to change how people think and talk and act about sex. Rather, the ordinance advocates relentlessly utilized and exploited traditional ideas and language regarding sex in all aspects of the campaign.

Let me give just a few examples.

First, the language and rhetorical style of campaign advocacy were characterized by stereotypically masculine attributes. The language and style were militant, authoritative, and riddled with the easy obscenities typical of male talk. (I've done a little male talk myself in this section.) This style was impressively successful—the advocates were powerful campaigners; but the use of additional, less masculine rhetorical styles, which can also be persuasive and moving, would have made the ordinance campaign less gendered.

The campaign also seemed gendered because the arguments of campaign advocates were typically structured by hierarchical dichotomies. Thus, advocates reduced arguments against the ordinance to dismissive epithets: they were "anti-feminist" or "individualistic." Similarly, advocates oversimplified the character of pornography, suggestively referring only to rip and slash material in their discussions rather than acknowledging the complex character of the pornographic genre. Like the style of their rhetoric, the content of their arguments was stirring; it was arousing. But like the ideology of gender, which rigidly divides the world into two sexes, the campaign argument was premised on an assumption that its listeners were divisible into only two camps—those who were pro-woman, and, therefore, pro-ordinance, or those who weren't.

I believe a less dichotomized approach to the problem of the oppression of women by sex would have been more likely to change the way we think and act about sex. By falsely simplifying the content of the pornography genre, the advocates overlooked the way in which some workers within the genre already thematically challenge the subordination of women by sex. Not all pornography is simply about women being fucked. There are some pornographic works in which women fuck, for example; some works in which the objectification of the orgasming penis is not repeatedly depicted and valorized; and many works in which the subjectivity of a female character is a dominant and successful thematic concern. These works do not depict what the ordinance advocates suggested pornography "is."

The ordinance advocates falsely simplified user responses to pornography, assuming in most of their arguments that pornography users mechanistically identify with same-sex characters and mechanistically seek to reproduce pornography scenes in their own lives. This singular reaction does not characterize reader responses to non-pornographic literature or viewer responses to non-pornographic films. Although many individuals may use pornography for sex instruction, it also seems likely that others use pornography as an implement of fantasy, seeking through their reading or viewing to escape lives characterized by chastity, by routinized sex, or by genderized sex. They may also use pornography to transform their lives by a more complicated reaction than simple imitation.

Users would not be interested in or sexually aroused by many forms of pornography if they reacted only by identifying with same-sex characters. Works like sexually explicit formula romances, for example, in which a woman is the principal sexual subject, would most likely be sexually arousing to a male user only if he identified with the female heroine, thereby relinquishing his sex-stereotyped desires to fuck and fantasizing himself instead as fuckee. Similarly, the appeal of lesbian and gay pornography seems to depend on more than mechanistic same-sex identification, in that users must select differences other than biological sex to identify with particular characters.

I hope I am not misunderstood here. I do not want to be understood as a pornography apologist, for I believe that the proliferation and character of the pornography genre is one of the most complicated cultural events of our time, an event whose meanings are still quite indeterminate.

I also do not want to be understood as anti-feminist. The polarization of the feminist legal community during the ordinance campaign was terrifying to me; I understand the instinct to condemn the opposition that caused such division among friends and colleagues. However, I believe the divisions the campaign produced among feminists constituted an important challenge to the polarization of the world by gender. The closing lesson I want to draw from the anti-pornography campaign about feminist organization is the observation that exploring, pursuing, and accepting differences among women and differences among sexual practices is necessary to challenge the oppression of women by sex. Only when sex means more than male or female, only when the word "woman" cannot be coherently understood, will oppression by sex be fatally undermined.

Notes

1
Sexual Equality and Sexual Difference in American Law

1. See, e.g., Grace Blumberg, De Facto and De Jure Discrimination Under the Equal Protection Clause: A Reconsideration of the Veterans' Preference in Public Employment, 28 Buffalo L. Rev. 1 (1977); Nancy S. Erickson, Kahn, Ballard, and Wiesenfeld: A New Equal Protection Test in "Reverse" Discrimination Sex Discrimination Cases? 42 Brook. L. Rev. 1 (1975); Ruth Ginsberg, Some Thoughts on Benign Classifications in the Context of Sex, 10 Conn. L. Rev. 813 (1978); Note, Challenges to Sex-based Mortality Tables in Insurance and Pensions, 6 Women's Rts. L. Rep. 59 (1979–80); Note, Women and the Draft: the Constitutionality of All-male Registration, 94 Harv. L. Rev. 406 (1980).

2. Joseph Tussman and Jacobus tenBroek, The Equal Protection of the Laws, 37 Cal. L. Rev. 341 (1949).

3. Thus, for example, the influential feminist interpretation of the proposed Equal Rights Amendment to the Federal Constitution proposed a "unique physical characteristic" exception to its otherwise absolute prohibition of sex-based classifications. See Barbara A. Brown, et al., The Equal Rights Amendment: A Constitutional Basis for Equal Rights for Women, 80 Yale L. J. 871, 893 (1971).

4. Frontiero v. Richardson, 411 U.S. 677 (1973) (plurality opinion stating that sex-based classifications should require strict scrutiny).

5. See, e.g., Personnel Adm'r of Massachusetts v. Feeney, 442 U.S. 256 (1979) (refusal to extend impact analysis to sex-based classifications); and General Elec. Co. v. Gilbert, 429 U.S. 125 (1976) (refusal to find that pregnancy constituted a disability under the sex discrimination prohibition of the Equal Employment Opportunity Act).

6. See, e.g., Nancy S. Erickson, Pregnancy Discrimination: An Analytical Approach, 5 Women's Rts. L. Rep. 83 (1979).

7. Roe v. Wade, 410 U.S. 113 (1973).

8. Harris v. McRae, 448 U.S. 297 (1980).

9. See, e.g., Lucinda M. Finley, Transcending Equality Theory: A Way Out of the Maternity and the Workplace Debate, 86 Colum. L. Rev. 1118 (1986); Ann E. Freedman, Sex Equality, Sex Differences, and the Supreme Court, 92 Yale L. J. 913 (1983); Sylvia A. Law, Rethinking Sex and the Constitution, 132 U. Pa. L. Rev. 955 (1984); Nadine Taub, From Parental Leaves to Nurturing Leaves, 13 N.Y.U. Rev. L. & Soc. Change 381 (1984–85).

10. Wendy W. Williams, Equality's Riddle: Pregnancy and the Equal Treatment/Special Treatment Debate, 13 N.Y.U. Rev. L. & Soc. Change 325 (1984–85).

11. Mary Joe Frug, Securing Job Equality for Women: Labor Market Hostility to Working Mothers, 59 B.U. L. Rev. 55 (1979).

12. Christine A. Littleton, Reconstructing Sexual Equality, 75 Cal. L. Rev. 1279 (1987).

13. Catharine A. MacKinnon, Feminism Unmodified: Discourses on Life and Law 32–45 (1987); Ann C. Scales, The Emergence of Feminist Jurisprudence: An Essay, 95 Yale L. J. 1372 (1986).

14. California Federal Savings & Loan v. Guerra, 479 U.S. 272 (1987).

15. See, e.g., Williams, supra note 10.

16. See, e.g., Linda J. Krieger and Patricia N. Cooney, The Miller-Wohl Controversy: Equal Treatment, Positive Action, and the Meaning of Women's Equality, 13 Golden Gate U. L. Rev. 513 (1983).

17. Although the Supreme Court held in Cal. Fed. that California did not discriminate by requiring employers to extend pregnancy benefits to employees, in another decision during the same term the Court held that refusing unemployment compensation to a woman who is not working because of her pregnancy does not constitute discrimination. See Wimberly v. Labor & Indus. Relations Comm'n, 479 U.S. 511 (1987).

18. See, e.g., Finley, supra note 9; Law, supra note 9.

19. See Catharine MacKinnon, supra note 13.

20. Catharine A. MacKinnon, Toward a Feminist Theory of the State 219 (1989).

21. See, e.g., Martha Minow, The Supreme Court, 1986–Forward: Justice Engendered, 101 Harv. L. Rev. 10 (1987); see also Scales, supra note 13.

22. A representative selection of essays that have influenced my thinking about the construction of gender include: Luce Irigaray, Psychoanalytic Theory: Another Look, and When Our Lips Speak Together, in This Sex Which Is Not One (Catherine Porter trans. 1985); Jane Gallop, Lip Service, in Thinking Through the Body (1988); Donna C. Stanton, Difference on Trial: A Critique of the Maternal Metaphor in Cixous, Irigaray,

and Kristeva, in The Poetics of Gender (Nancy K. Miller ed. 1986); and Linda Alcoff, Cultural Feminism Versus Post-Structuralism: the Identity Crisis in Feminist Theory, 13 Signs 405 (1988).

23. See Teresa de Lauretis, The Essence of the Triangle or, Taking the Risk of Essentialism Seriously: Feminist Theory in Italy, the U.S., and Britain, 1 Differences 3 (1989).

24. Cultural feminism has promoted an important degree of self-pride and some degree of political power for women by celebrating feminine commonalities. I want to raise, however, a strong word of concern regarding the eager embrace this approach to sexual difference has received. Cultural feminism has many sources of support and inspiration, but in my judgment Carol Gilligan's book, In a Different Voice (1982), has had a large role in cultural feminism's current popularity. To be quite clear, I believe the vulgarization of Gilligan's book has been a catastrophe for feminists. Ripped from the context of a debate among moral developmentalists, In a Different Voice seems to have lost its edge as a disruption of previous research methods or a challenge to existing normative hierarchies. Read and cited as an exaltation of relationships, of the relational self, of the self *in* relationship, a conservative interpretation of this book has not only validated humanistic skills and values often linked with women but it has also promoted, as if she were a new invention, a model of female subject which has been the traditional excuse for the oppression women have suffered. Thus, although I urge here that both negative feminism and cultural feminism be transformed by a nondualistic, antiessentialist approach to sexual difference, I believe that cultural feminism has more dangerous implications for the cause of women than negative feminism. See chapter 3.

25. Catharine MacKinnon's work, for example, has tended to emphasize the politics of gender at the expense of epistemology, so that despite its significant influence it has come under increasing attack for its implicitly essentialist image of women. See, e.g., Marlee Klein, Race, Racism and Feminist Legal Theory, 12 Harv. Women's L. J. 115 (1989). But see Frances Olsen, Feminist Theory in Grand Style, 89 Colum. L. Rev. 1147 (1989) (book review).

26. Examples of feminist doctrine include, e.g., Elizabeth M. Schneider, Equal Rights to Trial for Women: Sex Bias in the Law of Self-Defense, 15 Harv. C.R.-C.L. L. Rev. 623 (1980); Frances Olsen, Statutory Rape: A Feminist Critique of Rights Analysis, 63 Tex. L. Rev. 387 (1984); Clare Dalton, An Essay in the Deconstruction of Contract, 94 Yale L. J. 997 (1985); Patricia J. Williams, Alchemical Notes: Reconstructing Ideals from Deconstructed Rights, 22 Harv. C.R.-C.L. L. Rev. 401 (1987); Marie Ashe, Law-Language of Maternity: Discourse Holding Nature in Contempt, 22 New Eng. L. Rev. 521 (1988); Kimberlé Crenshaw, Demarginalizing the Intersection of Race and Gender, 1989 U. of Chi. Legal F. 139.

2
Feminist Doctrine

1. EEOC v. Sears, Roebuck & Co., 628 F. Supp. 1264, 1288 (N.D. Ill. 1986), aff'd, 839 F.2d 302 (7th Cir. 1988).
2. 628 F. Supp. at 1276.
3. EEOC v. Sears, Roebuck & Co., 839 F.2d 302 (7th Cir. 1988).
4. 628 F. Supp. at 1294–1301.
5. Id. at 1279–85.
6. Id. at 1289–90.
7. Id. at 1290.
8. Id. at 1305–15.
9. Id. at 1308 and nn. 42, 43, 1314–15.
10. Id. at 1314 and nn. 60–63.
11. Id. at 1314–15.
12. Dr. Rosalind Rosenberg is an historian from Barnard College and author of Beyond Separate Spheres: Intellectual Roots of Modern Feminism (1982).
13. Offer of Proof Concerning the Testimony of Dr. Rosalind Rosenberg, EEOC v. Sears, Roebuck & Co., 628 F. Supp. 1264 (N.D. Ill. 1986), aff'd, 839 F.2d 302 (7th Cir. 1988), reprinted in 11 Signs 757, 758, 765–66 (1986).
14. Id. at 762–64.
15. Id. at 766.
16. Id. at 763.
17. Alice Kessler-Harris is an historian from Hofstra University and author of Out to Work: A History of Wage-Earning Women in the U.S. (1982).
18. Written Testimony of Alice Kessler-Harris, reprinted in 11 Signs 767 (1986).
19. Id. at 768.
20. Id. at 768–72.
21. Id. at 771.
22. See supra text accompanying note 7.
23. Jean Baker Miller writes about women:

    > People who are most attuned to psychological growth are those most closely in touch with it, those who are literally forced to keep changing if they are to continue to respond to the altering demands of those under their care. . . . [I]n a very immediate and day-to-day way women *live* change. It is amazing, in view of this, that women have been portrayed as the traditionalists, the sex that upholds the past while men march on to "progress." Here is perhaps one of the major places we have fallen into a terrible twisting of reality, for

if anything women are *closer* to change, real change. They have always been closest to direct involvement in the most important growth of all. (Jean Baker Miller, Toward a New Psychology of Women 54 [1976].)

24. In her concluding observations regarding the difference between men's and women's historical expectations and experiences in the labor force, Rosenberg stated, "It is naive to believe that the natural effect of these differences is evidence of discrimination by Sears." Offer of Proof Concerning the Testimony of Dr. Rosalind Rosenberg, 11 Signs 757, 766 (1986).

25. In her concluding observations regarding women's historical participation in the paid labor force, Kessler-Harris stated, "Failure to find women in so-called nontraditional jobs can thus only be interpreted as a consequence of employers' unexamined attitudes or preferences, which phenomenon is the essence of discrimination." Written Testimony of Alice Kessler-Harris, 11 Signs 767, 779 (1986).

26. See Jennifer Wicke, Postmodern Identity and the Legal Subject, 62 U. Colo. L. Rev. 455 (1991).

27. Wisconsin v. Peterson (Winnebago County Cir. Ct. Wis. Jan. 17 1991) (No. 90-Cf-280); Wicke, supra note 26 at 460.

28. Id. at 467.

29. See, e.g., In re Estate of Cooper, 564 N.Y.S.2d 684 (N.Y. Sup. Ct. 1990); Anonymous v. Anonymous, 67 Misc. 2d 982, 325 N.Y.S.2d 499 (N.Y. Sup. Ct. 1971); Frances B. v. Mark B., 78 Misc. 2d 112, 355 N.Y.S.2d 712 (N.Y. Sup. Ct. 1974).

30. Mashpee Tribe v. Town of Mashpee, 447 F. Supp. 940 (D. Mass. 1978); aff'd sub. nom. Mashpee Tribe v. New Seabury Corp., 592 F.2d 575 (1st Cir. 1979), cert. denied, 444 U.S. 866 (1979). See Wicke, supra note 26, at 465.

31. Id. at 455.

32. Id. at 471, 456, 462.

33. Id. at 471.

34. Id. at 457.

35. Id. at 472.

36. Id. at 473.

37. Id. at 455.

38. Id.

39. Id.

40. Id.

41. Id. at 471.

42. Id. at 464.

43. Id. at 457.

44. Frances Olsen, Statutory Rape: A Feminist Critique of Rights Analysis, 63 Tex. L. Rev. 387 (1984) (Having criticized the treatment of statutory rape pursuant to a rights analysis, this piece proposes a series of solutions that I characterize as postmodern.)

45. Wicke, supra note 26, at 456.

46. James White, Women in the Law, 65 Mich. L. Rev. 1051 (1967).

47. The survey indicates that women lawyers had greater long-term government employment than the men and worked in fewer medium-sized firms (id. at 1057–60).

48. More women specialized in trusts and estates, domestic relations, and tax and fewer women described their work as a "general practice" (id. at 1062–64).

49. The article reports that fewer women were married. Although the questionnaire Professor White circulated asked both men and women whether they had children (id. at 1117), the survey only provides data regarding the parental status of the women who returned questionnaires (id. at 1065–66).

50. Id. at 1085–87. Professor White does speculate, in a single sentence, about structural changes the profession might undertake to make legal "positions . . . [more] compatible with a mother's other responsibilities" (id. at 1092), but his other recommendations all relate to eliminating any discrimination against women which "cannot be shown to be functional" (id. at 1098).

51. Thus, he recommends litigation under the Civil Rights Acts, further research to confirm the abilities of women lawyers, and leadership by example in law schools where, in 1967, women were still radically underrepresented (id. at 1113–14).

52. There are several ways in which Professor White indicates his openness to whatever results the survey might yield. For example, he states at the outset of the article that his purpose is "to *report* data about what women do and what opportunities are open for them" (id. at 1052, emphasis added). When his findings do not confirm his own preconceived ideas or conventional views about what women lawyers are like, he discloses such findings but also confesses his surprise at what he has learned. Thus, for example, he writes, the data "do not support the *common* expectation that there is a vast difference between male and female performance on this point. Rather, the *striking* thing . . . is that both men and women changed jobs quite frequently" (id. at 1090, emphasis added). He is exacting and skeptical in his reporting of existing studies which claim there are psychological differences between the sexes, and yet he calls for more research on the question of whether such differences do in fact exist (id. at 1099).

53. Id. at 1118.

54. Id.

55. "P.S. You are part of a *male* control group. Because we are attempting to elicit the same data from our male control group as we get from the females, the questionnaire will seem more appropriate for a female" (id. at 1116).

56. Id. at 1115 (emphasis added).

57. Id. at 1116.

58. Id. at 1087–98. In order to cap the amount of economic gain considered functional, White introduces the concept of "primary" and "secondary" levels of discrimination, arguing that the lesser gains from secondary discrimination should not permit employers to discriminate against women lawyers (id. at 1095–98).

59. The questionnaire also assumes that parenting responsibilities must be shouldered by individual parents. There is no indication in the Michigan survey that the institutions of the legal profession should undertake any responsibility for child care issues.

60. White, supra note 46, at 1052.

61. In 1967, for example, this image may have encouraged employers to prefer male applicants to female applicants, if all other factors in their applications were the same. Professor White contemplates, with no apparent concern, just this practice (id. at 1096). Even today the image of women as primary childrearers may discourage female lawyers from having children or from seeking legal careers which are presently considered hard to combine with family responsibilities.

62. Elizabeth Nehls, Women in Law School, 33 Law School Record 14 (Spring 1987).

63. "The principal impediment to women's achievement," she writes, "lies . . . in the attitudes, values, and priorities that women . . . hold" (id.).

64. For example, in her discussion of women's selflessness Ms. Nehls writes, "Men, by contrast, are typically raised to accept an ethic of self-assertion, limited only by a negative duty of noninterference" (id. at 15). In her discussion of the passive behavior which parents encourage in girls, Ms. Nehls states "Boys, however, are actively discouraged from the dependent forms of relating, which are considered 'sissyish' in male children" (id. at 16). In explaining why women are insecure, or expect to fail, she writes "Parents tend to feel and express more anxiety, more apprehension of hurt, over a girl's activities than over a boy's" (id. at 17).

65. Id. at 18.

66. Since the Alumna letter was written twenty years after the Michigan survey, at a time when, as Ms. Nehls asserts, "institutional barriers to women's advancement have been almost entirely dismantled," one should not assume that Professor White would have approached the particular situation Ms. Nehls is addressing differently than she did. He

is more ambiguous (or flexible) about sex differences, as I have stated, but he was also writing in a different context than Ms. Nehls.

67. I believe that the sex-specific attitude which Ms. Nehls adopts in her letter poses a significant epistemological issue for scholars. Therefore I do not think Ms. Nehls could have avoided the criticism I have just made had she only been more careful to qualify her generalizations or tone down the oppositions.

3
Progressive Feminist Legal Scholarship

1. Mississippi University of Women v. Hogan, 458 U.S. 718 (1982). (*Hogan* was decided during O'Connor's first term on the Supreme Court.)

2. In using the phrase "formal equality" I mean only to refer to the extent of equal protection extended to gender classifications under current Constitutional law. The Court not only declined to adopt a gender-blind interpretation of the equality guarantee in *Hogan*, but it also refused to regard sex as a suspect classification. Nevertheless, the Court did state that gender classifications are subject to "exceedingly persuasive justification" (id. at 724), and it refused to dilute this standard of review either because the challenged law discriminated against males, rather than females, or because the purpose of the statute was to compensate women for past discrimination (id. at 723, 728–30).

3. See Comment, Gender Discrimination in Education, 96 Harv. L. Rev. 110, 116 (1982). The finality of *Hogan's* statement regarding the scope of the federal equality guarantee is emphasized by the fact that the year of its decision also marked the expiration of the deadline for the ratification of the federal Equal Rights Amendment.

4. See, e.g., Catharine A. MacKinnon, Feminism Unmodified 32–45 (1987).

5. *Hogan*, 458 U.S. 718, 739 n.5 (Powell, J. dissenting). Feminists admittedly have conflicting views regarding sex-segregated education, but the feminist critique of formal equality cannot be ascribed to the debate surrounding that particular issue.

6. See, e.g., Nancy E. Dowd, Work and Family: The Gender Paradox and the Limitations of Discrimination Analysis in Restructuring the Workplace, 24 Harv. C.R.—C.L. L. Rev. 79 (1989); Lucinda M. Finley, Transcending Equality Theory: A Way Out of the Maternity and the Workplace Debate, 86 Colum. L. Rev. 118 (1986); Mary Joe Frug, Securing Job Equality for Women: Labor Market Hostility to Working Mothers, 59 B.U. L. Rev. 55 (1979). For other critiques of formal equality, see, e.g., Christine A. Littleton, Reconstructing Sexual Equality, 75 Cal. L. Rev. 1279 (1987); Martha Minow, The Supreme Court, 1986 Term—Forward: Justice Engendered, 101 Harv. L. Rev. 10 (1987); and Ann C. Scales, The

Emergence of Feminist Jurisprudence: An Essay, 95 Yale L. J. 1373 (1986).

7. See Roberts v. United States Jaycees, 468 U.S. 609, 625 (1984) (rejecting an attempt by a private association to defend sex-based classifications on First Amendment grounds). See also Board of Directors of Rotary Int'l v. Rotary Club of Duarte, 481 U.S. 537 (1987); and New York State Club Ass'n v. City of New York, 487 U.S. 1 (1988).

8. *Hogan*, 458 U.S. at 724.

9. "That this statutory policy discriminates against males ... does not exempt it from scrutiny or reduce the standard of review" (id. at 723).

10. There is some confusion within *Hogan* about the scope of the decision. Because Hogan sought admission only to the nursing school, both O'Connor (458 U.S. at 723 n.7) and Justice Powell in dissent (id. at 745 n.18) claim that the Court's opinion does not address whether MUW schools other than the nursing school may not be restricted to women. As Justice Powell points out, however, "the logic of the Court's entire opinion ... appears to apply sweepingly to the entire University" (id. at 745 n.18). The Court's rejection of Mississippi's claim that the woman-only admissions' policy is compensatory appears to have been partly predicated on the suspicion that racism underlay the founding of MUW, as a single-sex institution. Justice O'Connor explains: "Apparently, the impetus for founding MUW came not from a desire to provide women with advantages superior to those offered men, but rather from a desire to provide white women in Mississippi access to state-supported higher learning" (id. at 727 n.13). (At the time MUW supporters initially sought to charter the university, the University of Mississippi did not admit women.)

11. Id. at 729.

12. Id. at 725–26.

13. See Personnel Administrator of Mass. v. Fenney, 442 U.S. 256 (1979); Roe v. Wade, 410 U.S. 113 (1973).

14. See text accompanying note 6, *supra*.

15. See Lenore J. Weitzman, The Divorce Revolution: The Unexpected Social and Economic Consequences for Women and Children in America (1985); Martha L. Fineman, Implementing Equality: Ideology, Contradiction and Social Change, 1983 Wis. L. Rev. 789.

16. See, e.g., Catharine A. MacKinnon, Feminism, Marxism, Method, and the State: Toward Feminist Jurisprudence, 8 Signs 635 (1983); Ann C. Scales, supra note 6; Lucinda M. Finley, supra note 6; Ann E. Freedman, Sex Equality, Sex Differences and the Supreme Court, 92 Yale L. J. 913 (1983); Sylvia A. Law, Rethinking Sex and the Constitution, 132 U. Pa. L. Rev. 955 (1984); Nadine Taub and Elizabeth M. Schneider, Women's Subordination and the Role of Law, in The Politics of Law: A Progressive Critique (David Kairys ed. 1982); Robin West, Jurisprudence and Gender, 55 U. Chi. L. Rev. 1 (1988); Mary Joe Frug, supra note 6; Frances

Olsen, Statutory Rape: A Feminist Critique of Rights Analysis, 63 Tex. L. Rev. 387 (1984).

17. This qualification has been an articulated aspect of the equality standard since Joseph Tussman and Jacobus tenBroek published their influential article, The Equal Protection of the Laws, 37 Cal. L. Rev. 341, 344 (1949).

18. See, e.g., General Electric v. Gilbert, 429 U.S. 125 (1976); Geduldig v. Aiello, 417 U.S. 484 (1974).

19. UAW v. Johnson Controls, 111 S. Ct. 1196 (1991).

20. Bureau of National Affairs, Pregnancy and Employment 57 (1987), noted in UAW v. Johnson Controls, 886 F.2d 871, 915 n.7 (1989) (Easterbrook, J., dissenting).

21. Frances Olsen, supra, note 16.

22. Martha Minow, Learning to Live With the Dilemma of Difference: Bilingual and Special Education, 48 Law & Contemp. Probs. 157 (1985).

23. See, e.g., Felice N. Schwartz, Management Women and the New Facts of Life, 1989 Harv. Bus. Rev. 65 (arguing that because the majority of women, unlike men, are "career-and-family" oriented, companies should create special roles for them in middle management, an area the author describes as normally filled with "people on their way up and people who have stalled." Schwartz does not consider trying to restructure top management jobs to make them compatible with parenting duties.)

24. For historical accounts and assessments of divorce law reforms, see Lenore Weitzman and Martha L. Fineman, supra note 15. Both divorce systems referred to in the text are, admittedly, formally sex-neutral, or at least they were mostly so by the early eighties. See Orr v. Orr, 440 U.S. 268 (1979). Nevertheless, since formal marriage is presently confined to heterosexual couples, a shift in the ideological impact of marriage dissolution laws is bound to affect sex-role choices. My views of the ideological effect of law have been particularly influenced by Louis Althusser, Lenin and Philosophy, and Other Essays (Ben Brewster trans. 1971) (articulating an ideological function of law), and Michelle Barrett, Ideology and the Cultural Production of Gender, in Feminist Criticism and Social Change 65–85 (Judith Newton and Deborah Rosenfelt eds. 1985) (arguing that ideology must be linked to material conditions in a particular time and place).

25. Marie Ashe's recent definition of *ecriture feminine*. Marie Ashe, Inventing Choreographies: Feminism and Deconstruction, 90 Colum. L. Rev. 1123, 1133 n.42 (1990) (reviewing Zillah Eisenstein, The Female Body and the Law [1988]).

26. Robin West's recent recommendation for the liberal dissenters on the Supreme Court, a recommendation that echoes the description of a different voice that Gilligan argues is more associated with women than men. Robin West, Forword: Taking Freedom Seriously, 104 Harv. L. Rev. 43, 105–6 (1990).

27. See, e.g., Hogan 458 U.S. at 725 n.10, where Justice O'Connor states that "History provides numerous examples of legislative attempts to exclude women from particular areas simply because legislators believed women were less able than men to perform a particular function." The note also cites and quotes from Bradwell v. Illinois 16 Wall. 130 (1873) and Goesaert v. Cleary 335 U.S. 464, 466 (1948). In the body of the opinion O'Connor refers to past discrimination in her discussion of the three cases decided since 1971 in which the Supreme Court has permitted sex-based classifications on the grounds that the challenged statutes compensated women for past discrimination (Hogan, 458 U.S. at 728).

28. Some women support a single-sex educational option as Justices Blackmun and Powell do; others maintain that all education should be coeducational. This conflict among women is indicated by Justice O'Connor's citation of testimony by American Nurses Association officials regarding the impact of excluding men from nursing on nurses' wages (Hogan, 458 U.S. at 729–30 n.15), and by Justice Powell's dissent citing evidence that students and alumnae of MUW wanted the university to remain a woman's institution (id. at 739 n.5). Moreover, Justice Powell's defense of single-sex education is so grounded in the rationale of allowing women to choose, he under-represents the role which discrimination played in the founding of women's colleges.

29. Of course there's no *ecriture feminine*, no moral concern for the "responsibilities as well as the rights of liberalism." Justice O'Connor wouldn't have been appointed to the Supreme Court if she talked like a French feminist or a Gilliganite. But there is plenty of sex talk, in this opinion, and O'Connor's text is different from the dissents in relationship to it.

30. Among the many factors that account for this shift, feminist reactions to *Hogan*'s standard of review are probably not particularly significant. I am using *Hogan* to label the turn in feminist legal scholarship because it did coincide with a shift in the feminist legal agenda and because of its symbolism as the culmination of the feminist campaign for formal (constitutional) equality.

31. Elizabeth M. Schneider, Describing and Changing: Women's Self Defense Work and the Problem of Expert Testimony on Battering, 9 Women's Rts. L. Rep. 195 (1986).

32. See, e.g., Lucinda M. Finley, A Break in the Silence: Including Women's Issues in a Torts Course, 1 Yale J. L. & Feminism 41 (1989); Regina Austin, Employer Abuse, Worker Resistance, and the Tort of Intentional Infliction of Emotional Distress, 41 Stan. L. Rev. 1 (1988); Leslie Bender, A Lawyer's Primer on Feminist Theory and Tort, 38 J. Legal Ed. 3 (1988); Carl Tobias, Gender Issues and the Prosser, Wade and Schwartz Torts Casebook, 18 Golden Gate U. L. Rev. 495 (1988); Clare Dalton, An Essay in the Deconstruction of Contract, 94 Yale L. J. 997 (1985); Mary Joe Frug, Re-Reading Contracts: A Feminist Analysis of a Contracts Casebook, 34 Am. U. L. Rev. 1065 (1985).

33. See, e.g., Susan Estrich, Real Rape (1987); Catharine A. MacKinnon, supra note 16; Frances Olsen, supra note 16.

34. Catharine A. MacKinnon, supra note 4 at 163–97.

35. See, e.g., Marie Ashe, Law-Language of Maternity: Discourse Holding Nature in Contempt, 22 New Eng. L. Rev. 521 (1988); and Kimberle Crenshaw, Demarginalizing the Intersection of Race and Sex: A Black Feminist Critique of Anti-Discrimination Doctrine, Feminist Theory and Anti-Racist Politics, 1989 U. of Chi. Legal F. 139.

36. Although I employ the essentialism/constructivism binarism to discuss the problem of difference, I do not think the danger of the difference strategy is the same as the question of whether gender differences are socially constructed or biologically linked. Rather, like Diana Fuss, I believe the danger of the difference strategy lies in the kind of social construction it advances. For Fuss's views, see Diana Fuss, Essentially Speaking: Feminism, Nature and Difference (1989); see also The Essential Difference, Another Look at Essentialism, differences (1989) (collected essays).

37. Lenore Weitzman and Martha Fineman, supra note 15.

38. Carol Gilligan, In a Different Voice 25–31 (1982) (hereinafter cited as Gilligan).

39. Although subsequent sections of this paper develop an argument that Gilligan's stance toward gender difference and her attitude toward women is more complicated than this statement suggests, neither interpretation of the book which I elaborate is inconsistent with the claim that despite criticisms of the commonalities attributed to women, the book also celebrates these commonalities.

40. See, e.g., Judith Areen, 1988 Survey of Books Relating to the Law; 1. Law and Society: A Need for Caring, 86 Mich. L. Rev. 1067, 1073 (1988) (book review); Leslie Bender, supra note 32, at 18–19, 28–32; Lucinda Finley, supra note 32; Carrie Menkel-Meadow, Portia in a Different Voice: Speculations on a Women's Lawyering Process, 1 Berkeley Women's L. J. 39, 41–42 (1985); Elizabeth M. Schneider, The Dialectic of Rights and Politics: Perspectives from the Women's Movement, 61 N.Y.U. L. Rev. 589, 613–18 (1986).

41. See, e.g., Deborah Rhode, The "Woman's Point of View", 38 J. Legal Ed. 39, 42–44 (1988); Joan C. Williams, Deconstructing Gender, 87 Mich. L. Rev. 797, 802–9 (1989).

42. Carol Gilligan, supra note 38, at 2–3.

43. The ethic of care is most fully and persuasively described in "Concepts of Self and Morality" (id. at 64–105), the chapter primarily concerned with the results of Gilligan's abortion decision study.

44. Id. at 170.

45. The ethic of rights is described in "Woman's Place in Man's Life Cycle" (id. at 5–23); see also, id. at 164–65.

46. Id. at 21.

47. Id. at 18.

48. Id. at 6–7, 10–13, 15, 18, 19–20, 107–8.

49. Suzanna Sherry, Civic Virtue and the Feminine Voice in Constitutional Adjudication, 72 Va. L. Rev. 543, 580 (1986).

50. Joan C. Williams, supra note 41.

51. The conservative reading of Gilligan has been so persuasive, and alternative sources informing the danger of the difference strategy are so intriguing that, like me, progressive feminist legal scholars have tended to give Gilligan's book short shrift in their work. The progressive interpretation I offer here is therefore more dependent on my own reading of Gilligan than the conservative interpretation.

52. Marie Ashe, supra note 35, at 522–23.

53. See chapters 5–7.

54. Gilligan, supra note 38, at 3.

55. Id. at 156.

56. For example, statements such as "*For women*, the integration of rights and responsibilities takes place through an understanding of the psychological logic of relationships" (id. at 100, emphasis added), and "*Thus women* not only reach mid-life with a psychological history different from men's and face at that time a different social reality having different possibilities for love and for work, but they also make a different sense of experience, based on their knowledge of human relationships" (id. at 172, emphasis added), seem to generalize the experience of women. On the other hand, the statement immediately following five quotations from interviews: "*Thus in all of the women's descriptions*, identity is defined in a context of relationship and judged by a standard of responsibility and care" (id. at 160, emphasis added), suggests that the experiences described pertain to the women in the study. Furthermore, a summarizing statement late in the book: "Thus, starting from very different points . . . *the men and women in the study* come . . . to a greater understanding of both points of view and thus to a greater convergence in judgment" (id. at 167, emphasis added), also limits the views described to those of the study's participants.

57. Id. at 2.

58. Id. at 25.

59. Id. at 39–44.

60. These statements occur in the first sentence of each paragraph: "While the truths of psychological theory have blinded psychologists to the *truth of women's experience*, that experience illuminates a world which

psychologists have found hard to trace, a territory where violence is rare and relationships appear safe" (id. at 62, emphasis added); "The reinterpretation of *women's experience* in terms of their own imagery of relationships thus clarifies that experience and also provides a nonhierarchical vision of human connection" (id. at 62, emphasis added).

61. These paragraphs, which summarize the model of rights as well as the ethics of care, are rhetorically critical because they use the images of web and hierarchy to contrast the models. This imagery has drawn much attention. See, e.g., Paul J. Spiegelman, Integrating Doctrine, Theory and Practice in the Law School Curriculum: The Logic of Jake's Ladder in the Context of Amy's Web, 38 J. Legal Ed. 243 (1988); see also Kenneth L. Karst, Woman's Constitution, 1984 Duke L. J. 447 (extensive use of the imagery).

62. See, e.g., Carol Gilligan, supra note 38, at 71, 79, 105; see also, id. at 173 ("[I]n the different voice of woman lies the truth of an ethic of care.")

63. I do not mean to imply here that Gilligan's title wins the day for a conservative interpretation of her book. Gilligan did not, after all, entitle her book *In THE Different Voice*. On the other hand, progressive readers may believe that *Different Voices* would more aptly describe the book they read.

64. Gilligan, supra note 38 at 74.

65. Id.

66. Id.

67. See, e.g., id. at 96.

68. Id. at 65–105.

69. Id. at 24–63.

70. Id. at 62.

71. Id. at 32–33.

72. Id. at 32–33.

73. See, e.g., id. at 94 ("Once obligation extends to include the self as well as others, . . . the moral problem is reconstructed in the light of the realization that the occurrence of the dilemma itself precludes nonviolent resolution"); id. at 166 (relating the discovery by a male college graduate that his "logical hierarchy" of absolute moral values "came to seem a barrier to intimacy rather than a fortress of personal integrity").

74. Suzanna Sherry, supra note 49, at 583.

75. Id. at 582.

76. See id. at 591.

77. Id. at 613.

78. Id. at 613.

79. Bowers v. Hardwick, 478 U.S. 186 (1986).

80. City of Richmond v. J. A. Croson Company, 488 U.S. 469 (1989).

81. EEOC v. Sears, 628 F. Supp. 1264, 1308 (N.D. Ill. 1986), *aff'd*, 839 F.2d 302 (7th Cir. 1988).

82. See chapter 2.

4
A Feminist Analysis of a Casebook

1. J. Dawson, W. Harvey, and S. Henderson, Cases and Comment on Contracts (4th ed. 1982) (hereinafter cited as J. Dawson).

2. For two essays that elaborated this idea for me, see M. Foucault, Two Lectures, in Power/Knowledge 78 (1980); and Griffin, The Way of All Ideology, in Feminist Theory: A Critique of Ideology 273 (N. Keohane, M. Rosaldo, and B. Gelpi eds. 1982).

3. For all of these reasons, some form of gender exploration is a major characteristic of feminist work. Feminists differ from one another in the ways they explore gender and in the significance the focus on gender has in their work. For many, feminist analysis consists of studying the social and psychological construction of the differences between men and women. Some of these scholars want to learn why more women than men take primary care of children. See, e.g., N. Chodorow, The Reproduction of Mothering: Psychoanalysis and the Sociology of Gender (1978); D. Dinnerstein, The Mermaid and the Minotaur: Sexual Arrangements and Human Malaise (1976). Others want to learn why housework is so dramatically undervalued. See, e.g., Gardiner, Women's Domestic Labor, in Capitalist Patriarchy and the Case for Socialist Feminism 173 (Z. Eisenstein ed. 1979); Feminism and Materialism: Women and Modes of Production (A. Kuhn and A. Wolpe eds. 1978). Still others want to learn why the objectification of women's sexuality takes the particular, violent form it takes in some kinds of pornography. See, e.g., A. Dworkin, Woman Hating (1974); Benjamin, The Bonds of Love: Rational Violence and Erotic Domination, in The Future of Difference 41–70 (H. Eisenstein and A. Jardine eds. 1985). Feminist literary theorists write about why women write and read differently than men do. See, e.g., J. Fetterley, The Resisting Reader: A Feminist Approach to American Fiction (1978); K. Ruthven, Feminist Literary Studies: An Introduction (1984). Feminist legal scholars, in part, have focused on the doctrinal and theoretical implications of treating women and men differently or similarly. See, e.g., Freedman, Sex Equality, Sex Differences, and the Supreme Court, 92 Yale L. J. 913 (1983); Olsen, The Family and the Market: A Study of Ideology and Legal Reform, 96 Harv. L. Rev. 1497 (1983); Olsen, Statutory Rape: A Feminist Critique of Rights Analysis, 63 Tex. L. Rev. 387 (1984); Minow, Rights of One's Own (Book Review), 98 Harv. L. Rev. 1084, 1089–93 (reviewing E. Griffith, In Her Own Right: The Life of Elizabeth Cady Stanton [1984]). See generally Bibliography of Feminist

Legal Scholarship (Dec. 28, 1984) (unpublished manuscript). Others have used gender as a way to draw on an aspect of experience more available to women than to men, such as a personal perspective on an issue or an outsider's unempowered perspective. See, e.g., Dalton, An Essay in the Deconstruction of Contract Doctrine, 94 Yale L. J. 997 (1985).

The present work is different from many of those I have just described in that my primary focus is an examination of the gendered nature of a specific text. Rather than examining gender itself as a phenomenon, or using a gender-related trait as a perspective from which to see something else, I am trying to work within gender categories, hoping to expose the way our ideas about the world are infected with our ideas about gender. My work is connected to other feminist projects, however, in that I will include investigations of the personal or silenced aspects of contract doctrine, references to the origins and nature of gender differences, and discussion of the legal questions gender poses for contract, as part of my undertaking. I believe my methodology is similar both to the conscious-ness-raising process feminists often describe and to the uncovering of submerged discourses that feminist literary theorists claim as their methodology. See, e.g., MacKinnon, Feminism, Marxism, Method, and the State: An Agenda for Theory, 7 Signs 515 (1982); Kolodny, Dancing Through the Minefield, in The New Feminist Criticism 144, 159–63 (E. Showalter ed. 1985).

4. See, e.g., S. Freud, Some Psychological Consequences of the Anatomical Distinction Between the Sexes and Female Sexuality, in Sexuality and the Psychology of Love, 183–93, 194–211 (P. Reiff ed. 1963).

5. C. Christ, Diving Deep and Surfacing 119–31 (1980); R. Johnson, She: Understanding Feminine Psychology (1976).

6. Joan Kelly's essay discussing the shift in feminist theory away from dualistic analyses is useful in pursuing this point. See J. Kelly, The Doubled Vision of Feminist Theory, in Women, History and Theory 51–64 (1984); see also K. Leahy, "until women themselves have told all they have to tell . . ." (1985) (unpublished paper).

7. See L. Davidson and L. Gordon, The Sociology of Gender 1–33 (1979); S. De Beauvoir, The Second Sex 1–47 (1953).

8. This claim is similar to that made by feminist literary critics regarding their work, see J. Fetterley, supra note 3, at vii–xxiv; J. Radway, Reading the Romance 3–18 (1984). It is also similar to Robert Gordon's description of Critical Legal Studies scholarship. See R. Gordon, Critical Legal Histories, 36 Stan. L. Rev. 57, 117–24 (1984).

9. For examples of feminist writing that can inform this definition of feminism, see J. Miller, Toward a New Psychology of Women (1976); Minow, supra note 3; Leahy, supra note 6.

10. Cf. A. Kolodny, supra note 3. The embrace of diversity implied here is similar to Annette Kolodny's normative description of feminist literary criticism as pluralistic (id.). I think Kolodny's use of "pluralistic" is

an unfortunate choice of adjective, however. Pluralism as commonly understood is not what I understand her to be saying, and it's not what I mean in suggesting that analyses which differ from mine may also be feminist. I think there is some "there" in feminism, not just anything goes.

11. For examples of this effort undertaken outside legal education, see Gappa, Sex and Gender in the Social Sciences (1980) (produced under grant from Women's Educational Equity Act Program, United States Department of Education); Ruth, Methodocracy, Misogyny and Bad Faith: The Response of Philosophy, in Men's Studies Modified: The Impact of Feminism on the Academic Disciplines (D. Spender ed. 1981). Efforts to eliminate overt sexism are now underway within legal education as well. Nancy S. Erickson at the Ohio State University College of Law was awarded an Ohio State University Affirmative Action grant for the 1984–85 academic year to complete a project "Sex Bias in the Criminal Law Course: Bringing the Law School Curriculum into the 1980s." Erickson, with the assistance of Nadine Taub (Rutgers/Newark) as primary consultant, and others, examined whether gender-related issues have become an integral part of the traditional first-year criminal law course as it is taught throughout the country.

The study proceeded in three concurrent steps: a review of major casebooks currently being used in the first-year criminal law courses; a survey of all law professors currently teaching the course; and a bibliography and compilation of supplementary materials recommended to compensate for inadequacies in traditional materials. The criminal law study was designed to serve as a model for a comprehensive study involving the entire law school curriculum. While this project focused on eliminating sex bias in the criminal law casebooks, it also overlapped with aspects of my project. Moreover, any effort to eliminate overt sexism will require feminist analysis as I have broadly defined it here, and I hope my work will further such pursuits.

12. I agree with Catharine MacKinnon's eloquent claim that "the male point of view [is] fundamental to the male power to create the world in its own image." MacKinnon, Feminism, Marxism, Method, and the State: Toward Feminist Jurisprudence, 8 Signs 635, 640 (1983). As long as our ideas about gender permit us to divide our views dualistically between male and female viewpoints, gender will continue to influence profoundly the nature of our lives.

13. I do not think that "professional necessity" is any more determinate than I suggest the contents of a casebook need to be. I use the phrase here, however, simply to acknowledge that there are some (arguable) limits within which a casebook editor functions in selecting the contents of a casebook which is to be used for legal education.

14. S. Fish, Is There a Text in this Class?: The Authority of Interpretive Communities 9 (1980) (emphasis added).

15. P. Atiyah, Rise and Fall of Freedom of Contract (1979).

16. R. Meslar, ed., Legalines: Contracts (1983).

17. It may seem paradoxical to seek to further our understanding of the content of gender when my stated objective is to "diminish the power that ideas about gender exercise over our lives." However, because I think that gender distinctions are nurtured and perpetuated by their continuing impact on our consciousnesses, I believe that we cannot diminish their power without first exposing them and discussing the effect they have on us.

5
An Overview of the Contracts Casebook

1. J. Russ, Magic Mommas, Trembling Sisters, Puritans and Perverts: Feminist Essays (1985).

2. Department of Labor reports indicate that women earn only 59 percent as much as men. See Women's Bureau, Office of the Secretary, U.S. Department of Labor, The Earnings Gap between Women and Men 6 (1979) (table 1). This discrepancy has been linked to the undervaluation of the kinds of work women do. See A. Blumrosen, Wage Discrimination, Job Segregation, and Title VII of the Civil Rights Act of 1964, 12 U. Mich. J. L. Reform 397, 421 (1979); Note, Equal Pay for Comparable Worth, 15 Harv. C.R.-C.L. L. Rev. 475, 478–79 (1980); Note, Equal Pay, Comparable Work, and Job Evaluation, 90 Yale L. J. 657, 663 (1981); see also, M.J. Frug, Securing Job Equality for Women: Labor Market Hostility to Working Mothers, 59 B.U. L. Rev. 55 (1979).

3. In contrast, other readers, readers who identify with the Feminist and the Reader with a Chip on Her Shoulder, are likely to realize the casebook's support for the ideology of gender immediately upon learning that the concept of the reasonable man is utilized in the first case in the book as a standard by which to judge the "objective" interpretation of contractual language. See Hawkins v. McGee, 84 N.H. 114, 115, 146 A. 641, 643 (1929), excerpted in J. Dawson, W. Harvey, and S. Henderson, Cases and Comment on Contracts 1,2 (4th ed. 1982) (hereinafter cited as J. Dawson).

4. This approach is similar to the first "moment" or stage of feminist literary criticism which K. Ruthven describes as "dismantling androcentric assumptions." K. Ruthven, Feminist Literary Studies: An Introduction 59–82 (1984).

5. Although the first part focuses on women as characters and the second on male characteristics, the first part will implicate the casebook treatment of men as characters, just as the second will implicate female characteristics. In the next chapter I will discuss the implications of this approach for contesting gender in the casebook.

6. The major cases in the book that involve parties who are women are: Williams v. Walker-Thomas Furniture Co., 350 F.2d 445 (D.C. Cir. 1965),

excerpted in J. Dawson at 697; Rouse v. United States, 215 F.2d 872 (D.C. Cir. 1954), excerpted in J. Dawson at 906; Kirksey v. Kirksey, 8 Ala. 131 (1845), excerpted in J. Dawson at 192; Bleecher v. Conte, 29 Cal. 3d 345, 626 P. 2d 1051, 173 Cal. Rptr. 278 (1981), excerpted in J. Dawson at 660; Parker v. Twentieth Century Fox Film Corp., 3 Cal. 3d 176, 474 P.2d 689, 89 Cal. Rptr. 737 (1970), excerpted in J. Dawson at 46; Heyer v. Flaig, 70 Cal.2d 223, 449 P.2d 161, 74 Cal. Rptr. 225 (1969), excerpted in J. Dawson at 896; Davis v. Jacoby, 1 Cal.2d 370, 34 P.2d 1026 (1934), excerpted in J. Dawson, at 316; Fairfield Credit Corp. v. Donnelly, 158 Conn. 543, 264 A.2d 547 (1969), excerpted in J. Dawson at 946; Allied Van Lines, Inc. v. Bratton, 351 So.2d 344 (Fla. 1977), excerpted in J. Dawson at 448; Skendzel v. Marshall, 261 Ind. 226, 301 N.E.2d 641 (1973), excerpted in J. Dawson at 681; Brackenbury v. Hodgkin, 116 Me. 399, 102 A. 106 (1917), excerpted in J. Dawson at 331; Hoffman v. Chapman, 182 Md. 208, 34 A.2d 438 (1943), excerpted in J. Dawson at 410; Fitzpatrick v. Michael, 177 Md. 248, 9 A.2d 69 (1939), excerpted in J. Dawson at 128; Reigart v. Fisher, 149 Md. 336, 131 A. 568 (1925), excerpted in J. Dawson at 848; Taylor v. Barton-Child Co., 228 Mass. 126, 117 N.E. 43 (1917), excerpted in J. Dawson at 935; Fischer v. Union Trust Co., 138 Mich. 612, 101 N.W. 852 (1904), excerpted in J. Dawson at 160; Skelly Oil Co. v. Ashmore, 365 S.W.2d 582 (Mo. 1963), excerpted in J. Dawson at 601; Gartrell v. Stafford, 12 Neb. 545, 11 N.W. 732 (1882), excerpted in J. Dawson at 118; Ellsworth Dobbs, Inc. v. Johnson, 50 N.J. 528, 236 A.2d 843 (1967), excerpted in J. Dawson at 469; Henningsen v. Bloomfield Motors, Inc., 32 N.J. 358, 161 A.2d 69 (1960), excerpted in J. Dawson at 461; Timko v. Useful Homes Corp., 114 N.J. Eq. 433, 168 A. 824 (1933), excerpted in J. Dawson at 123; Cook v. Lum, 55 N.J.L. 373, 26 A. 803 (1893), excerpted in J. Dawson at 919; Weisz v. Parke-Bernet Galleries, Inc., 67 Misc.2d 1077, 325 N.Y.S.2d 576 (N.Y. Cir. Ct. 1971), rev'd, 77 Misc.2d 80, 351 N.Y.S.2d 911 (N.Y. App. Term. 1974), excerpted in J. Dawson at 453; Cohen v. Kranz, 12 N.Y.2d 242, 189 N.E.2d 473, 238 N.Y.S.2d 928 (1963), excerpted in J. Dawson at 787; Mitchill v. Lath, 247 N.Y. 377, 160 N.E. 646 (1928), excerpted in J. Dawson at 426; Allegheny College v. National Chautauqua County Bank, 246 N.Y. 369, 159 N.E. 173 (1927), excerpted in J. Dawson at 194; Seaver v. Ransom, 224 N.Y. 233, 120 N.E. 639 (1918), excerpted in J. Dawson at 863; Wood v. Lucy, Lady Duff-Gordon, 222 N.Y. 88, 118 N.E. 214 (1917), excerpted in J. Dawson at 231; Hamer v. Sidway, 124 N.Y. 538, 27 N.E. 256 (1891), excerpted in J. Dawson at 156; Hinson v. Jefferson, 287 N.C. 422, 215 S.E.2d 102 (1975), excerpted in J. Dawson at 575; Funk v. Baird, 70 N.D. 396, 295 N.W. 87 (1940), excerpted in J. Dawson at 916; Kabil Devs. Corp. v. Mignot, 279 Or. 151, 566 P.2d 505 (1977), excerpted in J. Dawson at 269; East Providence Credit Union v. Geremia, 103 R.I. 597, 239 A.2d 725 (1968), excerpted in J. Dawson at 203; Najarian v. Boyajian, 48 R.I. 213, 136 A. 767 (1927), excerpted in J. Dawson at 850; DeLeon v. Aldrete, 398 S.W.2d 160 (Tex. Civ. App. 1965), excerpted in J. Dawson at 114; Batsakis v. Demotsis, 226 S.W.2d 673 (Tex. Civ. App. 1949), excerpted in J. Dawson at 165; Jackson v. Seymour, 193 Va. 735, 71 S.E.2d 181 (1952), excerpted in J.

Dawson at 170; Hoffman v. Red Owl Stores, Inc., 26 Wis.2d 683, 133 N.W.2d 267 (1965), excerpted in J. Dawson at 355; Plante v. Jacobs, 10 Wis.2d 567, 103 N.W.2d 296 (1960), excerpted in J. Dawson at 812.

7. Indeed, the figure of thirty-nine women's cases is somewhat misleading because women are coupled with their husbands in eleven of those cases and do not have a significant separate presence as women. The eleven cases involving married couples are: Fairfield Credit Corp. v. Donnelly, 158 Conn. 543, 264 A.2d 547 (1969), excerpted in J. Dawson at 946; Hoffman v. Chapman, 182 Md. 208, 34 A.2d 438 (1943), excerpted in J. Dawson at 410; Skelly Oil Co. v. Ashmore, 365 S.W.2d 582 (Mo. 1963), excerpted in J. Dawson at 601; Ellsworth Dobbs, Inc. v. Johnson, 50 N.J. 528, 236 A.2d 843 (1967), excerpted in J. Dawson at 469; Henningsen v. Bloomfield Motors, Inc., 32 N.J. 358, 161 A.2d 69 (1960), excerpted in J. Dawson at 461; Weisz v. Parke-Bernet Galleries, Inc., 67 Misc.2d 1077, 325 N.Y.S.2d 576 (1971), rev'd, 77 Misc.2d 80, 351 N.Y.S.2d 911 (N.Y. App. Term. 1974), excerpted in J. Dawson at 453; Kabil Devs. Corp. v. Mignot, 279 Or. 151, 566 P.2d 505 (1977), excerpted in J. Dawson at 269; East Providence Credit Union v. Geremia, 103 R.I. 597, 239 A.2d 725 (1968), excerpted in J. Dawson at 203; DeLeon v. Aldrete, 398 S.W.2d 160 (Tex. Civ. App. 1965), excerpted in J. Dawson at 114; Hoffman v. Red Owl Stores, Inc., 26 Wis.2d 683, 133 N.W.2d 267 (1965), excerpted in J. Dawson at 355; Plante v. Jacobs, 10 Wis.2d 567, 103 N.W.2d 296 (1960), excerpted in J. Dawson at 812. In addition, the woman involved in Hamer v. Sidway is an assignee (and wife) of the nephew whose uncle promised him money for refraining from various activities; she is scarcely noticeable in the decision. Hamer v. Sidway, 124 N.Y. 538, 538, 27 N.E. 256, 256 (1891), excerpted in J. Dawson at 156.

8. E.g., Skelly Oil Co. v. Ashmore, 365 S.W.2d 582 (Mo. 1963), excerpted in J. Dawson at 601; Henningsen v. Bloomfield Motors, Inc., 32 N.J. 358, 161 A.2d 69 (1960), excerpted in J. Dawson at 461; Weisz v. Parke-Bernet Galleries, Inc., 67 Misc.2d 1077, 325 N.Y.S.2d 576 (N.Y. Civ. Ct. 1971), rev'd, 77 Misc.2d 80, 351 N.Y.S.2d 911 (N.Y. App. Term 1974), excerpted in J. Dawson at 453; East Providence Credit Union v. Geremia, 103 R.I. 597, 239 A.2d 725 (1968), excerpted in J. Dawson at 203; De Leon v. Aldrete, 398 S.W.2d 160 (Tex. Civ. App. 1965), excerpted in J. Dawson at 114; Hoffman v. Red Owl Stores, Inc., 26 Wis.2d 683, 133 N.W.2d 267 (1965), excerpted in J. Dawson at 355.

9. Brackenbury v. Hodgkin, 116 Me. 399, 102 A. 106 (1917), excerpted in J. Dawson at 331.

10. Kirksey v. Kirksey, 8 Ala. 131 (1845), excerpted in J. Dawson at 192.

11. Davis v. Jacoby, 1 Cal. 2d 370, 34 P.2d 1026 (1934), excerpted in J. Dawson at 316.

12. Hinson v. Jefferson, 287 N.C. 422, 215 S.E.2d 102 (1975), excerpted in J. Dawson at 575.

13. Gartrell v. Stafford, 12 Neb. 545, 11 N.W. 732 (1882), excerpted in J. Dawson at 118.

14. Fitzpatrick v. Michael, 177 Md. 248, 9 A.2d 639 (1939), excerpted in J. Dawson at 128.

15. Wood v. Lucy, Lady Duff-Gordon, 222 N.Y. 88, 118 N.E. 214 (1917), excerpted in J. Dawson at 231.

16. Allegheny College v. National Chautauqua County Bank, 246 N.Y. 369, 159 N.E. 173 (1927), excerpted in J. Dawson at 194.

17. Parker v. Twentieth Century Fox Film Corp., 3 Cal.3d 176, 474 P.2d 689, 89 Cal. Rptr. 737 (1970), excerpted in J. Dawson at 46.

18. Fischer v. Union Trust Co., 138 Mich. 612, 101 N.W. 852 (1904), excerpted in J. Dawson at 160.

19. Williams v. Walker-Thomas Furniture Co., 350 F.2d 445 (D.C. Cir. 1965), excerpted in J. Dawson at 696.

20. See, e.g., Kirksey v. Kirksey, 8 Ala. 131 (1845) (brother-in-law), excerpted in J. Dawson at 192; Brackenbury v. Hodgkin, 116 Me. 399, 102 A. 106 (1917) (son and son-in-law), excerpted in J. Dawson at 331; Hamer v. Sidway, 124 N.Y. 538, 27 N.E. 256 (1891) (nephew and uncle), excerpted in J. Dawson at 156.

21. Hoffman v. Chapman, 182 Md. 208, 34 A.2d 438 (1943), excerpted in J. Dawson at 410.

22. Id.

23. Faber v. Sweet Style Manufacturing Corp., 40 Misc. 2d 212, 242 N.Y.S.2d 763 (N.Y. Sup. Ct. 1963), excerpted in J. Dawson at 492.

24. Bright v. Ganas, 171 Md. 493, 189 A. 427 (1936) ("personal attendant and companion"), excerpted in J. Dawson at 111.

25. Hawkins v. McGee, 84 N.H. 114, 146 A. 641 (1929), excerpted in J. Dawson at 1.

26. Drennan v. Star Paving Co., 51 Cal. 2d 409, 333 P.2d 757 (1958), excerpted in J. Dawson at 346.

27. Boone v. Coe, 153 Ky. 233, 154 S.W. 900 (1913), excerpted in J. Dawson at 92.

28. Hadley v. Baxendale, 9 Exch. 341 (Ex. 1854), excerpted in J. Dawson at 67.

29. Illinois Central Railroad Co. v. Crail, 281 U.S. 57 (1930), excerpted in J. Dawson at 59.

30. Rockingham County v. Luten Bridge Co., 35 F.2d 301 (4th Cir. 1929), excerpted in J. Dawson at 41.

31. Tanner v. Merrill, 108 Mich. 58, 65 N.W. 664 (1895), excerpted in J. Dawson at 541.

32. Denney v. Reppert, 432 S.W.2d 647 (Ky. 1968), excerpted in J. Dawson at 558.

33. American Broadcasting Companies, Inc. v. Wolf, 52 N.Y.2d 394, 420 N.E.2d 363, 438 N.Y.S.2d 482 (1981), excerpted in J. Dawson at 667.

34. Chicago Coliseum Club v. Dempsey, 265 Ill. App. 542 (1932), excerpted in J. Dawson at 81.

35. Southwest Engineering Co. v. Martin Tractor Co., 205 Kan. 684, 473 P.2d 18 (1970), excerpted in J. Dawson at 290.

36. Sheets v. Teddy's Frosted Foods, Inc., 179 Conn. 471, 427 A.2d 385 (1980), excerpted in J. Dawson at 254.

37. Clark v. West, 193 N.Y. 349, 86 N.E. 1 (1908), excerpted in J. Dawson at 738.

38. See supra notes 15, 17.

39. There are, of course, exceptions to this generalization. See, e.g., C. Knapp, Problems in Contract Law: Cases and Materials xxi (1976) ("no study of law is adequate if it loses sight of the fact that law operates first and last *for, upon,* and *through* individual human beings"). I. MacNeil, Cases and Materials on Contracts, Exchange Transactions and Relationships xx (2d ed. 1978) ("The book contains a considerable amount of text, both original and borrowed, devoted to putting the legal materials into the economic, social, financial and commercial contexts in which they occur.")

40. One might argue, however, that a certain lack of realism should be encouraged in a casebook in order to obtain the beneficial effect on readers of an idealized image of how editors think the world should be for women and men.

41. See supra notes 1–2.

42. 177 Md. 248, 9 A.2d 639 (1939), excerpted in J. Dawson at 128.

43. Id. at 259, 9 A.2d at 643, excerpted in J. Dawson at 128, 131.

44. By providing that all income earned during marriage is marital property, the recently proposed Uniform Marital Property Act values the housework of a married woman who has no other source of income at half her wage earning spouse's income. See Unif. Marital Property Act § 4(d), 9A U.C.L.A. 19 (Supp. 1985). In the context of divorce, the nonmonetary contributions homemakers and parents make to their families have received increased recognition through state legislation passed since the early 1970s which provides that a homemaker's contribution to a marital unit may be or (in some states) should be considered when dividing marital property according to the equitable distribution systems now in effect in most jurisdictions. See, e.g., LaRue v. LaRue, 304 S.E.2d 312, 321–23 (1983); In re Marriage of Cornell, 550 S.W.2d 823, 826 (Mo. Ct. App. 1977). See generally, Freed, Equitable Distribution as of December 1982, 9 (Current Developments) Family Law Rep. (BNA) 4001 (Jan. 11

1983). See also Avner, Using the Connecticut Equal Rights Amendment at Divorce to Protect Homemakers' Contributions to the Acquisition of Marital Property, 4 U. Bridge. L. Rev. 265, 270–80 (1982) (arguing that homemakers' nonmonetary contributions should be equated with wage earners' contributions). The law also attributes value to a homemaker's services in personal injury actions, where courts have valued the loss of a homemaker to her family by using a "replacement costs" standard (valuing the homemaker's work by determining either the cost of replacing each of the various tasks she performed or by determining the costs of procuring a "substitute homemaker"), or by using a "lost opportunity costs" standard (valuing a homemaker's work by equating it with the estimated value of the work she could have performed had she not worked in the home). See Yale, The Valuation of Household Services in Wrongful Death Actions, 34 U. Toronto L. J. 283, 292–304 (1984); Annot., 47 A.L.R.3d 971 (1973) (collected cases involving death of housewives).

45. Dallas Cowboys Football Club, Inc. v. Harris, 348 S.W.2d 37, 42–44 (Tex. Civ. App. 1961), excerpted in J. Dawson at 132.

46. See chapter 6.

47. 222 N.Y. 88, 118 N.E. 214 (1917), excerpted in J. Dawson at 231.

48. Shirley MacLaine, Jack Dempsey, and Hiram Walker are the other parties whose photographs appear in the casebook. See J. Dawson at 47, 82, 87, 563. Although the Hiram Walker case in the book involved the sale of a cow, Walker's picture is probably included in the casebook because of his more well known business, a liquor concern that still distributes its products in his name. See Sherwood v. Walker, 66 Mich. 568, 33 N.W.2d 919 (1887) (overruled in Lenarver Co. Bd. of Health v. Misserly, 417 Mich. 17, 331 N.W.2d 203 [1982]), excerpted in J. Dawson at 561; Letter from Helen MacKenzie, Public Relations Department, Hiram Walker & Sons, Ltd., Ontario, Canada to author (Aug. 13, 1985).

49. J. Dawson at 232.

50. In addition, Cardozo's wording might permit the female Reader with a Chip on Her Shoulder to believe, in her paranoid mode, that the judge was skeptical about the reasons for Lady Duff-Gordon's success. His opinion states that she "*styles* herself 'a creator of fashions.' " Wood v. Lucy, Lady Duff-Gordon, 222 N.Y. 88, 90, 118 N.E. 214 (1917), excerpted in J. Dawson at 231. "Was she really a designer?" such phrasing hints. Although in a later sentence Cardozo states that Lady Duff-Gordon did, in fact design things—"fabrics, parasols and what not"—this creativity could seem to be undercut not only by the judge's "what not" but also by the hint of contempt he displays for the public, which ascribed "new value . . . [to products she designed] when issued in her name" (id. at 90, 118 N.E. at 214).

51. 193 Va. 735, 71 S.E.2d 181 (1952), excerpted in J. Dawson at 170.

52. Other cases in the book involving women who do not work outside the

home also characterize the women, as this case does, as victims. See, e.g., Williams v. Walker-Thomas Furniture Co., 350 F.2d 445 (D.C. Cir. 1965), excerpted in J. Dawson at 697; Brackenbury v. Hodgkin, 116 Me. 399, 102 A. 106 (1917), excerpted in J. Dawson at 410. It is not clear whether the victimized women in other cases worked outside the home. See, e.g., Kirksey v. Kirksey, 8 Ala. 131 (1845), excerpted in J. Dawson at 192; Reigart v. Fisher, 149 Md. 336, 131 A. 568 (1925), excerpted in J. Dawson at 848; Batsakis v. Demotsis, 226 S.W.2d 673 (Tex. Civ. App. 1949), excerpted in J. Dawson at 165. The victimized stereotype is not the only unflattering stereotype readers can find in this casebook, however. For the cases in which women are characterized exclusively in terms of their dependency on their husbands, see supra note 7.

53. 193 Va. 69 at 736, 71 S.E.2d at 182, excerpted in J. Dawson at 170, 172. At the time of the purchase, neither he nor Mrs. Jackson knew that there was valuable timber on the land. Seymour cut and sold the timber, however, realizing a substantial amount of money which he did not share with his sister (id.).

54. Id. at 736, 71 S.E.2d at 182–83, excerpted in J. Dawson at 170, 172, 173.

55. For articles asserting an objective rather than subjective approach to interpreting the doctrine of mutual assent, see Costigan, Implied-In-Fact Contracts and Mutual Assent, 33 Harv. L. Rev. 376, 398–400 (1920); Williston, Mutual Assent in the Formation of Contracts, 14 Ill. L. Rev. 525, 529–35 (1919).

56. Cf. Kennedy, Distributive and Paternalist Motives in Contract and Tort Law, with Special Reference to Compulsory Terms and Unequal Bargaining Power, 41 Md. L. Rev. 563, 624–31 (1982).

57. While this is my general impression of the characterization of women in this casebook, there are cases in the book which do not conform to the generalization stated here. See, e.g., Bleecher v. Conte, 29 Cal. 3d 345, 626 P.2d 1051, 173 Cal. Rptr. 278 (1981), excerpted in J. Dawson at 660, in which Judge Rose Bird describes the defendant as "an experienced businesswoman involved in real estate transactions" (id.). Although the defendant is unsuccessful in her legal claims, she has some dignity in Judge Bird's treatment.

58. 191 Ky. 559, 231 S.W. 45 (1921), excerpted in J. Dawson at 25.

59. Ky. Rev. Stat. § 404.030 (1972).

60. Ky. Rev. Stat. § 404.020(1) (1972) (repealed by implication by the 1942 amendment to § 404.030[1]) (permitting married woman to sell land without husband's consent). See Schaengold v. Behen, 306 Ky. 544, 545–46, 208 S.W.2d 726, 729–30 (1948) (stating that Act of 1942 allows married woman to convey land freely). See also Levy, Vestiges of Sexism in Ohio and Kentucky Property Law: A Case of De Facto Discrimination, 1 N. Ky. St. L. F. 193, 214–18 (1973) (discussing impact of 1942 amendments on § 404.020).

61. Adding this historical material to the *Crenshaw* presentation might counter the sex role stereotyping effect on readers of later cases in the book, such as Reigart v. Fisher, 149 Md. 336, 131 A. 568 (Ap. Md. 1925), excerpted in J. Dawson at 848, in which a husband not only formally brought suit with his wife, in a dispute regarding the sale of her land, but also "acted as spokesman" for her. Since Maryland's provisions regarding the capacity of married women were not as restrictive as Kentucky's at the time of the decision in *Reigart,* readers cannot blame Gulielma Fisher's subordinated conduct on a legal anachronism. See Vogel v. Turnet, 110 Md. 192, 193–94, 72 A. 661, 662–63 (1909) (interpreting Maryland Married Women's Property Act to give wives same control as husbands over their own property); Md. Ann. Code § 4-203 (1984) (Maryland provision regarding married woman's control over her property).

62. See, e.g., J. Dawson at 6–8 (discussing controls over jury verdicts); id. at 37–41 (discussing history of equity).

63. I recognize that my claim that Dawson, Harvey, and Henderson have not included contracts cases in their book which would be particularly interesting to women might seem difficult to substantiate to some of my readers. Not only must I ask you to look with me in the casebook for what's not there, but more problematically the claim assumes the questionable proposition that women have special interests, that are different from men's, and that they have utilized the legal system, including contract doctrine, to pursue them.

64. J. Dawson at 25 (editor's note).

65. While reproductive functions and sexuality are also important to men, many feminists assert, and I agree, that the lack of control women have had over these matters is a major cause of their historical oppression. See, e.g., S. Firestone, The Dialectic of Sex 1–14 (1970); MacKinnon, Feminism, Marxism, Method, and the State: An Agenda for Theory, 7 Signs 515 (1982).

66. Typically, statutes provide that if a husband and wife consent in writing to artificial insemination with semen donated by someone other than the husband, the husband is irrebutably presumed to be the father of the conceived child. See, e.g., Ga. Code Ann. § 19-7-21 (1982); Unif. Parentage Act § 5, 9A U.L.A. 592–93 (1979). See generally, Wadlington, Artificial Conception: The Challenge for Family Law, 69 Va. L. Rev. 465, 483–84 n. 84 (1983) (surveying state statutes on artificial insemination).

67. See, e.g., Wash. Rev. Code Ann. § 26.26.050(2) (Supp. 1986). The issue of whether donors are responsible for the support of children conceived by their sperm is often avoided by medical practices designed to preserve donor anonymity. See Curie-Cohen, Current Practice of Artificial Insemination by Donor in the United States, 300 New Eng. J. Med. 585, 588–89 (1979).

68. Provisions in surrogate contracts which provide for payment to the

surrogate mother beyond her expenses are considered unenforceable in the forty-nine states that prohibit payment to parents for the termination of parental rights. See Wadlington, supra note 66, at 479–82; and Note, Parenthood by Proxy: Legal Implications of Surrogate Birth, 67 Iowa L. Rev. 385, 389 (1982). Moreover, such contracts have been criticized on the grounds that contractual analysis does not adequately consider the best interests of the child. Note, supra, at 389. But see Restatement (Second) of Contracts §§ 178, 179 (1979) (promises may be unenforceable on grounds of public policy). There is some evidence, however, that contracts are being used successfully to structure surrogate parenting arrangements in some cases. See, e.g., Syrokowski v. Appleyard, 420 Mich. 367, 362 N.W.2d 211 (1985) (requiring circuit court to accept subject matter jurisdiction over biological father's request under Paternity Act for order of filiation declaring paternity of child conceived by surrogate mother under surrogate parent contract). See also Brophy, A Surrogate Mother Contract to Bear a Child, 20 J. Fam. L. 263 (1981–82) (presenting surrogate parenting contract used in author's practice with infertile couples).

69. The most commonly litigated dispute involving reproductive technology occurs in a divorce or support proceeding in which a woman who conceived a child by artificial insemination from a third party seeks support for the child from her husband. Courts address this issue by determining whether the husband consented to the insemination procedure and whether the form of consent was adequate to comply with the formality requirements imposed by statute. See R.S. v. R.S., 9 Kan. App. 39, 670 P.2d 923 (1983). See also, supra note 68 (discussing surrogate parenting contracts).

70. See R.S. v. R.S., 9 Kan. App. 39, 670 P.2d 923 (1983) (utilizing equitable estoppel and implied contract doctrines to interpret formality requirement of spousal consent provision imposed by state statute); see also, Karin T. v. Michael T., 484 N.Y.S.2d 780, 127 Misc.2d 14 (1985); Anonymous v. Anonymous, 246 N.Y.S.2d 835, 41 Misc.2d 886 (1964); Gursky v. Gursky, 242 N.Y.S.2d 406, 39 Misc.2d 1083 (1963).

71. Thus, there is a natural fit between the reproductive technology materials and a contracts course. Moreover, the family law context in which these cases arise is sufficiently accessible so that it should not be a barrier to using the cases in a contracts course.

72. Indeed, Grant Gilmore has described contract doctrine as "a residual category—what is left over after all the 'specialized' bodies of law have been added up." G. Gilmore, The Death of Contract 7 (1974). Editors generally not only leave domestic relations cases out of basic contract materials, but they also minimize the number of cases involving such subjects as insurance, labor relations, admiralty, and business organization. See, e.g., F. Kessler and G. Gilmore, Contracts: Cases and Materials

vii (2d ed. 1970) (explaining omission of materials on labor contracts and antitrust in second edition) (hereinafter cited as F. Kessler).

73. Excluding the section of cases on standard form contracts, which is extensively discussed later (see chapter 6), the thirty-five other major cases in the chapter on assent doctrine (J. Dawson at 261–486 [chapter 3, "The Consensual Basis of Obligation"]), include only four cases involving family relations or family transactions. In several of the cases in which one corporation is suing another, one has no sense of the people who acted for the corporations in the transactions that gave rise to the disputes. See, e.g., Idaho Power Co. v. Westinghouse Electric Corp., 596 F.2d 924 (9th Cir. 1979), excerpted in J. Dawson at 368; Allied Steel & Conveyors, Inc. v. Ford Motor Co., 277 F.2d 907 (6th Cir. 1960), excerpted in J. Dawson at 313; Humble Oil & Refining Co. v. Westside Investment Corp., 428 S.W.2d 92 (Tex. 1968), excerpted in J. Dawson at 375.

    In contrast, the unit of six cases on promissory estoppel includes no cases involving sale of goods or construction contracts. There are two cases involving family disputes, Kirksey v. Kirksey, 8 Ala. 131 (1845), excerpted in J. Dawson at 192 (brother-in-law's breach of agreement to help sister-in-law "raise her family"), and Seavey v. Drake, 63 N.H. 393 (1882), excerpted in J. Dawson at 192 (father's failure to give son deed to land son had farmed). A third case involves a woman's promise to leave money for a scholarship fund in her name to a college. Allegheny College v. National Chatauqua County Bank, 246 N.Y. 369, 159 N.E. 173 (1927), excerpted in J. Dawson at 194, and a fourth case involves a married couple's dispute with a bank over insurance payments on their ranch wagon. East Providence Credit Union v. Geremia, 103 R.I. 597, 239 A.2d 725 (1968), excerpted in J. Dawson at 203. The two cases involving employment contract disputes convey a concrete sense of the individuals involved. See Goodman v. Dicker, 169 F.2d 684 (D.C. Cir. 1948), excerpted in J. Dawson at 217; Forrer v. Sears, Roebuck & Co., 36 Wis. 2d 388, 153 N.W.2d 587 (1967), excerpted in J. Dawson at 214.

74. One could argue that there is a discriminatory tilt in this area in favor of men. Thus, male spouses with sterility problems are protected against unwanted parental responsibility by statutes requiring their written consent to the artificial insemination procedures, even though these requirements may make parenthood somewhat more difficult for women whose husbands are sterile. See supra notes 66, 67. Similarly, male donors who wish to sell their sperm and avoid any further responsibility for children who are conceived are permitted to use contracts for those purposes, while women have not been permitted to contract for the use of their wombs and the sale of their ova. See supra notes 67, 68. However, these materials can also be understood as discriminating against sterile married men or men who are married to infertile women, for the decisions make siring and fathering children of their own difficult for these men. This reversed understanding of the discriminatory tilt of the deci-

sions is one of the reasons they would be interesting to add to a contracts casebook; the results in these cases cannot be explained by our traditional ideas of what women and men are like.

75. See supra notes 52–56 and accompanying text.

76. By sexualizing these materials through the selective use and organization of women's cases, the editors obstruct connections readers might usefully make between them. Cf. Dalton, An Essay in the Deconstruction of Contract Doctrine, 94 Yale L. J. 997, 999 (1985) (describing how doctrines constitute other doctrines generally understood to stand in opposition to or in conflict with them).

77. For an essay by a linguist discussing the relationship between language and gender formation, see McConnell-Ginet, Difference and Language: A Linguist's Perspective, in The Future of Difference, 157–66 (H. Eisenstein and A. Jardine eds. 1985).

78. Although I write as if readers in general will notice the observations elaborated here about women as authors and in the language of the casebook, typically only readers who are conscious of gender issues are likely to notice such things. I believe, however, that most readers are influenced by these gender-related factors.

79. U.C.C. § 1-102(5)(b) (1977), quoted in J. Dawson at 977.

80. See, e.g., Parker v. Twentieth Century Fox Film Corp., 3 Cal.3d 176, 474 P.2d 689, 89 Cal. Rptr. 737 (1970), excerpted in J. Dawson at 46, where the dissenting judge states that the general principle that "governs the obligations of an employee after *his* employer has wrongfully repudiated or terminated the employment contract ... requires *him* to make a reasonable effort to secure other employment. *He* is not obliged, however, to seek or accept any and all types of work which may be available." Id. at 185, 474 P.2d at 695, 89 Cal. Rptr. at 743, excerpted in J. Dawson at 46, 51 (emphasis added, footnote omitted).

81. See, e.g., Fuller and Perdue, The Reliance Interest in Contract Damages, 46 Yale L. J. 52, 56–57 (1936), quoted in J. Dawson at 4–5. In the reproduced portion of this influential description of the three purposes served by contract damages, promisors and promisees are consistently referred to as men. This passage is pivotal for readers, since it conceptually frames and organizes the lengthy materials on damages that follow.

82. Consider, for example, two passages placed relatively early in the book with the apparent intention of directing the readers' attention beyond the development of legal doctrine. Thus, in a portion of the stirring Holmes essay which includes the phrase, "If you want to know the law and nothing else, you must look at it as a bad man," the clear and personal voice of the justice speaks directly to readers who want to know the law, but he speaks to the readers quite specifically as men. Holmes, The Path of the Law in Collected Legal Papers 168–76 (1920), quoted in

J. Dawson at 30–33. Similarly, later in the book, having advised readers that they should know something about judicial style, the editors reproduce several paragraphs from The Bramble Bush, where Karl Llewellyn links clarity, consistency, craft, knowledge, beauty, and vision with the needs and aspirations of "a man," "a man," and "a man." K. Llewellyn, The Bramble Bush 157–58 (1951), quoted in J. Dawson at 110–11. Like the passage by Holmes, this piece reaches directly to readers with ambitious goals for themselves, but one knows from the many references to men that the readers Llewelyn addresses here are decidedly not women.

83. J. Dawson, at 98 (contract between "*s*" and "*b*"); id. at 133 (dealings between "vendor" and "vendee"); id. at 227 (contract between "seller" and "buyer"); id. at 304 (claims of "*a*" and "*b*"); id. at 353 (bids of "sub" and "general"); id. at 365 (negotiations between "offeror" and "offeree," "*v*" and "*p*"); id. at 640 (sale of land by "*s*" to "*b*"); id. at 855 (conveyance from "vendor" to "vendee").

84. J. Dawson at 284–85 (referring to purchaser attempting to buy fur coat, supermarket purchaser, medical school applicant, homeowner, and auctioneer by male pronouns).

85. In addition to the nine problems Dawson, Harvey and Henderson have written for the casebook, they have also included a much larger number of shorter "questions" which are dispersed throughout the book. Like the problems, the questions do not use feminine names or pronouns to refer to persons generically. However, a few questions which refer to cases involving women do use feminine pronouns to refer to those parties (e.g., id. at 125, 233, 918). Indeed, one of the few examples of blatant sexism I have found in the book involves one such question. Immediately following the note case of Ricketts v. Scothorn, 57 Neb. 51, 77 N.W. 365 (1898), excerpted in J. Dawson at 193, the editors challenge that court's use of equitable estoppel in a case in which a granddaughter is suing her grandfather's estate to enforce his promise to give her money so that she could stop working. Although the granddaughter had returned to work after a year, and the court found that in her year of not working she had "altered her position for the worse on the note being paid in full," Dawson, Harvey, and Henderson ask "Was Katie's position altered very much 'for the worse'?" (id. at 193). I doubt they would have asked such a question if Katie had been a male grandchild, for whom work would have been understood as important for his feelings of self-respect. Indeed, I also doubt that the court or Dawson, Harvey, and Henderson would have referred to a male grandchild by his first name.

86. Dawson, Harvey, and Henderson state in their preface that in addition to "substantive knowledge and analytical skills," their book aspires to pass on "a language and a culture" (id. at xvii).

87. In fact at least several cases in the casebook were written by women. See, e.g., Sheets v. Teddy's Frosted Foods, 179 Conn. 471, 427 A.2d 385

(1980) (Ellen Peters, J.), excerpted in J. Dawson at 254; Bleecher v. Conte, 29 Cal. 3d 345, 626 P.2d 1051, 173 Cal. Rptr. 278 (1981) (Rose Bird, C.J.), J. Dawson at 660.

88. See, e.g., J. Dawson at 4 (discussing work of "Lon" Fuller); id. at 40 (discussing rebellion against chancery led by "Sir Edward" Coke).

89. See J. Dawson at 589 (reference to Kronman, Mistake, Disclosure, Information, and the Law of Contracts, 7 J. Legal Studies 1 [1978]).

90. Id. at 31 (illustration of Oliver Wendell Holmes, Jr.); id. at 772 (illustration of Earl of Mansfield); id. at 709 (photograph of Arthur Corbin); id. at 459 (photograph of Karl Llewellyn); id. at 195 (illustration of Benjamin Cardozo); id. at 344 (Photograph of Judge Learned Hand).

91. One feminist commentator has described the psychological differences between men and women by making a similar point about the basis for male self-confidence:

> All oppressed people must be controlled. Since open force and economic coercion are practical only part of the time, ideology—that is, internalized oppression, the voice in the head—is brought in to fill the gap. . . . Vast numbers of men can be allowed to experience some power as long as they expend their power against other men and against women. . . .
> The Masculine Imperative means that men avoid the threat of failure, inadequacy, and powerlessness—omnipresent in a society built on competition and private property—by existing against others. But the Feminine Imperative allows of no self-help at all. We exist *for* others. (J. Russ, supra note 1, at 44).

92. See supra note 73 and accompanying text.

93. For example, Lon Fuller's use of remedies at the beginning of his casebook is frequently cited as an example of the use of casebook organization to affect readers' views regarding legal formalism. See Klare, Contracts Jurisprudence and the First-Year Casebook (Book Review), 54 N.Y.U. L. Rev. 876, 882–84 (1979) (reviewing C. Knapp, supra note 39).

94. There are at least a half dozen times in *Dawson, Harvey, and Henderson* where a woman's case is paired with a contradictory case involving a man. Compare Parker v. Twentieth Century Fox Film Corp., 3 Cal.3d 176, 474 P.2d 689, 89 Cal. Rptr. 737 (1970), excerpted in J. Dawson at 46 (restrictive application of general mitigation rule in case involving female employee) with Rockingham County v. Luten Bridge Co., 35 F.2d 301 (4th Cir. 1929), excerpted in J. Dawson at 41 (broad application of mitigation rule in case involving a male contractor); compare Brackenbury v. Hodgkin, 116 Me. 399, 102 A. 106 (1917), excerpted in J. Dawson at 331 (applying rule that offeror may not terminate offer for unilateral contract after performance begun in case involving female offeror) with Petterson v. Pattberg, 248 N.Y. 86, 161 N.E. 428 (1928), excerpted in J. Dawson at 323 (applying rule that offeror may terminate unilateral contract after performance begins in case involving male parties).

95. 84 N.H. 114, 146 A. 641 (1929), excerpted in J. Dawson at 1.

96. The *Restatement (Second) of Contracts* indicates that expectation is the primary standard for measuring contract damages. Restatement (Second) of Contracts § 347 (1979). The expectation measure, which gives an injured party damages measured by the value of the performance he or she was promised, is frequently contrasted with the reliance measure. The expectation measure puts an injured party where she would have been but for the breach, whereas the reliance measure puts an injured party where she would have been but for the contract. See generally, Fuller and Perdue, supra note 81, at 54, quoted in J. Dawson at 5.

97. The court concludes that the appropriate measure should be "the difference between the value . . . of a perfect hand . . . and the value of the hand in its present condition." Hawkins v. McGee, 84 N.H. 114, 117, 146 A. 641, 644 (1929), excerpted in J. Dawson at 1, 3.

98. The excerpt from Fuller's article on reliance damages includes his critique that there is less justification for the use of the expectation measure than the reliance or restitution measure. Fuller and Perdue, supra note 81, at 56–57, quoted in J. Dawson at 5.

99. Sullivan v. O'Connor, 363 Mass. 579, 586–89, 296 N.E.2d 183, 188–90 (1973), excerpted in J. Dawson at 5, 6.

100. Id. at 579–80, 296 N.E.2d at 184, excerpted in J. Dawson at 5.

101. See generally, L. Gilbert and P. Webster, Bound by Love: The Sweet Trap of Daughterhood 1–19 (1982).

102. Parker v. Twentieth Century Fox Film Corp., 3 Cal.3d 176, 474 P.2d 689, 89 Cal. Rptr. 737 (1970), excerpted in J. Dawson at 46. In fact there are two cases that involve women among the eighteen that precede the equitable remedies section, but readers may overlook the presence of a woman in De Leon v. Aldrete, 398 S.W.2d 160 (Tex. Civ. App. 1965), excerpted in J. Dawson at 114. Although the editors state in an opening note that the defendants are husband and wife, the court refers to the DeLeons throughout the opinion as "the defendants," thereby disguising their sex for the remainder of the opinion.

103. The three cases involving women are: Fitzpatrick v. Michael, 177 Md. 248, 9 A.2d 639 (1939), excerpted in J. Dawson at 128; Gartrell v. Stafford, 12 Neb. 545, 11 N.W. 732 (1882), excerpted in J. Dawson at 118; and Timko v. Useful Homes Corp., 114 N.J. Eq. 433, 168 A. 824 (1933), excerpted in J. Dawson at 123.

104. *Cf.* Restatement (Second) of Contracts §§ 347, 359(1) (1979). Section 359(1) provides: "(1) Specific performance or an injunction will not be ordered if damages would be adequate to protect the expectation interest of the injured party" (Id.). See also supra notes 111–16 and accompanying text.

105. See supra notes 98, 104.

106. See supra notes 77–85 and accompanying text.

107. See supra notes 86–91 and accompanying text.

108. See supra notes 6–37 and accompanying text.

109. See supra notes 47–50 and accompanying text.

110. Mills v. Wyman, 20 Mass. (3 Pick.) 207, 207 (1825), excerpted in J. Dawson at 181.

111. See supra notes 67–72 and accompanying text.

112. Britton v. Turner, 6 N.H. 481, 482 (1834), excerpted in J. Dawson at 104.

113. Hamer v. Sidway, 124 N.Y. 538, 540, 2 N.E. 256, 256 (1891), excerpted in J. Dawson at 156.

114. Fera v. Village Plaza, Inc., 396 Mich. 639, 646–47, 242 N.W.2d 372, 375–76 (1976), excerpted in J. Dawson at 76, 80.

115. Hoffman v. Red Owl, 26 Wis. 2d 683, 133 N.W.2d 267 (1965), excerpted in J. Dawson at 355.

116. Brackenbury v. Hodgkin, 116 Me. 399, 102 A. 106 (1917), excerpted in J. Dawson at 331.

117. Id.

118. Sheets v. Teddy's Frosted Foods, 179 Conn. 471, 427 A.2d 385 (1980), excerpted in J. Dawson at 254.

119. Boone v. Coe, 153 Ky. 233, 154 S.W. 900 (1913), excerpted in J. Dawson at 92.

120. Webb v. McGowin, 27 Ala. App. 82, 168 So. 196 (1935), cert. denied, 232 Ala. 374, 168 So. 199 (1936), excerpted in J. Dawson at 185.

121. See Chodorow, Gender, Relation, and Difference in Psychoanalytic Perspective, in The Future of Difference 3–19 (H. Eisenstein and A. Jardine eds. 1985) for an account of the construction of gender differences based on psychoanalytic, social, and cultural factors.

122. Although the attributions I have made accurately reflect how I think many people would characterize the sexes, I also believe that people attribute qualities to the sexes in a relational way. That is, when women exhibit the traits generally ascribed to men, we tend to think of these traits in comparison to opposing, differently formulated traits linked to men. We make the same comparative adjustments when men exhibit "feminine" characteristics. However, because of men's traditional dominance over women, the traits which were positive when they were linked with men may seem negative when they are attributed to women. Thus, women may be described as scheming, cold, selfish, and manipulative, when they appear intellectual, detached, autonomous, and in control, while men may be described as uninhibited, loyal, considerate, and easy-going, when they seem emotional, attached, compassionate, and spontaneous.

123. As long as we continue to identify characteristics by one sex or the

other, the only barrier to fully genderizing all our artifacts is whatever limits our imaginations impose on our willingness to personify things. My sturdy, dependable, capacious, cyclical washing machine is certainly an "old girl," rather than an "old boy" to me, while the computer on which I am composing these words is so logical and self-contained that I could never think of it as female. If I were able to anthropomorphize it at all, it would be male.

124. J. Dawson at 1–143.

125. See, e.g., L. Fuller and M. Eisenberg, Basic Contract Law (4th ed. 1981); C. Knapp, supra note 39; F. Kessler, supra note 72; A. Mueller, A. Rosett, and G. Lopez, Contract Law and Its Application (3d ed. 1983).

126. See Klare, supra note 93, at 882.

127. This form of organization probably seems natural because it is "chronological." See Klare, supra note 93, at 878. It also seems natural to students, however, because many contract study aids and contract treatises are organized chronologically. See, e.g., J. Calamari and J. Perillo, The Law of Contracts (2d ed. 1977); M. Eisenberg, Gilbert Law Summaries: Contracts (11th ed. 1984); S. Emanuel and S. Knowles, Emanuel Law Outlines: Contracts (2d ed. 1984); E. A. Farnsworth, Contracts (1982); G. Schaber and C. Rohwes, Contracts in a Nutshell (2d ed. 1984); Restatement (Second) of Contracts (1979); cf. Legalines: Contracts (R. Meslar ed. 1983) (adaptable to courses utilizing materials by Dawson).

128. Examples of the categories into which the editors divide the casebook are "Grounds for Enforcing Promises" and "The Consensual Basis of Obligation." See J. Dawson at xix (summary of Table of Contents).

129. My claim here should be familiar, in that the impersonality of legal study has been described and criticized elsewhere. See, e.g., J. Noonan, Jr., Persons and Masks of the Law vii–xii, 3–28 (1976). See also G. Frug, The Ideology of Bureaucracy in American Law, 97 Harv. L. Rev. 1276, 1293–95 (1984); Gabel, Intention and Structure in Contractual Conditions: Outline of a Method for Critical Legal Theory, 61 Minn. L. Rev. 601 (1977); Gabel, Book Review, 91 Harv. L. Rev. 302 (1977) (reviewing R. Dworkin, Taking Rights Seriously [1977]). What is different about my assertion, however, is the contention that impersonality seems male to gender-conscious readers.

130. See supra note 94 and accompanying text.

131. See, e.g., C. Knapp, supra note 39; T. Morgan and R. Rotunda, Problems and Materials on Professional Responsibility (2d ed. 1981); E. Rabin, Fundamentals of Modern Real Property Law (2d ed. 1982).

132. The illustrations that arguably are useful to the way readers understand the book accompany Rockingham County v. Luten Bridge Co., 35 F.2d 301 (4th Cir. 1929), excerpted in J. Dawson at 41; and Mitchill v. Lath, 247 N.Y. 377, 160 N.E. 646 (1928), excerpted in J. Dawson at 426. The

Luten Bridge illustration shows the photograph of a bridge, (id. at 43) that a construction company continued to build after county commissioners rescinded the contract for its construction and discontinued work on the connecting surface roads. Because the bridge looks quite substantial and unoccupied in the picture, it may reinforce the arguments in the decision regarding the value of mitigating damages. The Mitchill photographs (id. at 427, 430) show an elaborate summer house and the plain wooden ice house that blocked its view. The summer house purchaser claimed that the seller had agreed to tear the ice house down. The photograph of the buildings may help readers determine whether the parties were likely to have included such an agreement in the contract for sale of the house. I think I may be giving the editors the benefit of the doubt on the Mitchill photos, however, since they do not affect my own views of the case.

133. At best the illustrations may help readers remember the cases they accompany. At worst, perhaps inadvertently, they convey information to readers about the hierarchy of the legal profession. Thus, the illustrations of four celebrities, mentioned supra note 48, could suggest that only famous clients are sufficiently interesting to warrant illustrations, and most lawyers won't have the opportunity to represent such people. The six imposing photographs of legal heroes, mentioned supra note 90, are a visible reminder that women and minorities do not yet have a significant presence in the profession. The full-page picture of a cow that accompanies Sherwood v. Walker, 66 Mich. 568, 33 N.W. 919 (1887) (overruled in Lenawee Co. Bd. of Health v. Messerly, 417 Mich. 17, 331 N.W.2d 203 [1982], excerpted in J. Dawson at 561, 568), amusingly labeled "Black Angus in Pensive Mood," seems like an exception to the mulish, humorless charge of abstraction I have developed against the illustrations. The Black Angus seems to be the editors' joke on their own illustrations. Why is this in here except to make us laugh?

134. See supra notes 77–85 and accompanying text.

135. The editors' preface states:

> We point again to the attention given remedies for breach of contract—still at center stage but now even nearer the footlights. . . . Because contract is as much a social and economic concept as it is a set of rights and duties, we continue to believe that contract law is best understood, in function and societal impact, if it is approached through a remedy-centered study. The underlying purposes of contract law (what it seeks to do, and how it goes about doing it) are revealed most clearly when problems are looked at from the perspective of taking care of harms or losses, or gains held unjustly. (J. Dawson at xvii).

I maintain that this oblique discussion provides little information to readers regarding the editors' theory of rules or contract doctrine. Cf. F. Kessler, supra note 72, at 1–15 (casebook introduction discussing relationship between casebook organization and editors' theory of social function of contract).

136. See generally, J. Dawson at xix (summary of Table of Contents).

137. See, e.g., id. at 54, 67, 74 (posing questions changing facts of preceding cases), and id. at 242 (asking how plaintiff in preceding case would have fared under U.C.C.).

138. See id. at 37–41 (discussing history of equity); id. at 99–103 (discussing history of common counts and restitution).

139. See id. (discussing historical merger of law and equity).

140. See id. at 6–8 (commenting on controls over jury verdicts).

141. See, e.g., id. at 146–50 (commenting on legal formalities as introduction to chapter on consideration).

142. See, e.g., id. at 6–8 (commenting on controls over jury verdicts).

143. See Dawson, Economic Duress—An Essay in Perspective, 45 Mich. L. Rev. 253, 254 (1947). See generally, G. White, Patterns of American Legal Thought 116–32, 136–44 (1978) (describing development of Realist movement).

144. Llewellyn's excerpt on judicial style is an exception to this statement. The excerpt, however, is quite slight. J. Dawson at 110–11 (excerpting K. Llewellyn, supra note 82, at 157–58).

145. Kessler and Gilmore's casebook gives readers some sense of intellectual legal history by their extensive introduction, "Contract as a Principle of Order," and by their chapter and section titles, which indicate the relationship between the cases and moral, social, and political themes. F. Kessler, supra note 72, at 1–15. (Titles include such headings as "From Status to Contract," "Formalism in Our Law of Contracts," and "Mistake: Security of Transactions and the Objective Theory of Contracts.")

146. There are a few, very narrow exceptions to this assertion. See, e.g., J. Dawson at 56 (giving brief, apolitical description of price fixing and union organizing efforts during time of fluctuating coal prices, referred to in Missouri Furnace Co. v. Cochran, 8 F. 463 [W.D. Pa. 1881], excerpted in J. Dawson at 54); J. Dawson at 167–68 (noting starvation conditions in Greece after Nazi occupation, as historical setting for Batsakis v. Demotsis, 236 S.W.2d 673 [Tex. Civ. App. 1949], excerpted in J. Dawson at 165).

147. Cf. M. Horwitz, The Transformation of American Law, 1780–1860 (1977).

148. See, e.g., J. Dawson at 249–54 (description of congressional attempts to regulate automobile manufacturers' franchise transactions with dealers, following two cases involving claims of unjust termination of franchises, Bushwick-Decatur Motors, Inc. v. Ford Motor Co., 116 F.2d 675 [2d Cir. 1940], excerpted in J. Dawson at 243; and Corenswet, Inc. v. Amana Refrigeration, Inc., 594 F.2d 129 [5th Cir. 1979], excerpted in J. Dawson at 247). See also id. at 352–53 (comment on firm offer that

praises construction industry practices regarding revocability of sub-contractors' bids, following three cases in which issue was litigated, James Baird Co. v. Gimbel Bros., Inc., 64 F.2d 344 [2d Cir. 1933], excerpted in J. Dawson at 342; Drennan v. Star Paving Co., 51 Cal. 2d 409, 333 P.2d 757 [1958], excerpted in J. Dawson at 346; E. A. Coronis Associates v. M. Gordon Construction Co., 90 N.J. Super. 69, 216 A.2d 246 [1966], excerpted in J. Dawson at 350).

149. See, e.g., Forrer v. Sears, Roebuck & Co., 36 Wis. 2d 388, 153 N.W.2d 587 (1967), excerpted in J. Dawson at 214; Goodman v. Dicker, 169 F.2d 684 (D.C. Cir. 1948), excerpted in J. Dawson at 217; Sheets v. Teddy's Frosted Foods, Inc., 179 Conn. 471, 427 A.2d 385 (1980), excerpted in J. Dawson at 254.

150. See generally, Note, Protecting Employees at Will Against Wrongful Discharge: The Public Policy Exception, 96 Harv. L. Rev. 1931, 1931 n. 3 (1983) (citing extensive commentary on unfair employees' discharge that was available before casebook's fourth edition was published).

151. See supra note 73 and accompanying text. See also, Olsen, The Sex of Law (1985) (unpublished paper).

6
Challenging the Gender of Two Contract Decisions

1. 3 Cal. 3d 176, 474 P.2d 689, 89 Cal. Rptr. 737 (1970), excerpted in J. Dawson, W. Harvey, and S. Henderson, Cases and Comment on Contracts 46 (4th ed. 1982) (hereinafter cited as J. Dawson).

2. J. Dawson at 46 n. *. MacLaine won an academy award in 1984 for her role in the film *Terms of Endearment*.

3. In Rockingham County v. Luten Bridge Co., 35 F.2d 301 (4th Cir. 1929), excerpted in J. Dawson at 41, a contractor was denied his claim for the full contract price of an agreement to build a bridge. The plaintiff had completed the bridge after the defendant had repudiated the contract (id. at 303, excerpted in J. Dawson at 41, 42).

4. J. Dawson at 49 (emphasis added). The Restatement of Contracts chooses different wording, stating that "damages are not recoverable for loss that the injured party could have avoided without undue risk, burden or humiliation" (Restatement (Second) of Contracts § 350[1] [1979]).

5. In offering MacLaine *Big Country*, the studio asserted there was insufficient time to negotiate with her regarding choice of director and regarding the screenplay. The studio reminded her that she had "already expressed an interest in . . . 'Big Country, Big Man,' " and although she could not have the same approval rights she would have had in *Bloomer Girl* the studio did promise to consult with her regarding the choice of director for photoplay and regarding screenplay revisions (Parker v. Twentieth Century Fox Film Corp., 3 Cal. 3d 176, 180 n. 2, 474 P.2d 689,

691 n. 2, 89 Cal. Rptr. 737, 739 n. 2 [1970], excerpted in J. Dawson at 46, 47–48 n. 2).

6. Id., at 183–84, 474 P.2d at 693–94, 89 Cal. Rptr. at 741–42, excerpted in J. Dawson at 46, 50.

7. Id. at 188, 474 P.2d at 697, 89 Cal. Rptr. at 745 (Sullivan, Acting C.J., dissenting), excerpted in J. Dawson at 46, 52–53.

8. *Springtime for Hitler* was the musical comedy created within the film *The Producers* solely for the purpose of obtaining a financial loss for its originators. The producers designed the musical hoping it would be a commercial disaster. See N.Y. Times, Mar. 19, 1968, at 38, col. 1 (reviewing *The Producers*).

9. See Fatout, Amelia Bloomer and Bloomerism, 36 The New York Hist. Society Q. 361, 365 (1952). For recent histories of other prominent feminists that contain references to Amelia Bloomer, see L. Banner, Elizabeth Cady Stanton, a Radical for Women's Rights 35 (1980); E. Griffith, In Her Own Right: The Life of Elizabeth Cady Stanton 63–64 (1984); and E. DuBois, eds., Elizabeth Cady Stanton, Susan B. Anthony, Correspondence, Writings, Speeches 15 (1981).

10. Although the actress's decision to reject *Big Country, Big Man* may not have been politically motivated, feminists who read the case now may identify MacLaine as a feminist and they are likely to assume that her decision more than twenty years ago was politically motivated. MacLaine has written about her longstanding political activism, as well as her other interests, in several bestselling autobiographical books. See, e.g., S. MacLaine, Out on a Limb (1983); and S. MacLaine, You Can Get There from Here (1975). MacLaine has been a Civil Rights activist, a vigorous opponent of the Vietnam War, and a delegate to the Democratic National Convention. See J. Spada, Shirley and Warren 210 (1985). In 1984, when she received an honorary degree from Hunter College, she was praised for her "support of those who champion the victims of discrimination, particularly women" (id.).

11. Indeed, while the spirited campaign for bloomers was ultimately unsuccessful in reforming women's dress of the period, it contained themes familiar to modern feminists—bloomer advocates sought to free themselves from the confines of fashion constraints which they blamed men for imposing on them. Cf. S. Brownmiller, Femininity 77–102 (1984); K. Chernin, The Obsession: Reflections on the Tyranny of Slenderness (1981); Note, Gender-Specific Clothing Regulation: A Study in Patriarchy, 5 Harv. Women's L. J. 73 (1982).

12. It turns out that *Bloomer Girl* did have feminist themes, as Charles Knapp has pointed out in his contracts casebook. C. Knapp, Problems in Contract Law: Cases and Materials 1118 (1976). My own intuitions about *Bloomer Girl* were confirmed by reading John Gregory Dunn's review of a book by "Danny Santiago" in the *New York Review of Books* last year. Dunne, The Secret of Danny Santiago (Book Review), 31 N.Y. Rev. of

Books 17 (Aug 16, 1984) (reviewing D. Santiago, Famous all over Town [1984]). "Danny Santiago" was revealed in that review to be the *nom de plume* of Dan James, a Hollywood writer who was blacklisted during the fifties because of his past membership in the Communist party. Dunne mentioned that the Broadway musical *Bloomer Girl* was based on a play that James and his wife Lilith coauthored. The inspiration for the James' play stemmed from "a Party-endorsed workshop on women's rights" (id. at 20). Professor Stewart Macaulay, of the University of Wisconsin, who has extensively researched the production and reception of the Broadway *Bloomer Girl*, has kindly shared with me some of the fascinating details he has found about the Broadway play. A major character in the play was based on Amelia Bloomer, who is portrayed as having a brother who manufactures hoop skirts. One of his daughters refuses to marry a hoop salesman, as her five sisters have done before her, and joins her aunt in abolition activities. In the song "It was Good Enough for Grandma," lyricist E. Y. Harburg dashes off several bitingly feminist stanzas, including the verses:

> When Grandma was a lassie,
> That tyrant known as man
> Thought a woman's place
> Was just the space
> Around a frying pan. . . .
>
> We won the revolution
> In seventeen-seventy-six . . .
> Who says it's nix
> For us to mix
> Our sex with politics!
> We've bigger seas to swim in
> And bigger worlds to slice.
> Oh, Sisters, are we women
> Or mice?

L. Engel, Their Words Are Music 75 (1975). Descriptions of *Bloomer Girl* can be found in A. Laufe, Broadway's Greatest Musicals 77–79 (1970), and D. Ewen, New Complete Book of the American Musical Theater 11–12 (1958).

13. The court in *Parker* states that *Big Country* was a "'western type' story taking place in an opal mine in Australia." Parker v. Twentieth Century Fox Film Corp., 3 Cal.3d 176, 183, 474 P.2d 689, 693–94, 89 Cal. Rptr. 737, 741–42 (1970), excerpted in J. Dawson at 46, 50. Marlene Lasky, library assistant with the Academy of Motion Picture Arts and Sciences, stated in a telephone interview that although Sean Connery and Diane Cilento were signed to play the lead roles, the movie was probably never made. Telephone interview with Marlene Lasky, Library Assistant, Academy of Motion Picture Arts and Sciences (July 22, 1985). Ms. Lasky thinks the film was about the settlement of Australia.

14. These readers might also be able to find support for their views in other

language of the majority opinion. By describing the Big Man role as a *"female* lead as a dramatic actress in a western style motion picture," the majority may be indicating their awareness that women are traditionally given subordinate roles in western films. Parker v. Twentieth Century Fox Film Corp., 3 Cal.3d 176, 184, 474 P.2d 689, 694, 89 Cal. Rptr. 737, 742 (1970), excerpted in J. Dawson at 46, 50 (emphasis added). In contrast, the dissent describes the *Big Country, Big Man* role as "the leading female role in a dramatic motion picture." Id. at 189, 474 P.2d at 697, 89 Cal. Rptr. at 745, excerpted in J. Dawson at 46, 52. By not referring to the "dramatic motion picture" as a "western," the dissent seems insensitive to the issue of female subordination in westerns, thus suggesting that attitudes toward the importance of sex roles may explain the silent rationale of the majority opinion, as well as the distinctions between the two opinions in the case (id.).

15. Well before the fourth edition of *Dawson, Harvey, and Henderson* was published in 1982, Charles Knapp informed his readers that MacLaine had been connected to feminist causes and that one of the characters in *Bloomer Girl* was "Amelia Jenks ('Dolly') Bloomer . . . a leading advocate of women's rights in the United States during the nineteenth century" (C. Knapp, supra note 12, at 1118 n. 1). It is hard to believe that Dawson, Harvey, and Henderson were unaware of this casebook scholarship.

16. See Homans, "Her Very Own Howl": The Ambiguities of Representation in Recent Women's Fiction, 9 Signs 186 (1983) (describing views of French and American feminist literary critics regarding relationship between women's experiences and their interpretations and use of language).

17. J. Dawson. The illustration is a photograph of the widely reproduced Charles Hopkinson portrait which hangs in the Harvard Law School.

18. In addition to the negative pedagogical consequences of the editors' treatment of *Parker*, the choice and organization of the first three illustrations in the casebook are likely to diminish the general confidence of some feminist readers in the casebook. Insofar as the photograph of MacLaine signals such readers that the editors are insensitive to the opposition many harbor to the sexual subjugation of women, these readers may be on guard after reading the decision in *Parker* against what they understand as the editors' implicit misogyny. Think of how differently these readers might view the casebook if Shirley MacLaine were pictured making a campaign appearance for George McGovern, or if she were shown smoking a big cigar after a theater triumph. See, e.g., J. Spada, supra note 10, at 150, 164 (1985). Adding either of these photographs would be a plausible way for Dawson, Harvey, and Henderson to preserve the charm that illustrations give their casebook while eliminating the negative effect of the first three illustrations on a portion of their readers. The two illustrations accompanying Chicago Coliseum Club v. Dempsey, 265 Ill. App. 542 (1932), excerpted in J. Dawson at 81,

the case involving Jack Dempsey's breach of contract to fight Harry Wills, suggest to me that the editors may be sensitive to the power of some of their illustrations (J. Dawson at 82, 87). The first Dempsey illustration shows Dempsey fighting Gene Tunney, and the second shows Dempsey shaking hands with Wills, a black fighter (id.). Since the opinion is silent about the race of the parties, the additional photograph may alert readers to the question of whether race may have been a factor in Dempsey's breach of contract or in the court's decision (id. at 87).

19. As the dissenting judge in *Parker* states, the basic mitigation rule "embodies notions of fairness and *socially responsible* behavior which are fundamental to our jurisprudence . . . it is a rule requiring reasonable conduct in commercial affairs" (Parker v. Twentieth Century Fox Film Corp., 3 Cal. 3d 176, 183, 474 P.2d 689, 694, 89 Cal. Rptr. 737, 742 [1970] [Sullivan, Acting C.J., dissenting], excerpted in J. Dawson at 46, 50). The basic rule "minimizes the *unnecessary personal and social (e.g., nonproductive use of labor, litigation) costs* of contractual failure" (id. at 186 n. 5, 474 P.2d at 693 n. 5, 89 Cal. Rptr. at 744 n.5, excerpted in J. Dawson at 46, 52 n. 3 [emphasis added]).

20. Indeed, some readers may think the decision in *Parker* is irrational because the sex of the victorious plaintiff is inconsistent with the gender of the legal rationale supporting the decision, while other readers will be pleased that the decision reverses the usual assumption that men's problems will be resolved with "male" rules and women's with "female" rules. The kind of analysis of the sexualization of law presented here is developed in Fran Olsen's paper "The Sex of Law" (1985) (unpublished paper). While asserting that dualization occurs, Olsen also criticizes this process, arguing that each pole of a duality is constitutive of the other, rather than separate and different from the other. See generally, Kennedy, Form and Substance in Private Law Adjudication, 89 Harv. L. Rev. 1685 (1976) (describing fundamental conflict between individualism and altruism in common law and in political and economic discourse).

21. Parker v. Twentieth Century Fox Film Corp., 3 Cal.3d 176, 186–89, 474 P.2d 689, 696–97, 89 Cal. Rptr. 737, 744–45 (1970), excerpted in J. Dawson at 46, 52.

22. See chapter 5.

23. See, e.g., R. Scholes, Uncoding Mama: The Female Body as Text, in Semiotics and Interpretation 127 (1982) (describing restrictions on female sexuality achieved through particular forms of discourse); see also Vance, Pleasure and Danger: Toward a Politics of Sexuality, in Pleasure and Danger, Exploring Female Sexuality 1–29 (C. Vance ed. 1984) (describing relationship between "good" female behavior and protection against male violence).

24. Readers might also disparage the value of a male actor's work, but that attitude too would probably be affected by the gender-related notion that a *real* man wouldn't do that kind of work.

25. A footnote in the dissenting opinion, which informs readers that the mitigation rule "may have had its origin in the bourgeois fear of resubmergence in lower economic classes," may influence readers to adopt the kind of class bias analysis suggested here as an explanation for MacLaine's victory in the case. Parker v. Twentieth Century Fox Film Corp., 3 Cal.3d 176, 185 n. 2, 474 P.2d 689, 695 n. 2, 89 Cal. Rptr. 737, 743 n.2 (1970) (Sullivan, Acting C.J., dissenting), excerpted in J. Dawson at 46, 51 n. 2.

26. See chapter 5, notes 51–56 and accompanying text.

27. See chapter 5, notes 42–45 and accompanying text.

28. 351 So. 2d 344 (Fla. 1977), excerpted in J. Dawson at 448.

29. The other four major cases in the unit are Woodburn v. Northwestern Bell Telephone Co., 275 N.W.2d 403 (Iowa 1979), excerpted in J. Dawson at 476; Ellsworth Dobbs, Inc. v. Johnson, 50 N.J. 528, 236 A.2d 843 (1967), excerpted in J. Dawson at 469; Henningsen v. Bloomfield Motors, Inc., 32 N.J. 358, 161 A.2d 69 (1960), excerpted in J. Dawson at 461; Weisz v. Parke-Bernet Galleries, Inc., 67 Misc. 2d 1077, 325 N.Y.S.2d 576 (N.Y. Civ. Ct. 1971), rev'd, 77 Misc. 2d 80, 351 N.Y.S.2d 911 (N.Y. App. Term. 1974), excerpted in J. Dawson at 453.

30. In Weisz, Henningsen, and Ellsworth Dobbs, the challenged provisions were not enforced. Ellsworth Dobbs, Inc. v. Johnson, 50 N.J. 528, 236 A.2d 843, 858 (1967), excerpted in J. Dawson at 469, 474; Henningsen v. Bloomfield Motors, Inc., 32 N.J. 358, 408, 417, 461 A.2d 69, 97, 102 (1960), excerpted in J. Dawson at 461, 467; Weisz v. Parke-Bernet Galleries, Inc., 67 Misc. 2d 1077, 1082–84, 325 N.Y.S.2d 576, 582–83 (N.Y. Civ. Ct. 1971), rev'd, 77 Misc. 2d 80, 351 N.Y.S.2d 911 (N.Y. App. Term, 1974), excerpted in J. Dawson at 453. In *Woodburn* the case was remanded to determine if the plaintiff had an opportunity to see the restrictive provisions. Woodburn v. Northwestern Bell Tel. Co., 275 N.W.2d 403 (Iowa 1979), excerpted in J. Dawson at 476.

31. Although the decision reports that the jury at trial considered both mistake and assent in reaching its verdict for Mrs. Bratton, mistake is not discussed in the appellate opinion (Allied Van Lines, Inc. v. Bratton, 351 So.2d 344, 347–48 [Fla. 1977], excerpted in J. Dawson at 448, 451–52). This treatment of the enforceability issue is conventional. See Kessler, Contracts of Adhesion—Some Thoughts About Freedom of Contract, 43 Colum. L. Rev. 629, 630 (1943).

32. Allied Van Lines, Inc. v. Bratton, 351 So.2d 344, 346 (Fla. 1977), excerpted in J. Dawson at 448, 449.

33. Id.

34. Id. at 348, excerpted in J. Dawson at 448, 451.

35. The bill of lading reproduced in the decision provided:

    Unless the shipper expressly releases the shipment to a value of 60 cents per pound per article, the carrier's maximum liability for loss and damage shall be either the lump sum value declared by the shipper or an amount equal to $1.25 for each pound of weight in the shipment, whichever is greater. The shipment will move subject to the rules and conditions of the carrier's tariff. Shipper hereby releases the entire shipment to a value not exceeding. . . . Notice, the shipper signing this contract must insert in the space above, in his own handwriting either his declaration of the actual value of the shipment, or the words "60 cents per pound per article." Otherwise, the shipment will be deemed released to a maximum value equal to $1.25 times the weight of the shipment in pounds. (Id. at 346, excerpted in J. Dawson at 448, 448–49.)

36. Id. at 348, excerpted in J. Dawson at 448, 451.

37. Id.

38. "Mrs. McKnab's situation is different [from Mrs. Bratton's] . . . for she sought information [and] was misled by the carrier's agent as to available coverage" (id.). In addition, the court cites portions of the trial transcript in which Mrs. McKnab testified about her conversation with the agent in which she inquired about insurance (id. at 347 nn. 5–6, excerpted in J. Dawson at 448, 449–50 nn. 4–5).

39. Inequality of bargaining power is discussed in Ellsworth Dobbs, Inc. v. Johnson, 50 N.J. 528, 555–56, 236 A.2d 843, 857–58 (1967), excerpted in J. Dawson at 469, 473–74; Henningsen v. Bloomfield Motors, Inc., 32 N.J. 358, 389–91, 161 A.2d 69, 86–88 (1960), excerpted in J. Dawson at 461, 463–64; Weisz v. Parke-Bernet Galleries, Inc., 67 Misc. 2d 1077, 1081–82, 325 N.Y.S.2d 576, 581–82 (N.Y. Civ. Ct. 1971), rev'd, 77 Misc. 2d 80, 351 N.Y.S.2d 911 (N.Y. App. Term. 1974), excerpted in J. Dawson at 453, 456–57.

40. Recent feminist scholarship has addressed the distinctions between male and female notions of personhood. See e.g., N. Chodorow, The Reproduction of Mothering: Psychoanalysis and the Sociology of Gender (1978); C. Gilligan, In a Different Voice: Psychological Theory and Women's Development (1982). Feminist legal scholars are beginning to use this scholarship in their work. See, e.g., Dalton, Remarks on Personhood, AALS panel (Jan. 5, 1985) (unpublished manuscript on file with author); Salter, Extended Identity, A Feminist Intuition of Self/Other and Its Implications for Theories of Justice and Rights (1984) (unpublished manuscript on file with author).

41. Woodburn v. Northwestern Bell Telephone Co., 275 N.W.2d 403 (Iowa 1979), excerpted in J. Dawson at 476, is the only major case in the unit on standardized contracts in which a woman is not a party.

42. Recall that 39 of the 183 major cases in the casebook involve women parties, in contrast to 4 out of 5 in this unit. See chapter 5, notes 6–7 and accompanying text.

43. It is interesting to note that other contracts casebooks also begin standard form contract units with cases involving women. See, e.g., O'Callaghan v. Waller & Beckwith Realty Co., 15 Ill. 2d 436, 155 N.E.2d 545

(1958), excerpted in E. Farnsworth, Contracts 442 (1982); L'Estrange v. Graucob, Ltd., 2 K.B. 394 (1934), excerpted in F. Kessler and G. Gilmore, Contracts: Cases and Materials 1075 (2d ed. 1970).

44. The female Reader with a Chip on Her Shoulder, thinking, perhaps, in her paranoid mode, may be alerted to gender messages in the *Allied* decision by the quotation marks placed around the word "shipper" whenever it is used next to the names of the plaintiffs in the decision. While quotation marks could indicate someone else's words are being used, or while they might reflect the stylistic custom of using quotation marks to identify a person by his role, these plausible explanations for the use of quotation marks in *Allied* fail. There is nothing in the text to suggest the quotation marks note a quotation, and since the opinion writer does not use quotation marks when the word "carrier" is placed next to the defendant's name, it is unlikely that the quotation marks around the word "shipper" represent customary usage. Moreover, the diligent reader who looked beyond the text would learn that other cases involving householders which are cited in the opinion do not use quotation marks when referring to those parties as shippers. See Brannon v. Smith Dray Line & Storage Co., 456 F.2d 260 (6th Cir. 1972), noted in J. Dawson at 451–52; Chandler v. Aero Mayflower Transit Co., 374 F.2d 129 (4th Cir. 1967), noted in J. Dawson at 451. Thus, it is likely, at least for some readers, that the quotation marks function in *Allied* as a wink, conveying a message other than the ordinary meaning of the word they surround. While the judge's wink in *Allied* might simply indicate sympathy for the parties, some readers are likely to assume instead that the judge is communicating his view that since these shippers are women, and probably only housewives or widows, they are not shippers as someone in the public world understands the term. If the traditional readers who are undisposed to favor women notice the quotation marks, they will be assured that they are correct in their opinion that Mrs. Bratton, rather than the carrier or the court, is at fault in *Allied*.

45. Allied Van Lines, Inc. v. Bratton, 351 So.2d 344, 346 n. 3 (Fla. 1977), excerpted in J. Dawson at 448, 449 n. 2.

46. See generally, Rakoff, Contracts of Adhesion: An Essay in Reconstruction, 96 Harv. L. Rev. 1173 (1983) (expansive description and criticism of past and current presumption that standardized agreements are enforceable).

47. I am not referring here to the inequality of bargaining power argument which often surfaces in standardized agreement cases. See supra note 39 (referring to bargaining power); see also Kennedy, Distributive and Paternalist Motives in Contract and Tort Law, with Special Reference to Compulsory Terms and Unequal Bargaining Power, 41 Md. L. Rev. 563, 614–20 (1982) (criticizing inequality of bargaining power as an "appropriate" test for determining enforceability of compulsory terms).

48. The emphasis on knowledge occurs in the third subsection of section 211. Restatement (Second) of Contracts, § 211(3) (1979), reprinted in J. Dawson at 479.

    > Section 211. Standardized Agreements
    > (1) Except as stated in Subsection (3), where a party to an agreement signs or otherwise manifests assent to a writing and has reason to believe that like writings are regularly used to embody terms of agreements of the same type, he adopts the writing as an integrated agreement with respect to the terms included in the writing.
    > (2) Such a writing is interpreted whenever reasonable as treating alike all those similarly situated without regard to their knowledge or understanding of the standard terms of the writing.
    > (3) Where the other party has reason to believe that the party manifesting such assent would not do so if he knew that the writing contained a particular term, the term is not part of the agreement.

    Professor Rakoff argues that subsection three of the Restatement § 211 broadens traditional exceptions to the presumption that standardized agreements are enforceable (Rakoff, supra note 46, at 1190–91).

49. Other analyses of standardized contracts also raise the issue of power in such contracts. See, e.g., Kessler, supra note 31, at 640.

50. See generally, M. Foucault, Two Lectures, in Power/Knowledge (1980); see also G. Frug, The Language of Power (Book Review), 84 Colum. L. Rev. 1881 (1984) (reviewing B. Ackerman, Reconstructing American Law [1984]).

51. See supra notes 17–18 and accompanying text. While the photograph could be understood as an overtly sexist part of *Dawson, Harvey, and Henderson,* I believe that class discussions of the more subtle, gender-related aspects of the casebook, such as the stereotypical roles of the casebook parties, the silence regarding women judges, or the predominance of masculine pronouns in the opinions and in the editorial material, would receive the same mixed reception I project here for the discussion of material which some readers will construe as overtly sexist. There are, of course, a number of other strategies this book suggests that instructors could utilize in class in order to challenge the gendered stance of *Dawson, Harvey, and Henderson.* In addition to discussing some of the observations presented here, instructors could also add material to the casebook that would challenge the links the casebook makes between gender and the law. By adding material to the course of special interest to women, instructors could challenge the restricted idea that contracts courses are limited to traditionally "masculine" interests.

52. For example, my class discussions of Parker v. Twentieth Century Fox Film Corp., 3 Cal.3d 176, 474 P.2d 689, 89 Cal. Rptr. 737 (1970), excerpted in J. Dawson at 46; Allied Van Lines, Inc. v. Bratton, 351 So.2d 344 (Fla. 1977), excerpted in J. Dawson at 448; Crenshaw v. Williams, 191 Ky. 559, 231 S.W. 45 (1921), excerpted in J. Dawson at 25; and Fitzpatrick v. Michael, 177 Md. 248, 9 A.2d 639 (1939), excerpted in J. Dawson at

128, are influenced by this essay. In contrast, my discussions of Wood v. Lucy, Lady Duff-Gordon, 222 N.Y. 88, 118 N.E. 214 (1917), excerpted in J. Dawson at 231; and Jackson v. Seymour, 193 Va. 735, 71 S.E.2d 181 (1952), excerpted in J. Dawson at 170, tend not to be.

53. See Pickard, Experience as Teacher: Discovering the Politics of Law Teaching, 33 U. Toronto L. J. 279 (1983) (criticizing effect of such power and authority on students). See also D. Kennedy, Legal Education and the Reproduction of Hierarchy 58–65 (1983).

54. See chapter 5, notes 121–123 and accompanying text.

7
A Postmodern Feminist Analysis of Contract Law

1. Letter from W. David Slawson, Professor of Law, University of Southern California, to Mary Joe Frug, Professor of Law, New England School of Law 1–2 (June 24, 1988) (circulated to the members of Professor Slawson's advisory committee).

2. Id. at 2.

3. Id.

4. Jacques Derrida, Spurs: Nietzsche's Styles 71 (Barbara Harlow trans. 1978) (emphasis added).

5. Id. (emphasis added).

6. Richard A. Posner and Andrew M. Rosenfield, Impossibility and Related Doctrines in Contract Law: An Economic Analysis, 6 J. Legal Studies 83 (1977).

7. Robert A. Hillman, An Analysis of the Cessation of Contractual Relations, 68 Cornell L. Rev. 617 (1983).

8. Robert A. Hillman, Court Adjustment of Long-Term Contracts: An Analysis Under Modern Contract Law, 1987 Duke L. J. 1.

9. See Frances Olsen, The Sex of Law 1–2 (Dec. 14, 1988) (unpublished manuscript).

10. See chapter 5.

11. See, e.g., Jane Gallop, The Daughter's Seduction: Feminism and Psychoanalysis (1982) [hereinafter Gallop, Seduction]; Jane Gallop, Thinking Through the Body (1988) [hereinafter Gallop, Thinking]; Luce Irigaray, Speculum of the Other Woman (Gillian C. Gill trans. 1985); Luce Irigaray, This Sex Which is Not One (Catherine Porter trans. 1985) [hereinafter Irigaray, This Sex]; Barbara Johnson, The Critical Difference (1980); Barbara Johnson, A World of Difference (1987) [hereinafter Johnson, A World]; Julia Kristeva, Desire in Language: A Semiotic Approach to Literature and Art (Thomas Gora et al. trans. 1980); Julia Kristeva, The Kristeva Reader (Toril Moi ed. 1986) [hereinafter Kristeva, Reader].

12. See, e.g., Friedrich Kessler et al., Contracts: Cases & Materials 861–976

(1986) (discussing the "jurisprudential misfortune" of courts treating mistakes differently from impossibilities or frustrations); Hillman, supra note 7, at 617–18 (arguing that the various doctrines for cessation are treated similarly by the courts); Hillman, supra note 8, at 31 (arguing that court intervention should be standardized for certain "impracticable" circumstances); Posner and Rosenfield, supra note 6, at 85–86 (asserting that treating contract-discharging doctrines alike for purposes of analysis is most useful).

13. See generally Jacques Derrida, Differance, in Margins of Philosophy 1–27 (Alan Bass trans. 1982).

14. Posner and Rosenfield, supra note 6, at 100.

15. Id. at 90.

16. See id. at 90–92.

17. Id. at 100.

18. Id.

19. See id. at 102, 108.

20. See id. at 90.

21. See, e.g., id. at 98 (using the economically based discharge doctrine "to supply those contract terms that the parties would have adopted if they had negotiated expressly over them").

22. See, e.g., id. at 110 (comparing the breach/discharge dichotomy to the strict/no liability choice).

23. See Hillman, supra note 7, at 629–39.

24. See Ian R. Macneil, The New Social Contract: An Inquiry into Modern Contractual Relations 44–47 (1980).

25. See, e.g., Richard E. Speidel, Court-Imposed Price Adjustments Under Long-Term Supply Contracts, 76 Nw.U. L. Rev. 369, 370 (1981) (discussing the appropriateness of court-imposed adjustments of contract terms); Richard E. Speidel, Excusable Nonperformance in Sales Contexts: Some Thoughts About Risk Management, 32 S.C.L. Rev. 241, 270–71 (1980) (arguing that there is a role for court adjustment in impracticable circumstances).

26. See generally, Hillman, supra note 8, at 19–33 (describing the circumstances under which court adjustment may be appropriate).

27. See Carol Gilligan, In a Different Voice 18, 30, 62–63 (1982). For an analysis of Gilligan's influence in legal scholarship, see chapter 3.

28. See Posner and Rosenfield, supra note 6, at 86: "Since the typology is empty . . . [it] has led legal scholars to despair of generalizing fruitfully about the discharge problem."

29. See id. at 87–88: "thus far the insight has been a sterile one."

30. See id. at 88.

31. See Hillman, supra note 7, at 620.

32. See id. at 620–29 (discussing express and implied desires of contracting parties); id. at 629–42 (describing a model of "fairness in contract cessation").

33. See id. at 620: "In the conclusion, I present some brief observations based on the survey in Part II." See also id. at 617: "My first goal is to demonstrate that the courts generally have taken a common approach to the issue of cessation."

34. See id. at 627 (discussing, under the subheading "Gaps," failures of certain contracts to "consider and plan for contingencies that will arise").

35. See Gallop, Thinking, supra note 11.

36. Johnson, A World, supra note 11, at 15.

37. See Posner and Rosenfield, supra note 6, at 110–11.

38. Id. at 110.

39. See id.

40. See Hillman, supra note 7, at 659.

41. Letter from John Keats to George and Tom Keats (Dec. 22, 1818), in 1 The Letters of John Keats: 1814–1821, at 193 (Hyder Edward Rollins ed. 1958).

42. See Hillman, supra note 7, at 618–19: "My second goal is to explain the common approach to cessation. . . . Four interrelated fairness norms figure prominently in such analysis."

43. Id. at 626.

44. Id. at 640.

45. Id. at 640–41.

46. Id. at 641.

47. Id.

48. Id. (emphasis added) (citation omitted).

49. See 1 Theophilus Parsons, The Law of Contracts 384 (1980) (impossibility defense); 11 id. at 556 (marriage contracts).

50. Impossibility doctrine was purportedly "formed" in the early or mid-nineteenth century. See Grant Gilmore, Death of Contract 138 n. 206 (1974) (crediting Tarling v. Baxter, 108 Eng. Rep. 484 [1827] as the early leading case); Leon E. Trakman, Winner Take Some: Loss Sharing and Commercial Impracticability, 69 Minn. L. Rev. 471, 475 (1985) (crediting Taylor v. Caldwell, 122 Eng. Rep. 309 [1863]). Paradine v. Jane, 82 Eng. Rep. 897 (1647), is conventionally cited as evidence that impossibility doctrine did not exist earlier. See, e.g., Kessler, et al., supra note 12, at 913. This case raises for me, however, the possibility that the doctrine in fact predates the nineteenth century, since such a "rejection" could

202 / Postmodern Legal Feminism

be understood as a recognition of the doctrine coupled with a refusal to utilize it.

51. See Frances Olsen, Statutory Rape: A Feminist Critique of Rights Analysis, 63 Tex. L. Rev. 387, 399 n. 56 (1984): "Until the passage of the married women's property acts in the late 19th century, married women were legally incompetent to bind themselves by contract."

52. The methodology of this section is consistent with the long-standing feminist practice of analyzing the consequences for a particular discourse of omitting women or topics which particularly interest or involve women.

53. See Joel P. Bishop, Commentaries on the Law of Marriage and Divorce, and Evidence in Matrimonial Suits §§ 548–90 (1852).

54. See supra note 24 and accompanying text.

55. See 5 Samuel Williston, A Treatise on the Law of Contracts 668–69 (Walter Jaeger ed., 3d ed. 1961): "Where . . . the law itself has imposed the condition . . . it can . . . shap[e] the boundaries of the constructive condition in such a way as to do justice and avoid hardship."

56. Bishop, supra note 53, § 297.

57. See id.

58. See e.g., Cal. Civ. Proc. Code § 1760 (West 1982) (providing that the family conciliation court shall have jurisdiction over "any controversy . . . between spouses [who have a minor child in their household whose welfare might be affected by the controversy] . . . which may . . . result in the dissolution or annulment of the marriage"); Mass. Ann. Laws ch. 208, § 1A (Law. Co-op. 1981 & Supp. 1991) (providing that in deciding on a couple's efforts to obtain divorce on the ground of irretrievable breakdown of their marriage, "the court shall . . . make a finding as to whether or not an irretrievable breakdown of the marriage exists").

59. See e.g., This Bridge Called My Back: Writings by Radical Women of Color (Cherríe Moraga and Gloria Anzaldúa eds. 1983) (challenging feminist claims from the perspective of both lesbian feminists and women of color).

60. See generally, Gallop, Seduction, supra note 11, at 124 (noting that female theorists merely reverse the bipolar gender characterization of male theorists); Kristeva, Reader, supra note 11, at 81–82 (discussing the Marxist view of wealth as resulting from the bipolar elements of work, which is male, and matter, which is female).

61. See, e.g. Irigaray, This Sex, supra note 11, at 81–85 (discussing how "the double demand—for both equality and difference—[can] be articulated").

62. Postmodern feminists are increasingly charged with claims that their work is depoliticized, or antipolitical, or post-feminist. See, e.g., Karen Offen, The Use and Abuse of History, Women's Review of Books, April

1989, at 15–16 (asking "Must the postmodernist be necessarily post-feminist?"). But see Johnson, A World of Difference, supra note 11, at 25–31 (discussing whether "writerliness" is "conservative").

63. Jane Gallop is particularly adept at challenging the male/female opposition at the same time she disrupts it. See generally, Gallop, Seduction supra note 11.

64. See Gilligan, supra note 27.

8
A Postmodern Feminist Legal Manifesto

1. See Catharine A. MacKinnon, Feminism, Marxism, Method and the State: An Agenda for Theory, 7 Signs 515 (1982); Catharine A. MacKinnon, Feminism, Marxism, Method and the State: Toward Feminist Jurisprudence, 8 Signs 635 (1983).

2. Andrea Dworkin, Letters From a War Zone 65 (1989).

3. Andrea Dworkin, Right-Wing Women 20 (1983).

4. For the radical feminist focus on male domination, see Andrea Dworkin, Pornography: Men Processing Women 14–18, 53–56 (1989); Andrea Dworkin, supra note 3, at 77–87 (1983); Catharine MacKinnon, Feminism Unmodified 40–45, 171–74 (1987); MacKinnon, Agenda for Theory, supra note 1, at 530–34; and MacKinnon, Toward Feminist Jurisprudence, supra note 1, at 643. For the cultural feminist focus on the ethic of care, see Carol Gilligan, In a Different Voice 64–105 (1982); and Leslie Bender, A Lawyer's Primer on Feminist Theory and Tort, 38 J. Legal Educ. 3, 28–37 (1988) (suggesting the incorporation of Gilligan's ethic into tort law's standard of care).

5. For a race-conscious critique of liberal, radical, and cultural feminism for overlooking minority women concerns, see Angela P. Harris, Race and Essentialism in Feminist Legal Theory, 42 Stan. L. Rev. 581, 585–86 (1990); Marlee Kline, Race, Racism, and Feminist Legal Theory, 12 Harv. Women's L. J. 115, 120–23, 144–50 (1989); and Kimberlé Crenshaw, Demarginalizing the Intersection of Race and Sex: A Black Feminist Critique of Antidiscrimination Doctrine, Feminist Theory and Antiracist Politics, 1989 U. of Chi. Legal F. 139, 140, 152–60 (1989). For the lesbian feminist critique of heterosexist assumptions in liberal, radical, and cultural feminisms, see Audre Lorde, Sister Outsider 114–23 (1984); Adrienne Rich, Compulsory Heterosexuality and Lesbian Existence, in Powers of Desire: The Politics of Sexuality 177, 178–82 (Ann Snitow, Christine Stansell, and Sharon Thompson eds. 1983). For a class-conscious feminist critique of the class bias inherent in liberal, radical, and cultural feminisms, see Kristin Luker, Abortion and the Politics of Motherhood 192–215 (1984).

6. Cf. Louis Althusser, Lenin and Philosophy and Other Essays 127–86 (Ben

204 / Postmodern Legal Feminism

Brewster trans. 1971) (demonstrating the role of ideology and social structure in shaping personality); Michel Foucault, 1 The History of Sexuality (Robert Hurley trans. 1978) (discussing the power-sex relationship in terms of affirmation).

7. Even sex workers who are "in the life" feel interrogated by the sexualization question; they too struggle against acting like whores. Consider, for example, one sex worker's description of the discomfort she experienced because she sexually responded to her customer during an act of prostitution. Her orgasm in those circumstances broke down a distinction she sought to maintain between her work and the sexual pleasure she obtained from her non-work-related sexual activity. See Judy Edelstein, In the Massage Parlor, in Sex Works: Writings by Women in the Sex Industry 62, 62–63 (Frederique Delacoste and Priscilla Alexander eds. 1987) (hereinafter Sex Work). Consider also the many accounts of sex workers who feel degraded or angry about their work; this is an experience of sexual division, a fear that, in their work as whores, they are acting like whores. See, e.g., Jean Johnson, Speaking in Tongues, in Sex Work at 70; Sharon Kaiser, Coming Out of Denial, in Sex Work at 104–5; Rosie Summers, Prostitution, in Sex Work at 113–15.

8. MacKinnon, Agenda for Theory, supra note 1, at 533–34.

9. "Nightline": Interview with Madonna (ABC News broadcast, Dec. 3, 1990).

10. MacKinnon, Agenda for Theory, supra note 1, at 534.

11. See, e.g., Veazy v. Blair, 86 Ga. App. 721, 726 (1952) (holding that a cause of action existed when the defendant had stated that "the plaintiff, a pure and chaste lady of unblemished character, was a 'public whore' "); Mullins v. Mutter, 287 Ky. 164, 173–74 (1941) (upholding large slander award when the defendant called the plaintiff a "damned whore"). In *Mullins*, the court noted that:

> In this case plaintiff is an orphaned girl, bearing—so far as the record discloses—a good reputation. . . . Up to the time complained of no breath of suspicion had been leveled against her chastity. But, so emphatically repeated charges by defendant was calculated to leave a scar upon her reputation that might follow her to her grave. (Id.)

12. See Commonwealth v. Joyce, 415 N.E.2d 181 (Mass. 1981).

13. Id.

14. Id. at 184.

15. See Mass. Gen. L. ch. 233, § 21B (1991).

16. Joyce, 415 N.E.2d at 186.

17. Id. at 186.

18. Id. at 187 (citations omitted).

19. Id. (citations omitted).

20. See Kathleen Barry, Female Sexual Slavery 226–37 (1979).

21. See Margaret Jane Radin, Market-Inalienability, 100 Harv. L. Rev. 1849, 1921–25 (1987) (favoring limited decriminalization of prostitution, at least for the short term). But see Jody Freeman, The Feminist Debate Over Prostitution Reform: Prostitutes' Rights Groups, Radical Feminists, and the (Im)possibility of Consent, 5 Berk. Women's L. J. 75 (1989–90) arguing that "the best short-term approach to reform entails removing prostitution from the criminal realm . . . and, at the same time taking affirmative steps to destroy the conditions that create consumption and drive women to the trade").

22. Not all sex workers seek to legalize as well as decriminalize their work, but many do. See e.g., Gail Pheterson, A Vindication of the Rights of Whores 33–34 (1989); Draft Statements from the 2nd World Whores' Congress (1986), in Sex Work at 307; International Committee for Prostitutes' Rights World Charter, in Sex Work at 305.

23. Since teenage women are still subject to contraceptive restrictions, despite Eisenstadt v. Baird, 405 U.S. 438 (1972), these rules are not in desuetude.

24. At least fifty cases have been brought against women for "fetal abuse" in giving birth to drug-exposed babies. See Dorothy E. Roberts, The Future of Reproductive Choice for Poor Women and Women of Color, 12 Women's Rts. L. Rep. 59, 64 n. 40 (1990). Some states have expanded the definition of neglected children to include babies who are born addicted to certain classes of drugs. See Fla. Stat. Ann. § 415.503(9)(a)(2) (West Supp. 1991); Mass. Gen. L. ch. 119, § 51A (1991). Women have also been charged with vehicular homicide for the death of their fetuses. See State v. McCall, 458 So.2d 875 (Fla. Ct. App. 1984) (count dismissed).

25. See, e.g., American Nurses' Ass'n v. Illinois, 783 F.2d 716, 725 (7th Cir. 1986) (holding that a state's refusal to adopt the principle of comparable worth was not actionable); American Fed'n of State, County, Mun. Employees v. Washington, 770 F.2d 1401, 1408 (9th Cir. 1985) (rejecting a union's claim that the state was compelled to restructure its compensation system based on the results of a comparable worth study); Christensen v. Iowa, 563 F.2d 353, 355 (8th Cir. 1977) (finding no prima facie case under title VII, 42 U.S.C. §2000e to 2000e-17 [1988], in a state university's practice of paying male physical plant workers more than female clerical workers of equivalent seniority and grade).

26. See, e.g., Hayes v. Shelby Memorial Hosp., 726 F.2d 1543, 1552 (11th Cir. 1984); Wright v. Olin Corp., 697 F.2d 1172, 1188–91 (4th Cir. 1982).

27. See 111 S.Ct. 1196, 1203 (1991).

28. See EEOC v. Sears, 628 F. Supp. 1264, 1352–53 (N.D. Ill. 1986), aff'd, 839 F.2d 302 (7th Cir. 1988); Vicki Schultz, Telling Stories About Women and Work: Judicial Interpretations of Sex Segregation in the Workplace in Title VII Cases Raising the Lack of Interest Argument, 103 Harv. L. Rev. 1749, 1754–56 (1990).

29. See Wimberly v. Labor & Indus. Relations Comm'n., 479 U.S. 511, 514, 522 (1987).

30. American Booksellers Ass'n v. Hudnut, 771 F.2d 323, 324 (7th Cir. 1985), aff'd, 475 U.S. 1001 (1986) (quoting Indianapolis, Ind. Code § 16-3[q] [1984]).

31. MacKinnon, supra note 4, at 205 (1987).

32. Id.

33. 410 U.S. 111 (1973).

34. James Jones, From Here to Eternity (1951).

35. See Park Elliott Dietz and Alan E. Sears, Pornography and Obscenity Sold in "Adult Bookstores": A Survey of 5132 Books, Magazines, and Films in Four American Cities, 21 Mich. J. L. Ref. 7, 10–11 (1987–88).

36. Pauline Réage, The Story of O (Sabine d'Estreé trans. 1965).

37. Georges Bataille, Histoire de L'Oeil (1967).

38. American Booksellers Ass'n v. Hudnut, 771 F.2d at 324 (7th Cir. 1985), aff'd, 475 U.S. 1001 (1986) (quoting Indianapolis, Ind. Code § 16-3[q] [1984]).

Index